Praise for
African Safari Journal

As someone who has visited Africa over 40 times, I can say without hesitation that the *African Safari Journal* is the best single resource one can have with them on what is sure to be an adventure of a lifetime. Its easy-to-read style and wide variety of information make it a "must have" for anyone on safari!

—RON MAGILL
COMMUNICATIONS & MEDIA
MIAMI METROZOO

Mark Nolting has done it again! Clearing out the clutter from the safari experience, making sense of what is good and what is bad, getting prepared once you have decided are all often overlooked and sometimes overwhelming aspects of the safari. Thanks to *African Safari Journal* it's all done for you, and all that is left is to engulf yourself in our continent's pleasures.

—DERECK JOUBERT, EXPLORER IN RESIDENCE AT THE
NATIONAL GEOGRAPHIC SOCIETY, CONSERVATIONIST, FILMMAKER

If *Africa's Top Wildlife Countries* is the first book to grab when planning your safari, then the *African Safari Journal* is the first book to grab when you're headed to the airport to go on your safari! Nolting has got you covered from planning your safari, to living it, and reliving it again through the notes in your own personal safari journal. Packed full of information, maps, hundreds of color illustrations, and space for your own notes, it's the only book you'll ever need while on safari!

—GENE ECKHART – PROFESSIONAL PHOTOGRAPHER AND AUTHOR OF
"MOUNTAIN GORILLAS: BIOLOGY, CONSERVATION AND COEXISTENCE"

Mark Nolting's *African Safari Journal* has accompanied our family on each of our sojourns to Africa. Incorporating an abbreviated guide to the African bush, a planner and a personal journal in a compact format, the *African Safari Journal* has been an indispensable tool accompanying our travels. Upon return, it remains a keepsake of treasured memories and mementos secreted within its pages.

—TERRI WILLIAMS-JAKWAY
WHITE BEAR LAKE, MN

I refer to the *African Safari Journal* while I'm on my journey on a daily basis. I use it for reference as well as to keep track of all I've seen, felt, photographed...all my thoughts and activities in one place. I find it to be a handy reference when I return home and arrange my photos and share my experiences with family and friends. I've even referred friends to Mark to travel to particular places after reviewing my *African Safari Journals*...I keep a new one for each trip...along with my photo albums. The journal is just one of the many advantages of traveling with the very client-oriented Africa Adventure Company!!

—*ABBY LAZAR*
JAMESVILLE, NY

We found the *African Safari Journal* to be an invaluable tool. When we left home, we had no appreciation for how many animals, or how many different kinds of animals we would see. Each night we would record our adventure and learn more about what we had seen. When we got home, it was a great tool to recreate our journey and make a scrapbook to share with our friends.

—*BOB AND DENISE BLACKNEY*
UPLAND, CA

Initially I intended to use the *African Safari Journal* as something to simply wrap up as a Christmas present for my children prior to our trip in July. As it turned out, I probably enjoyed the book even more than the kids and refer to it frequently at our travel agency. It was a wealth of information prior to our departure and during our trip. I loved having the maps and a place to take notes. The animal illustrations with descriptions and check-list in the back are terrific.

—*ANN TUTWILER WEST*
NASHVILLE, TN

We observed a family using the *African Safari Journal* at an airport. We asked to see it and were impressed at the amount of useful information your company provided in the *Journal*. We followed up and began planning our next trip with The Africa Adventure Company. Your company provided us with such a unique trip, tailored specifically to our interests.

—*SUSIE AND JIM DOYLE*
TACOMA, WA

African
SAFARI JOURNAL

Mark W. Nolting

African Safari Journal
(Fifth edition, completely revised and updated)
ISBN-10: 0-939895-11-0
ISBN-13: 978-0-939895-11-3

Photo credits:
lion – Wilderness Safaris
leopard cub and running zebras – Michael Poliza
elephant – Dave Christiansen

Graphic Design by Nature Works and 1106 Design
Printed by Taylor Books
Printed in the United States of America
Distributed by Publishers Group West

Illustrations and natural history texts © Duncan Butchart 2007

Publisher's Notes
Although every effort has been made to ensure the accuracy of the information in this book, the author and publisher do not assume and hereby disclaim any liability to any party for any loss or damage caused by errors, omissions, misleading information or any potential travel problem caused by information in this book, even if such errors or omissions are a result of negligence, accident or any other cause.

Special Sales

Discounts for bulk purchases available.

Special Offer

Have the name and/or logo of your travel agency, tour company, safari group, organization, etc. printed on the cover!

For details please contact the publisher at
phone: 954-491-8877 or 1-800-882-9453, fax: 954-491-9060
e-mail: safaribooks@aol.com

or write to:

Global Travel Publishers, 5353 N. Federal Highway, Suite 300
Ft. Lauderdale, FL 33308 USA

This is the
African Safari Journal
of:

_____

About the Author

Mark W. Nolting has had the pleasure to explore and research the African continent for over 30 years. He expanded his passion for Africa into a successful tour company called The Africa Adventure Company, now celebrating its' 22nd Anniversary. One of the top leaders in the safari industry, The Africa Adventure Company (www.africanadventure.com) specializes in customized adventures appealing to all budgets. Beyond the traditional safari destinations of Eastern and Southern Africa, AAC is expanding travelers' horizons to new frontiers such as Ethiopia and Madagascar.

Mark recognized a need for a comprehensive travel book about the various safari destinations within Africa and from that *Africa's Top Wildlife Countries* was born. This book is the perfect resource for uncovering the diverse wildlife reserves, attractions and safari camps and lodges, and stands alone as the quintessential "must read" for anyone preparing for a safari.

For several consecutive years now, Condé Nast *Traveler* magazine has recognized Mark as one of the World's Top African Travel Specialists. Mark continues to travel to Africa yearly to update his books and explore new areas. One of Mark's special passions is speaking to individuals and groups about Africa and planning a safari for them to this magical continent. His enthusiasm is contagious and he loves talking about the epic game viewing, gorgeous accommodations and scenery that is unmistakably Africa. In the end clients have a personalized safari that will exceed their expectations and fulfill their dreams!

About the Illustrator

Duncan Butchart was born in England and has lived in South Africa since 1970. He has traveled and worked in numerous African countries and has authored and edited a host of books, booklets, periodicals and manuals.

His illustrations have appeared in a variety of magazines, books and other publications, including *The Vultures of Africa*.

Foreword

Dear Safarier:

You are about to depart on the adventure of a lifetime! If this is your first safari or your twentieth, there is one thing we can guarantee — Africa will inspire you! It is impossible to not be touched in some way by the magic of Africa. The sights and sounds will leave you breathless and the people you'll encounter will leave an imprint on your spirit.

Over the past three decades I have had the privilege of exploring Africa on countless safaris. Having spent hours of preparation for each of my earlier safaris, and carrying with me several heavy resource books on mammals, reptiles, birds and trees, as well as maps, phrase books and a diary, the idea of consolidating all this into one book was formed. Also, seeing the need for an easy-to-use comprehensive travel guide covering all the top wildlife regions, I authored *Africa's Top Wildlife Countries* — now in its 7th edition.

Why do so many people wish to go to Africa, and why do so many return time and time again after experiencing a well-planned safari? One of the main allures of Africa is that you can find adventure there. When you go on a game-viewing activity, you never know what you're going to see or what is going to happen. Every safari is exciting.

With so many changes taking place in the realm of travel, it is imperative to book your safari with a company whose expertise and passion are in sync with your own. From my very first safari I had a dream to establish a safari company unlike any other. From that dream, The Africa Adventure Company was born in 1986. For the past several years we have been honored to have been selected as one of Conde Nast *Traveler's* Top Specialists in the World. As a company we have steered clear of the cookie cutter itineraries and focused on what we love the most, remote Africa. My passion has always been to have people experience the "real Africa". If you have traveled on one of our trips you know what I am referring to; small out-of-the way camps, top notch guiding, incredible game viewing and memories to last a lifetime.

Africa is going through its own evolution of eco-conservation. More and more of the continent's wildlife is becoming threatened. We may be the last generation to see Africa in its true glory — huge herds of wildlife and tribal cultures living unaffected lifestyles. Going on a photographic safari is a donation, in itself, toward conserving African wildlife and habitats. A safari could be the most enjoyable and rewarding environmental contribution you will ever make and there is no better time to venture to Africa than the present!

Sincerely,

Mark W. Nolting

The Africa Adventure Company
5353 N. Federal Highway, Suite 300
Ft. Lauderdale, FL 33308
Tel: 800-882-WILD (9453)
Tel: 954-491-8877
Fax: 954-491-9060
Email: safari@africanadventure.com
Website: *www.africanadventure.com*

An invitation

Before booking your trip to Africa, contact us at
The Africa Adventure Company
to discuss the many safari options we have to offer.
Call today — my expert staff and I would love to
assist you in planning your safari!

The *African Safari Journal* differs from other books on the wildlife of the continent in that it is designed for you to write down your experiences and observations while you are traveling. While there is a great deal of interesting and useful information on the following pages, the book will really come to life when you add your own notes and stories. Most travelers are used to recording their safaris and other holidays through photographs, but there is nothing quite like the immediacy of a personal travel diary to complement these images. This book has been designed in such a way that it will encourage and help you to record the highlights, events and dramas of your African safari, as well as providing a means of noting activities and lists of the mammals and birds which you encounter.

There is space for you to record all of your important personal details, as well as the contact details of traveling companions, safari guides and other people who you will meet. Introductory information on the landscapes and habitats of Africa will set the scene for your own notes. The descriptive accounts of the animals highlight interesting behavior which you should look out for, as well as identification tips. The checklist provides a convenient place for recording your sightings of mammals, reptiles, birds, insects and trees, and also serves as an index to the illustrations themselves. The detailed Map Directory will help you to orient yourself and follow the route of your safari, while the section on languages will provide key words and phrases to help you communicate with the people you meet on safari. A list of recommended books, including comprehensive field guides which are essential traveling companions, is also provided, and there is a glossary of unfamiliar terms that you'll hear on safari.

So, get started now by writing down your own name on page v and recording your important details, flight schedule and safari itinerary on pages 16 to 23.

Enjoy your safari!

Mark W. Nolting

African Facts at a Glance

Area: 11,635,000 square miles (30,420,000km^2)

Approximate size: More than three times the size of the United States; larger than Europe, the United States and China combined; the second largest continent, covering 20% of the world's land surface

Population: 625,000,000 (approx.)

Largest waterfall: Victoria Falls (the world's largest waterfall by volume), twice the height of Niagara Falls and one-and-a-half times as wide

Longest river: Nile River (world's longest), 4,160 miles (6,710km)

Largest crater: Ngorongoro Crater (largest intact caldera/crater in the world), 12 miles (19km) wide with its rim rising 1,200–1,600 feet (366–488m) off its expansive 102-square-mile (264km^2) floor

Highest mountain: Mt. Kilimanjaro (highest mountain in the world not part of a range), 19,340 feet (5,895m)

Largest lake: Lake Victoria (world's third largest), 26,828 square miles (69,485km^2)

Largest freshwater oasis: Okavango Delta (Botswana), over 6,000 square miles (15,000km^2)

Largest desert: Sahara (world's largest), larger than the continental United States

Largest land mammal: Elephant (world's largest), over 15,000 pounds (6,800kg)

Largest bird: Ostrich (world's largest), over 8 feet (2.5m) tall

Deepest lake: Lake Tanganyika (world's second deepest), over 4,700 feet (1,433m)

Longest lake: Lake Tanganyika (world's longest), 446 miles (714km)

Longest rift valley: The Great Rift Valley, a 5,900 mile (9,500km) gash from the Red Sea to Lake Malawi, with 30 active volcanoes

Most species of fish: Lake Malawi (500 species)

Tallest people: The Dinka of southern Sudan (world's tallest) generally reach on average 71 inches (180cm)

Shortest people: The pygmies of the Congo (world's shortest) reach only 49 inches (125cm)

Contents

While on safari, you will enjoy the attention and input of one or more guides whose job is to make sure that you have a safe, enjoyable and enlightening experience. But although you will be in capable hands, the more you know before setting off, the more you will get out of the experience.

Background reading is perhaps the most important, although speaking to somebody who has been to the area you intend to visit can be invaluable. The *African Safari Journal* is aimed at providing you with an advance overview, as well as being a guide and field book to record your observations. As such, it should be a constant companion on your travels.

Your desire to visit Africa may well have been triggered by National Geographic documentaries or Animal Planet. This is all very well, but you should not expect to see everything in the way in which these films depict. The best wildlife films take years to create, and involve weeks or months of waiting for acton to happen. Part of enjoying your safari is having a realistic expectation, and you should always remember that wildlife is just that, it's wild! With the exception of the most common birds and herbivorous mammals, nothing can be guaranteed on safari — and that, really, is the thrill of it. It is anticipation and chance which makes getting up early each morning, and driving around each bend in the road, so enthralling.

It is vital to develop a good relationship with your guide from the outset. Bear in mind that he or she will not only know the area and its wildlife, but also the best ways to reveal this to you. Make sure that you state your expectations clearly from the word go, and don't be shy to get involved in each day's routine. If you have seen enough lions for one day, for example, let your guide know that they should perhaps just park at a scenic lookout so that you can enjoy the space and serenity of the wilderness.

Rather than spending your whole safari charging about looking only for big game, aim to get an understanding and appreciation for the whole ecosystem, of which termites and fig trees play as big a role as elephants and lions. Developing an interest in birds, reptiles and trees means that you'll have a captivating experience at all times. Perhaps the saddest thing to come across on safari is someone who has spent all day in the bush and says that he has "seen nothing!"

Sensitivity towards wildlife is paramount. Your guide will know the correct distance to approach each individual species without causing stress, but in the rare instances where this may not be so, it is up to you to dictate the distance. The most enthralling wildlife encounters are often those in which the animals that you are viewing are unaware or unafraid.

What is a typical day on safari? Most safaris are centered on guests participating in two activities per day, such as morning and afternoon game drives in four-wheel-drive (4wd) vehicles or minivans. Most game drives consist of having your guide drive you around a reserve, national park or wilderness area in search of wildlife, while helping you to interpret and understand what you encounter. Virtually all wildlife is most active in the cooler hours of early morning or late afternoon and evening, although some species are nocturnal and only seen after dark. Night game drives with spotlights are often very exciting, but permitted only in particular reserves.

Being on safari generally puts you at less risk than you would be when traveling on busy roads in your own neighborhood, but many animals are potentially dangerous and some simple precautions are advisable. A good guide will naturally avert any risky situations, but as already mentioned, respecting animals' space by not attempting to get too close is paramount. Almost all large mammals are frightened of humans, and generally run or move off when confronted with the upright form of a person. This can never be taken for granted, however, and you should not be tempted to leave the safety of a safari vehicle to approach an animal. It is equally important to remain seated while in open safari vehicles, because lions, for example, appear to regard safari vehicles as one entity, rather than a collection

of edible primates! Many of the best wildlife lodges are not fenced and allow free movement of all wildlife, so you can expect to be escorted to and from your room or tent after dinner by an armed guard. Most large mammals may explore lodge surroundings after dark, but typically keep well clear during daylight hours. Exceptions include impala, bushbuck and some other herbivores which realise that the lodge offers protection from predators. Opportunistic vervet monkeys, and sometimes baboons, frequently raid kitchens and table fruit. Monkeys can become aggressive once they are accustomed to handouts, so the golden rule is to never feed them, or any other animal.

Naturally, most people will want a record of their safari, so tips on photography are provided on page 42–44. Perhaps the most important piece of equipment, however, is a pair of binoculars which are not only essential for watching birds but also for looking at larger mammals in detail. Apart from the usual casual clothing one would pack for a holiday in a warm region, you should bear in mind that morning and night game drives in open vehicles can be cool to very cold, so it is advisable to pack a good jacket and woollen hat. A baseball cap or wide-brimmed hat are also recommended; sun protection cream, and anti-malarial medication (check with your doctor) are essential.

PERSONAL DETAILS

Name: _____

Nationality _____

Passport #: _____ Date of issue: _____

Date of expiration: _____ Place of issue: _____

My home address: _____

My e-mail address: _____

My telephone: _____

My spouse/traveling companion: _____

Date of birth: _____ Blood type: _____

Medications: _____

_____

Allergies: _____

Personal physician: _____

Optometrist: _____

Additional information: _____

_____

_____

In case of emergency, contact:

Name: _____

Address: _____

Bus. tel.: _____ Home tel.: _____

Fax: _____ E-mail: _____

Relationship: _____

TRAVEL INSURANCE

Company: _____

Policy number: _____

Group number: _____

Telephone: _____

(Collect call): _____

Contact: _____

Trip cancellation coverage: _____

Travel delay: _____

Baggage loss coverage:_____

Medical: _____

Emergency medical transportation/evacuation: _____

_____

HEALTH INSURANCE:

Company: _____

Policy number: _____

Group number: _____

Telephone: _____

(Collect call): _____

Contact: _____

HEALTH HISTORY:

_____

_____

_____

_____

CONTACT DETAILS OF YOUR TRAVEL CONSULTANT, TOUR OPERATOR AND AFRICAN GROUND OPERATORS

CONTACT DETAILS OF YOUR TRAVEL CONSULTANT, TOUR OPERATOR AND AFRICAN GROUND OPERATORS

CONTACT DETAILS OF TRAVEL COMPANIONS
AND NEWFOUND FRIENDS

CONTACT DETAILS OF TRAVEL COMPANIONS
AND NEWFOUND FRIENDS

FLIGHT SCHEDULE AND SAFARI ITINERARY

FLIGHT SCHEDULE AND SAFARI ITINERARY

_____

_____

_____

_____

_____

_____

_____

_____

_____

_____

_____

_____

_____

_____

_____

_____

_____

_____

_____

_____

_____

_____

_____

_____

_____

_____

PACKING CHECKLIST AND LUGGAGE INVENTORY

1. Check the items listed below to be taken with you on your trip. Add additional items in the blank spaces provided. Use this list as a guide. In case of baggage loss, assess the value of items lost and file a claim with your baggage-loss insurance company.

2. Safari clothing can be any comfortable cotton clothing and should be neutral in color (tan, brown, khaki, light green). Avoid dark blue and black, as these colors attract tsetse flies. Note that cotton clothing is also much cooler on safari than synthetic fibers.

3. Please note that all clothes washed on safari may be ironed, so cotton clothing is preferable. Synthetic clothing may be damaged.

4. Please read your itinerary carefully as you may have a strict baggage weight limit (i.e. 33 pounds/15kg per person), so please pack accordingly.

5. Virtually all safari camps and lodges provide daily laundry service and many provide complimentary shampoo and conditioner, so you can travel with much less clothing and toiletries than you might imagine!

WOMEN'S CLOTHING

- ❑ Sandals or lightweight shoes
- ❑ Walking shoes or lightweight hiking shoes (not white for walking safaris)
- ❑ Wide-brimmed hat
- ❑ Windbreaker
- ❑ Sweater or fleece
- ❑ 3 pr. safari* pants
- ❑ 3 pr. safari* shorts
- ❑ 5 pr. safari/sport socks
- ❑ 3 short-sleeve safari* shirts
- ❑ 3 long-sleeve safari* shirts
- ❑ Swimsuit/cover-up
- ❑ 1 pr. casual slacks or skirt
- ❑ 1 or 2 blouses
- ❑ Belts
- ❑ 6 sets underwear
- ❑ 3 bras

OPTIONAL

- ❑ 1 cocktail dress

- ❑ 1 pr. dress shoes and nylons/panty hose
- ❑ 1 sports bra (for rough roads)

MEN'S CLOTHING

- ❑ Sandals or lightweight shoes
- ❑ Walking shoes or lightweight hiking shoes (not white for walking safaris)
- ❑ Wide-brimmed hat
- ❑ Windbreaker
- ❑ Sweater or fleece
- ❑ 3 pr. safari* pants
- ❑ 3 pr. safari* shorts
- ❑ 5 pr. safari/sports socks
- ❑ 3 short-sleeve safari* shirts
- ❑ 3 long-sleeve safari* shirts
- ❑ Swim trunks
- ❑ 1 pr. casual slacks
- ❑ 1 sports shirt
- ❑ 6 sets underwear
- ❑ Belts

* Any comfortable cotton clothing for safari should be neutral in color *(tan, brown, light green, khaki)*. Evening wear can be any color you like!

❑ Large handkerchief

OPTIONAL

❑ 1 pr. dress slacks, shoes and dress socks
❑ 1 dress shirt/jacket/tie

TOILETRIES AND FIRST AID

❑ Anti-malaria pills (prescription)
❑ Vitamins
❑ Aspirin/Tylenol/Advil
❑ Motion sickness pills
❑ Decongestant
❑ Throat lozenges
❑ Laxative
❑ Anti-diarrhea medicine
❑ Antacid
❑ Antibiotic
❑ Cortisone cream
❑ Antibiotic ointment
❑ Anti-fungal cream or powder

SUNDRIES

❑ Passport (with visas, if needed)
❑ International Certificates of Vaccination
❑ Air tickets/vouchers
❑ Money pouch
❑ Credit cards
❑ Traveler's checks
❑ Personal checks
❑ Insurance cards
❑ Pocket calculator
❑ Sunglasses/guard
❑ Spare prescription glasses/contacts
❑ Copy of prescription(s)
❑ Eyeglass case
❑ Travel alarm clock
❑ Small flashlight (torch) and extra batteries

❑ Prescription drugs
❑ Medical summary from your doctor (if needed)
❑ Medical alert bracelet or necklace
❑ Band-Aids (plasters)
❑ Thermometer
❑ Insect repellent
❑ Sunscreen/sun block
❑ Shampoo (small container)
❑ Conditioner (small container)
❑ Deodorant
❑ Toothpaste
❑ Toothbrush
❑ Hairbrush/comb
❑ Razor
❑ Q-tips/cotton balls
❑ Nail clipper
❑ Emery boards
❑ Makeup
❑ Tweezers

❑ Binoculars
❑ Sewing kit
❑ Small scissors
❑ Tissues (travel packs)
❑ Handiwipes (individual)
❑ Anti-bacterial soap
❑ Laundry soap (for washing delicates)
❑ Large ziplock bags for damp laundry
❑ Copy of *Africa's Top Wildlife Countries*
❑ Maps
❑ Business cards
❑ Pens
❑ Deck of cards
❑ Reading materials
❑ Decaffeinated coffee/herbal tea
❑ Sugar substitute

CAMERA EQUIPMENT

- ❏ Lenses
- ❏ Digital memory cards/Film
- ❏ Camera bag or backpack
- ❏ Lens cleaning fluid
- ❏ Lens tissue/brush
- ❏ Extra camera batteries
- ❏ Flash
- ❏ Flash batteries
- ❏ Battery charger and adapters
- ❏ Plastic bags for lenses and camera body
- ❏ Beanbag, small tripod or monopod
- ❏ Extra video camera batteries
- ❏ Video charger
- ❏ Outlet adapters (3-prong square and round plugs)
- ❏ Cigarette lighter charger (optional)

GIFTS & TRADES

- ❏ T-shirts
- ❏ Pens
- ❏ Inexpensive watches
- ❏ Postcards from your area/state
- ❏ Children's magazines and books
- ❏ Small acrylic mirrors
- ❏ Balloons
- ❏ School supplies

OTHER

❏ _____ ❏ _____

❏ _____ ❏ _____

❏ _____ ❏ _____

❏ _____ ❏ _____

❏ _____ ❏ _____

❏ _____ ❏ _____

❏ _____ ❏ _____

❏ _____ ❏ _____

❏ _____ ❏ _____

❏ _____ ❏ _____

❏ _____ ❏ _____

❏ _____ ❏ _____

❏ _____ ❏ _____

❏ _____ ❏ _____

❏ _____ ❏ _____

SHOPPING LIST

Item: _____

Best places
to shop for it: _____

_____

_____

_____

_____

Item: _____

Best places
to shop for it: _____

_____

_____

_____

_____

Item: _____

Best places
to shop for it: _____

_____

_____

_____

_____

Item: _____

Best places
to shop for it: _____

_____

_____

_____

_____

Africa is a continent of incredible diversity. Straddling the equator, and stretching beyond both the tropic of Cancer and Capricorn, almost every conceivable landscape and climate is present on the giant landmass. From snow-capped peaks to parched deserts, and from dripping rainforests to expansive savannahs, each habitat has its own particular community of plants and animals. No other parts of the world contain as much unaltered habitat, and nowhere are large mammals still so numerous and widespread. All African countries have extensive networks of protected areas and — in many cases — these are actually increasing in size as nature-based tourism becomes an ever more important component of local economies. Nevertheless, Africa's wild places face innumerable threats and challenges as human populations increase, and development goes unchecked. The impact of man-induced climate change is of growing concern here, as it is around the world.

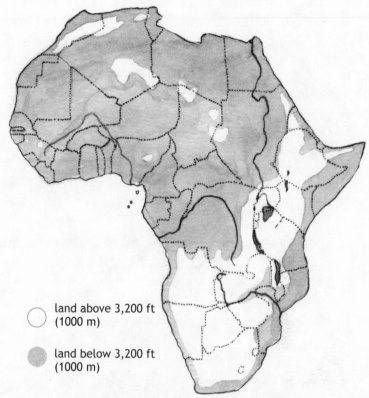

land above 3,200 ft
(1000 m)

land below 3,200 ft
(1000 m)

Altitude above sea level is a major factor in terms of Africa's climate, as it determines the vegetation types and distribution of wildlife, as well as the patterns of human settlement. The continent can be divided into "high" and "low" regions, with the land above 3,200 feet being more temperate even on the equator. European colonists chose to establish settlements on the higher plateaus, where wheat, tea and livestock such as cattle and sheep were able to thrive. Malaria and most livestock diseases are prolific in hot lowlands, so these areas were spared from much development and still contain some extensive wilderness areas. The Congo Basin and most of west Africa is a steamy wet lowland, while the majority of countries of east and southern Africa enjoy the benefits of both temperate and tropical or subtropical climates. The southern African highveld plateau experiences bitterly cold night temperatures during winter (May to August), while towns that are at high altitude such as Nairobi experience cool nights throughout much of the year.

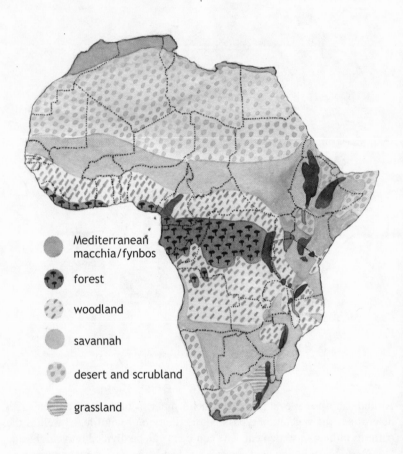

Mediterranean macchia/fynbos

forest

woodland

savannah

desert and scrubland

grassland

Africa can be divided into several broad categories of landscape which are a result of climate (particularly rainfall), altitude, topography and soils, all of which are interlinked. Geographers refer to these landscapes as vegetation zones (or biomes), and they include well-known types such as forest, desert and grassland. In most cases, these and other vegetation zones do not have well defined boundaries but merge into adjacent habitats to create zones of transition. On the following pages, the more conspicuous vegetation types, and their characteristic wildlife, are briefly described.

Savannah

The African landscape so often depicted in films — and imagined by travelers — is a park-like vista of grassland dotted with flat-topped trees. This is the savannah, a mosaic of woodland and grassland. The ratio of trees to grass, and the dominant species of trees is determined by rainfall and soil type. This is the dominant habitat in most of the large wildlife reserves in southern and east Africa, with thorny acacia trees being conspicuous. Seasonal grass fires are an important mechanism in the maintenance of

savannah ecosystems, as they encourage grass growth and limit the spread of woody plants. Large herbivores including giraffe, elephant, zebra, buffalo and wildebeest favor the savannah which also supports the highest density of lions and other large predators. Bird diversity is great with eagles, vultures, bustards, rollers, hornbills, larks, shrikes, starlings and weavers among the conspicuous families.

Woodland

Woodland generally occurs in higher rainfall areas but often merges with savannah. Trees are taller and more closely spaced, sometimes with their canopies touching. Much of southern Tanzania, Zambia and Zimbabwe is blanketed in moist *miombo woodland*, while swathes of dry *mopane woodland* occur in northern Botswana and the low-lying parts of Zimbabwe and northeastern South Africa. Browsing herbivores such as kudu live in woodlands, while roan and sable favor grassy clearings. African elephant may be seasonally abundant in mopane woodland. Birds such as woodpeckers, cuckoos, turacos, tits, orioles, warblers and sunbirds are well represented in woodlands.

Scrublands and Semidesert

In low rainfall areas such as the Kalahari and northern Kenya, short thorny trees and shrubs (particularly *acacia* and *commiphora*) are interspersed with hardy grasses. Termite mounds may be a conspicuous feature of these landscapes. Bands of taller trees occur along seasonal streams (drainage lines) where they typically tap into an underground water supply. Aloes, euphorbias and other succulents may occur on well-drained slopes. These landscapes are transformed after good rainfall and typically explode with life for short periods. Gazelles, oryx, cheetah, bat-eared fox and black-backed jackal are often resident, while gerbils and other rodents can be seasonally abundant. Bustards, sandgrouse and larks are typical birds, while eagles, goshawks, falcons and other raptors are often conspicuous.

Desert

Africa has two true deserts. The Sahara is undoubtedly the world's most famous but it is not known for its wildlife and is not dealt with here. In contrast, the Namib Desert (after which the country of Namibia is named) is an extraordinary wilderness with a host of unique arid-adapted plants and animals. Deserts are characterized by extremely low annual rainfall, although brief periods of bounty follow uncharacteristic thunderstorms. Large mammals are few and mostly nomadic, but a variety of interesting arid-adapted birds and reptiles are present.

Forest

Forest may be defined as an area with total tree cover where tree canopies interlock. There are several kinds of forest in Africa, ranging from equatorial/lowland rain forest, coastal forest, temperate montane forest and bands of riverine forest in savannah habitats. The temperate montane forests of Rwanda and Uganda are home to mountain gorillas, while chimpanzees and various other primates occur in forest pockets of Uganda and Tanzania. African elephant, buffalo and various species of duiker are typical forest mammals. A large number of bird species are restricted to forests of one kind or another throughout Africa; some are canopy feeders while others skulk on the forest floor. The Congo Basin is the second largest rainforest on the planet, after the Amazon.

Lowland forests contain hardwood trees attractive to loggers and extensive areas have been cleared or are currently under threat.

High Altitude Grassland

On the highveld plateau of South Africa, a prarie-like grassland once dominated the landscape but intensive agriculture and coal mining have now reduced this to a fragment of its former extent and many grassland specialist species are now endangered. Indigenous trees are largely absent due to winter frosts and regular fires, but hardy alien species such as eucalyptus and weeping willow are now conspicuous. The upland regions of Ethiopia, Kenya, Malawi and Tanzania have smaller but usually more pristine areas of high altitude grassland. Large mammals are few but birds are abundant and conspicuous.

Rivers, Lakes and Wetlands

Africa has several major rivers, including the north-flowing Nile — the world's longest — which empties into the Mediterranean. The Congo River is second only to the Amazon in terms of volume as it drains west into the Atlantic. The Zambezi, Limpopo, Ruvuma, Rufiji, Galana and Tana are the major river systems draining southern and eastern Africa into the Indian Ocean. These rivers are all fed by smaller tributaries, many of which are seasonal. All of these waterbodies are essential for people and wildlife but many are threatened by inappropriate agriculture, deforestation and erosion of catchments and the impacts of global warming. A chain of great lakes occurs in the two arms of the Rift Valley, and the world's third largest — Lake Victoria — is sandwiched in between. Botswana's Okavango Delta is formed by the river of the same name spilling out into the Kalahari Basin; the Rufiji and Zambezi deltas are important coastal wetlands. Hippo are restricted to rivers and wetlands, while elephant, buffalo and many other large mammals are water dependent. A vast array of birds including pelicans, flamingos, storks, herons, ducks, geese, cormorants, kingfishers, jacanas, plovers and migratory sandpipers inhabit wetlands of various types.

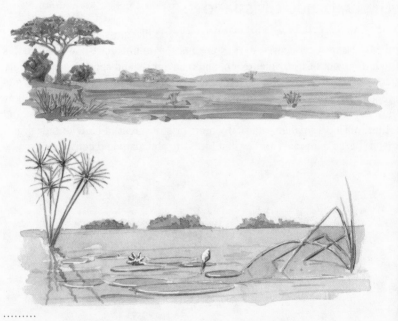

Coast and Reefs

The shore and seas off Africa's coast support diverse wildlife communities in habitats ranging from kelp beds and coral reefs, to mangroves and pristine beaches. The deep pelagic waters beyond the continental shelf are home to whales, dolphins, sea turtles and great white shark, as well as birds such as albatrosses, petrels and shearwaters.

There is a vast difference between the east and west coasts of the continent. The cold Benguela current sweeps north from the Antarctic to bring cool, nutrient rich water to the western Cape and Namibia, with large numbers of fur seals and gannets thriving in the productive waters which are, however, threatened by commercial fishing fleets. In contrast, the Indian Ocean is warmed by equatorial waters, with coral reefs off the Kenyan, Tanzanian and Mozambican coasts, and palm-fringed islands such as Zanzibar and Seychelles. Fish and other wildlife have been heavily harvested along this tropical coast which has been exploited and fought over by traders, settlers and locals for centuries. Fortunately, marine reserves in Kenya, Tanzania and South Africa protect extensive areas.

A few days on an island or beach is a perfect way to end an African safari, with the splendour of a healthy coral reef surpassing most terrestrial habitats in terms of diversity and color.

ANIMALS BY HABITAT AND DIET

The animals listed below are classified according to the habitat where most of their time is spent. The animals are listed in order of size by weight.

SAVANNAH/SAVANNAH WOODLAND		
GRAZERS	BROWSERS	CARNIVORES
White Rhino	Elephant	Lion
Eland	Giraffe	Hyena (three species)
Zebra	Nyala	Cheetah
Roan Antelope	Bushbuck	African Wild Dog
Gemsbok (Oryx)	Gerenuk	Jackal (three species)
Topi	Duiker, Grey	Serval
Hartebeest	Dikdik	Bat-Eared Fox
Wildebeest		Mongoose (many species)
Tsessebe		Genet (two species)
Warthog		Caracal
Reedbuck		
Grant's Gazelle	Grant's Gazelle	
Impala	Impala	
Springbok	Springbok	
Thomson's Gazelle	Thomson's Gazelle	
Klipspringer	Klipspriinger	
Steenbok	Steenbok	
FOREST		
OMNIVORES	BROWSERS	CARNIVORES
Gorilla	Elephant	Leopard
Chimpanzee	Colobus Monkey	Serval
Syke's Monkey	Bongo	Genet
	Bushbuck	
	Duiker (several species)	

WETLANDS	
BROWSERS	CARNIVORES
Hippopotamus	Crocodile
Buffalo	Otter
Sitatunga	
SCRUBLANDS, SEMIDESERTS AND DESERTS	
See savannah grazers, browsers and carnivores above	

MAJOR WILDLIFE AREAS BY HABITAT
P-Primary Habitat S-Secondary Habitat (R)-Riverine (L)-Lake
EAST AND CENTRAL AFRICA

COUNTRY	WILDLIFE AREA	WOODLAND/ SAVANNAH	FOREST	WETLAND
Tanzania	Arusha (N.P.)		P	S
	Lake Manyara	S	S	P (L)
	Ngorongoro Crater	P	S	S (L)
	Serengeti	P		S (R)
	Tarangire	P		S (R)
	Mt. Kilimanjaro		P	
	Selous	P		S (R)
	Ruaha	P		S (R)
	Mikumi	P		
	Gombe Stream		P	S (L)
	Mahale Mountains		P	S (L)
Kenya	Nairobi (N.P.)	P		
	Amboseli	P		S
	Tsavo	P		
	Masai Mara	P		S (R)
	Mt. Elgon		P	
	Aberdare		P	
	Mt. Kenya		P	
	Meru	P	S	
	Lake Navaisha			P (L)
	Lake Nakuru			P (L)
	Lake Bogoria			P (L)
	Lake Baringo			P (L)
	Samburu	P		S (R)
	Lewa Downs	P		
	Laikipia	P		
Uganda	Murchison Falls	P	S	S (R)
	Queen Elizabeth N.P.	P	S	S(L)
	Bwindi		P	
	Kibale Forest		P	
Rwanda	Volcano N.P.		P	
Congo	Virunga (Rwindi area)	P		S (L)
	Virunga (other areas)	S	P	
	Kahuzi-Biega		P	

MAJOR WILDLIFE AREAS BY HABITAT
P-Primary Habitat S-Secondary Habitat (R)-Riverine (L)-Lake
SOUTHERN AFRICA

COUNTRY	WILDLIFE AREA	WOODLAND/ SAVANNAH	FOREST	WETLAND	DESERT
Botswana	Okavango Delta	S		P	
	Moremi	P		S	
	Linyanti/Selinda/Kwando	S		P	
	Savute	P			
	Chobe	P		S(R)	
	Makgadikgadi	S		P	
	Nxai Pan	S	P		
	Kalahari Desert	S			P
Zimbabwe	Hwange	P			
	Matusadona	S		P (L)	
	Mana Pools	S		P (R)	
	Matobo Hills	P			
	Chizarira	P			
	Ghonorhezo	P			
Zambia	South Luangwa	P		S(R)	
	North Luangwa	P		S(R)	
	Lower Zambezi	S		P(R)	
	Kafue	P		S	
	Lochinvar	S		P	
Malawi	Liwonde	S		P	
Namibia	Etosha	P			S
	East Caprivi	P		S	
	Damaraland	P			
	Skeleton Coast	P			
	Namib-Naukluft	P			
South Africa	Kruger	P		S(R)	
	Private Reserves (Kruger)	P			
	Hluhluwe Umfolozi	P			
	St. Lucia	S	S	P(L)	
	Phinda	P	S	S(R)	
	Kgalagadi Trans-Frontier Pk.	S			P

The modern safari has its origin in the expeditions of European hunters and naturalists who traveled to hitherto uncharted parts of the continent in search of unusual animals for scientific description or as trophies during the early part of the 19th century. Among the better known explorers and hunters of the 1800s were William Burchell, Cornwallis Harris and Frederick Courtney Selous. Although Selous was undoubtedly in pursuit of macho adventure, thrill and bounty, he eventually proposed that wanton destruction of large mammals ought to be tempered with the British concept of "sportsmanship". This was in contrast to the African hunters armed by Arab merchants, and the Boer settlers in South Africa, who had set about decimating virtually all large mammals. Within a few decades of the publication of Selous's famous book *A Hunter's Wanderings in Africa* the first game control laws were established in most African countries which, in the early part of the 20th century, were European colonies. It is perhaps fitting that Africa's largest protected area — the Selous Game Reserve in Tanzania — should be so named, although many conservationists remain horrified at the number of rhino and other animals Selous "bagged" over the years.

It was Kenya and other parts of East Africa that attracted a growing number of American and European trophy hunters. The extravagant and glamorous expeditions of Theodore Roosevelt and others became legendary, as did the often eccentric antics of the foreign and colonial participants. Safari outfitting companies such as Kerr & Downey sprung up to service the industry, and professional hunters became established. Needless to say, overland safaris relied heavily upon unheralded gun bearers and porters until the introduction of motorized transport.

By the 1970s, the idea of a safari based on looking at and photographing game — as opposed to shooting and skinning — had become established. In many national parks and other protected areas, overland safaris were organized, tented camps erected and lodges constructed. Over time, these tours and facilities have become increasingly sophisticated both in terms of the guided interpretation, and the quality of meals, accommodation and transportation which may rival a five-star luxury hotel.

Interestingly, many of the best wildlife-watching experiences still rely on the very same acute observational skills of trackers and patient naturalists upon which the early explorers were dependent. Another thing that has not changed about the safari is the marvellous sense of adventure and wondrous anticipation that comes with every walk or drive in Africa's wild places.

The word "safari" is an Arabic verb which means "to make a journey" — this word was infused into the Swahili language where it refers to an expedition or voyage, and subsequently into the English language.

Breathtaking views of the night sky are a typical feature of clear nights in African wilderness areas. A cloudless night provides a glorious opportunity to become familiar with several interesting constellations and noteworthy stars, as well as up to five planets in our own solar system. The position of the stars and the constellations is constant, but their place in the night sky is determined by the position of our own planet Earth which, of course, revolves around the sun, as well as the time of night at which observations are made. So it is, that the position of the stars appears different to us at different times of the night and throughout the year. Gazing up at the night sky certainly provides a clear indication of the Earth's mobile state, and an understanding of this was the foundation for the human-invented calendar.

Sophisticated computer programs now make it possible to obtain a precise picture of the night sky, based on any particular position, at any particular time. A revolving "planisphere" (two adjustable polyvinyl wheels) is another reliable way to read the night sky.

SUMMER

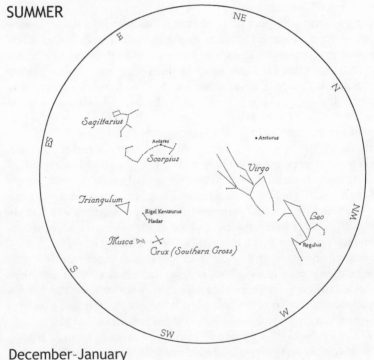

December-January

With so many hundreds of thousands of stars, it is quite impossible for the novice to gain anything but a general picture of the night sky, and most people will be happy to be able to locate and identify the Southern Cross (or Crux) and other major constellations such as Orion's Belt and Scorpio. One or more of the planets Venus, Jupiter or Mars will be visible at any given time of year.

Planets (including our own) do not emit light, but reflect light from the sun, around which all planets in our solar system revolve. Because of this, planets appear as constant, unblinking bright spots. Stars, on the other hand, are sources of light (like our sun) and appear as flickering bright spots when we view them (although in many cases we are viewing light from planet's which may have burned out decades ago!).

The diagrams on these pages provide a simplistic picture of the Southern Sky in summer (December-January) and winter (June-July). They are not intended as precise tools, but merely an indication of what you might look for.

WINTER

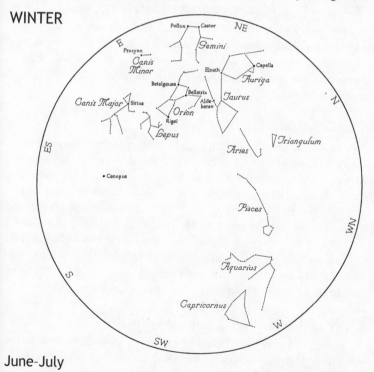

June-July

Many safari guides possess a good knowledge of the night sky and will be able to point out some of the constellations and planets, and perhaps even relate interesting fables and stories regarding the origin of their names.

A good pair of binoculars will greatly enhance sky watching, as you'll see up to ten times as many stars! Even seemingly "blank" or "sparse" parts of the sky will be seen to be filled with hundreds of distant stars when you use binoculars. Scanning the Milky Way can be truly astounding. To avoid tired arms and binocular shake when looking upwards for more than a few minutes, it is advisable to lie flat on the ground and brace your binoculars with your elbows.

The moon itself is magnificent to view through binoculars, as various craters and the Sea of Tranquillity are easily seen. Because it is so bright, detail on the surface of the moon is best viewed early in the evening before it becomes totally dark.

Photography on Safari

Most people will want to record their experiences on safari with photographs or video. In recent years, digital technology has advanced to such an extent that traditional 35mm cameras which use rolls of film have become almost extinct. There are some people who still use film cameras effectively, but they are in the minority.

CHOOSING A CAMERA

There are two basic kinds of digital camera (as there are conventional film cameras). One kind with a built-in lens (comparable to the old "instamatic") and the other kind with detachable lens. When choosing a digital camera, it is important to select a model which takes images of 4 MB, or larger, as this will enable clear prints to be made up to 8" x 10" format. For photographing wildlife, it is important to be able to zoom close to your subject, so you'll need a minimum of 10x "optical zoom," or — in the case of digital SLR — a lens of at least 300mm. Larger magnifications will be required for photographing birds. Many cameras now have "image stabilization" technology and this can be very valuable when shooting from vehicles on safari.

CHOOSING A CAMCORDER (VIDEO CAMERA)

As with digital cameras, the variety of camcorders on the market is not only bewildering, but constantly changing as technology advances. Most appropriate for use on safari are mini digital video (DV) camcorders which are small and lightweight. Some of these camcorders record onto miniDV tapes, but miniDVD and HDD (directly onto hard disc drive) are increasingly popular. Many camcorders have optical zoom of 20x or more which is ideal for shooting wildlife, but don't be fooled by high "digital zoom" statistics as these exaggerated magnifications produce images which are highly pixellated (broken up into small squares) and unsatisfactory. Some digital camcorders are also able to take still photographs, but the quality is never as good as with a dedicated still camera.

LIGHTING

The quality of any still photograph (or movie clip) is dependent upon lighting. For this reason, the best wildlife photographs are taken in the early morning or late afternoon when sunlight comes at an angle. In the middle of the day, sunlight comes from directly overhead which creates hard black shadows on and around your subject matter.

COMPOSITION

Choosing where to place your subject in the viewfinder of your camera is known as composition. This is a vital aspect of photography and separates great images from ordinary ones. Things to avoid are chopping off part of your subject (for example, feet), zooming in too tightly or placing your subject in the very center of your frame. It is much more pleasing on the eye if an animal is pictured off center and thus "looking-in" to a space. Likewise, placing the horizon of your landscape pictures in the bottom or top third of the frame (depending on whether the sky or foreground is of more interest), rather than in the very center, will create a more interesting perspective

CAMERA SHAKE

As already mentioned, some camera lenses now have "image stabilization" technology. Blurred photographs are caused mostly by camera shake, which is the result of not holding the camera firmly, or not selecting the correct exposure options and thus using long shutter speeds. The use of a tripod is hard to beat but this is not very practical on a safari. Some travelers will extend one leg of a tripod or use a monopod. Alternately, use a soft "bean-bag." Simply pack a small cloth bag in your travel kit and then fill it with dry beans (or rice) when you get to Africa. This will then provide you with a flexible yet solid support for your camera. In the absence of a tripod or beanbag, a rolled-up jacket or sweater placed on a seat or window ledge will provide decent support.

Vehicle vibrations are a major cause of blurred images, so ask your guide to turn off the vehicle engine for special shots.

BATTERIES and DATA CARDS

It is obviously necessary to have all the required battery chargers for your equipment when you travel. An electrical adaptor will also be important for connecting to local power supplies. Even the most remote safari camps usually have a generator capable of charging batteries. Consider taking two batteries for each camera, so that you always have a backup.

Data cards vary in size from 1GB to 8 or more GB. Take two or three cards and consider copying the data (i.e. your images) onto a compact disc (some safari camps do this) to enable you to delete them to free up space. Some travelers now carry iPods, or even a laptop, for copying image files onto; these instruments also allow you to better preview and edit photographs or video clips on the spot.

It is wise to store cameras and lenses in plastic ziplock bags to protect them from dust and humidity.

Safari Tips

Read the "Safari Glossary" to become familiar with the terminology used in the bush. Once on safari, you will notice that when you ask people what animals they saw on their game drive, they might reply, "elephant, lion, leopard and oryx," when in fact they saw several members of each species. This use of the singular form, when more than one of that species was seen, is common. However, one exception to this rule is saying *crocs* for *crocodile*. This form of "Safariese" will be used throughout this guide to help separate you from the amateur.

Put your valuables in a room safe or safety deposit box at your lodge or hotel.

Do not call out to a person, signaling with an index finger. This is insulting to most Africans. Instead, use four fingers with your palm facing downward.

During daytime game viewing activities, wear colors that blend in with your surroundings (brown, tan, light green or khaki). Do not wear perfume or cologne while game viewing. Wildlife can detect unnatural smells for miles and unnatural colors for hundreds of yards (meters), making close approaches difficult.

The very few tourists who get hurt on safari are almost always those travelers who ignore the laws of nature and most probably the advice and warnings of their guides. Common sense is the rule.

Do not wade or swim in rivers, lakes or streams unless you know for certain they are free of crocodiles, hippos and bilharzia (a snail-borne disease). Fast-moving areas of rivers are often free of bilharzia, but can still be a bit risky. Bilharzia, fortunately, is not the dreaded disease that it once was; if detected early it can be easily cured.

Do not walk along the banks of rivers near dawn, dusk or at night. Those who do so may inadvertently cut off a hippo's path to its water hole, and the hippo may charge.

Malaria is present in almost all the parks and reserves covered in this guide. Malarial prophylaxis (pills) should be taken and must be prescribed by a physician. Because most malaria-carrying mosquitoes come out from dusk until dawn, during this period you should use mosquito repellent and wear long pants and long-sleeve shirt or blouse, shoes (not sandals) and socks. For further information see the section on "Health" in the "Resource Directory" section of this book.

Because of the abundance of thorns and sharp twigs, wear closed-toed shoes or boots at night and also during the day if venturing out into the bush. Bring a flashlight and always have it with you at night.

Don't venture out of your lodge or camp without your guide, especially at night, dawn or dusk. Remember that wildlife is not confined to the parks and reserves in many countries, and, in fact, roams freely in and around many camps and lodges.

Resist the temptation to jog or walk alone in national parks, reserves or other areas where wildlife exists. To lion and other carnivores, we are just "meat on the hoof" like any other animal — only much slower and less capable of defending ourselves.

Birdwatching Tips

Many guides are avid birders and are only too delighted to have interested guests to show around. If your guide is not a keen birdwatcher and you are, you obviously need to let him know to ensure that you do not rush after large mammals all the time.

As many birdwatchers know, the number of species counted on a safari will depend directly on the number of habitats visited. This means that if you are a serious *twitcher* and want to log as many new "ticks" as possible, you should move a great deal throughout the safari. Africa, with its varying landscapes, lends itself well to this and in most cases you can visit two or three habitats while staying in the same camp. As mentioned before, some birding trips will take you to areas with less game and more birds — such as some of the forest areas, so a balance is important.

If you are a serious birder, it is very important to let your agent or tour operator know about it. Many companies have one or two guides who are particularly knowledgeable and, with prior notice, a private birding guide can be booked for your safari.

A lot of birding is very close range, so a close-focusing pair of binoculars is an important asset. A minimum of 8-power and preferably 10-power (10-by-40) works well for birds, as the finer details are important for identification. For the ultra keen, a spotting scope and tripod will definitely come in handy — especially for waders and bird life around lakeshores — but carrying this equipment can be cumbersome so it is recommended for only the specialist.

Checklists are very important but will most often be provided by your guide, but don't forget a reliable pencil to carry along with that. Many people take a small dictaphone to record sightings and then translate them to a written list each evening in the camp. This saves fumbling around with complicated checklists while the guide is rattling off all those new and exciting species!

If you are keen on photographing birds, a minimum of a 400mm lens, with a beanbag for the vehicle and a tripod for the land, should be used. See the previous section on "Photography on Safari" for more information.

There are several excellent illustrated field guides and references to the birds of Africa. The best identification guides are *Newman's Birds of Southern Africa* by Kenneth Newman (Struik); *Sasol Field Guide to Birds of Southern Africa* (Struik); *Birds of Kenya and Northern Tanzania* by Zimmerman, Turner and Pearson (A&C Black); and *Field Guide to the Birds of East Africa* by Terry Stevenson and John Fanshawe (Academic Press). The compact *Illustrated Checklist: Birds of Southern Africa* by von Perlo (Collins) is useful in that it covers Zambia and Malawi, as well as the region south of the Zambezi River. For visitors to Seychelles, Mauritius or Madagascar, the *Birds of the Indian Ocean Islands* by Sinclair and Langrand (Struik) is indispensable.

Among the groups of birds best represented in Africa are the herons (22 species), plovers (30), storks (8), bustards (21), francolins (36), eagles (23), vultures (11), doves (41), sandgrouse (12), turacos (23), barbets (44), hornbills (25), kingfishers (14) and shrikes (79).

Some of the most spectacular bird sights are the vast flocks of flamingos on East Africa's Rift Valley lakes, the hundreds of vultures which gather at the remains of kills, the breeding colonies of carmine bee-eaters on the Zambezi River, and the comical hornbills that often approach to within arm's reach. Add to this the world's largest bird (the ostrich), the world's heaviest flying bird (the kori bustard), jewel-like sunbirds, iridescent starlings and dazzling rollers, and you'll have an idea of what awaits you!

Between the months of November and March, Africa is visited by an estimated five million migratory birds from Europe and Asia. Among these are swallows, storks, kestrels, waders and warblers. At the same time, the majority of Africa's resident birds are breeding so they are most vociferous, and may often be seen at their nests or with young. It follows that this is the best time to visit if you are specifically interested in birds, but a trip at any time of year may yield sightings of hundreds of different species.

Safari Glossary

Ablution block: A building that contains showers, toilets and sinks, most often with separate facilities for men and women.

Acacia: Common, dry-country trees and shrubs armed with spines or curved thorns; they also have tiny, feathery leaflets.

Adaptation: The ability, through structural or functional characteristics, to improve the survival rate of an animal or plant in a particular habitat.

Aloe: A succulent plant of the lily family with thick, pointed leaves and spikes of red or yellow flowers.

Arboreal: Living in trees.

Avifauna: The birdlife of a region.

Banda: A basic shelter or hut, often constructed of reeds, bamboo, grass, etc.

Boma: A place of shelter, a fortified place, enclosure, community (East Africa).

Browse: To feed on leaves.

Calving season: A period during which the young of a particular species are born. Not all species have calving seasons. Most calving seasons occur shortly after the rainy season begins. Calving seasons can also differ for the same species from one park or reserve to another.

Camp: Camping sites; also refers to lodging in chalets, bungalows or tents in a remote location.

Canopy: The uppermost layer of a tree.

Caravan: A camping trailer.

Carnivore: An animal that lives by consuming the flesh of other animals.

Carrion: The remains of dead animals.

Crepuscular: Active at dusk or dawn.

Diurnal: Active during the day.

Endangered: An animal that is threatened with extinction.

Endemic: Native and restricted to a particular area.

Estrus: A state of sexual readiness in a female mammal when she is capable of conceiving.

Gestation: The duration of pregnancy.

Grazer: An animal that eats grass.

Habitat: An animal's or plant's surroundings that offers everything it needs to live.

Habituated: An animal that has been introduced to and has accepted the presence of human beings.

Herbivore: An animal that consumes plant matter for food.

Hide: A camouflaged structure from which one can view wildlife without being seen.

Home range: An area familiar to (utilized by) an adult animal but not marked or defended as a territory

Kopje (pronounced kopee): Rock formations that protrude from the savannah, usually caused by wind erosion (southern Africa).

Koppie: Same as kopje (east Africa).

Kraal: Same as boma (southern Africa).

Mammal: A warm-blooded animal that produces milk for its young.

Migratory: A species or population that moves seasonally to an area with predictably better food/grazing or water.

Midden: Usually, an accumulation of dung deposited in the same spot as a scent-marking behavior.

Nocturnal: Active during the night.

Omnivore: An animal that eats both plant and animal matter.

Pan: A shallow depression that seasonally fills with rainwater.

Predator: An animal that hunts and kills other animals for food.

Prey: An animal hunted by a predator for food.

Pride: A group or family of lions.

Rondavel: An African-style structure for accommodation.

Ruminant: A mammal with a complex stomach which therefore chews the cud.

Rutting: The behavioral pattern exhibited by male of the species during a time period when mating is most prevalent, e.g., impala, wildebeest.

Savannah: An open, grassy landscape with widely scattered trees.

Scavenger: An animal that lives off of carrion or the remains of animals killed by predators or which is dead from other causes.

Species: A group of plants or animals with specific characteristics in common, including the ability to reproduce among themselves.

Spoor: A track (i.e., footprint) or trail made by animals.

Symbiosis: An association of two different organisms in a relationship that may benefit one or both partners.

Tarmac: An asphalt-paved road.

Termitarium: A mound constructed by termite colonies.

Territory: An area occupied, scent-marked and defended from rivals of the same species.

Toilet, long-drop: A permanent bush toilet or "outhouse" in which a toilet seat has been placed over a hole that is dug about 6 feet (2m) deep.

Toilet, safari or short-drop: A temporary bush toilet, usually a toilet tent used on mobile tented safaris in which a toilet seat is placed over a hole that has been dug about 3 feet (1m) deep.

Tracking: Following and observing animal spoor by foot.

Tribe: A group of people united by traditional ties.

Troop: A group of apes or monkeys.

Ungulate: A hooved animal.

Veld: Southern African term for open land.

Wallow: The art of keeping cool and wet, usually in a muddy pool (i.e., rhinoceros, buffalo and hippopotamus).

Resource Directory

We have endeavored to make the information that follows as current as possible. However, Africa is undergoing constant change.

My reason for including the following information, much of which is likely to change, is to give you an idea of the right questions to ask — not to give you information that should be relied on as gospel. Wherever possible, a resource has been given to assist you in obtaining the most current information.

AIRPORT DEPARTURE TAXES

Ask your African tour operator, go on-line or call an airline that serves your destination, or the tourist office, embassy or consulate of the country(ies) in question, for current international and domestic airport taxes that are not included in your air ticket and must be paid with cash before departure. International airport departure taxes often must be paid in U.S. dollars or other hard currency, such as the Euro or British pounds. Be sure to have the exact amount required — often change will not be given. Domestic airport departure taxes may be required to be paid in hard currency as well, or in some cases may be payable in the local currency.

At the time of this writing, international airport departure taxes for the countries in this guide are listed below.

International Airport Departure Taxes

Country	Taxes due	Country	Taxes due
Botswana	*	Namibia	*
Burundi	$20.00	Rwanda	$20.00
Congo	$20.00	Seychelles	$40.00 approx
Egypt	*	South Africa	*
Ethiopia	*	Swaziland	$3.00
Kenya	*	Tanzania	$30.00
Lesotho	$30.00 approx	Uganda	$20.00
Madagascar	$20.00	Zambia	$30.00
Malawi	$20.00	Zimbabwe	*
Mauritius	$41.00 approx		
Mozambique	$20.00		

* Incuded in price of air ticket.

BANKS

Barclays and Standard Chartered Banks are located in most of these countries.

BANKING HOURS

Banks are usually open Monday-Friday mornings and early afternoons, sometimes on Saturday mornings, and closed on Sundays and holidays. Most hotels, lodges and camps are licensed to exchange foreign currency. Quite often, the best place to exchange money is at the airport upon arrival.

CREDIT CARDS

Major international credit cards are accepted by most top hotels, restaurants, lodges, permanent safari camps and shops. Visa and MasterCard are most widely accepted. American Express and Diner's Club are also accepted by most first-class hotels and many businesses. However, American Express is not often taken in more remote areas and camps. ATMs are in many locations in South Africa but are found in few other countries (except some major cities) covered in this book.

CURRENCIES

The currencies of Namibia, Lesotho and Swaziland are on a par with the South African Rand. The South African Rand may be accepted in Namibia, Lesotho and Swaziland; however, the currencies of Namibia, Lesotho and Swaziland are not accepted in South Africa.

Current rates for many African countries can usually be found on the Internet.

For U.S. dollars, bring only the newer "big faced" bills as the older bills are generally not accepted. Traveler's checks are *not* widely accepted.

CURRENCY RESTRICTIONS

A few African countries require visitors to complete currency declaration forms upon arrival; all foreign currency, travelers checks and other negotiable instruments must be recorded. These forms must be surrendered on departure. When you leave the country, the amount of currency you have with you must equal the amount with which you entered the country less the amount exchanged and recorded on your currency declaration form.

For some countries in Africa, the maximum amount of local currency that may be imported or exported is strictly enforced. Check for current restrictions by contacting the tourist offices, embassies or consulates of the countries you wish to visit.

In some countries, it is difficult (if not impossible) to exchange unused local currency back to foreign exchange (i.e., U.S. dollars). Therefore, it is best not to exchange more than you feel you will need.

The currencies used by the countries included in this guide are as follows:

Botswana	1 Pula	=	100 thebe
Burundi	1 Burundi Franc	=	100 centimes
Congo, D. R.	1 Zaire	=	100 makutas
Egypt	1 Egyptian Pound	=	100 piasers
Ethiopia	1 Birr	=	100 santim
Kenya	1 Kenya Shilling	=	100 cents
Lesotho	1 Loti	=	100 licente
Madagascar	1 Malagasy ariary	=	5 iraimbilanja
Malawi	1 Kwacha	=	100 tambala
Mauritius	1 Mauritius Rupee	=	100 cents
Namibia	1 Namibian Dollar	=	100 cents
Rwanda	1 Rwanda Franc	=	100 centimes
Seychelles	1 Seychelles Rupee	=	100 cents
South Africa	1 Rand	=	100 cents
Swaziland	1 Lilangeni	=	100 cents
Tanzania	1 Tanzania Shilling	=	100 cents
Uganda	1 Uganda Shilling	=	100 cents
Zambia	1 Kwacha	=	100 ngwee
Zimbabwe	1 Zimbabwe Dollar	=	100 cents

CUSTOMS

Australian Customs:

The Customs Information Centre: tel. (612) 6275 6666 (from outside Australia) and 1300 363 263 (from inside Australia); Monday–Friday, 8:30 a.m.–5:00 p.m.

Canadian Customs:

For a brochure on current Canadian customs requirements, ask for the brochure *I Declare* from your local customs office, which will be listed in the telephone book under "Government of Canada, Customs and Excise."

New Zealand Customs:

Custom House, Box 29, 50 Anzac Ave., Auckland; tel. 09 359 6655, fax 09 359 6735, www.customs.govt.az

United Kingdom:

HM Customs and Excise, Kent House, Upper Ground, London SE1 9PS

U.S. Customs:

For current information on products made from endangered species of wildlife that are not allowed to be imported, contact Traffic (U.S.A.), World Wildlife Fund, 1250 24th St. NW, Washington, DC 20037, tel. (202) 293-4800, and ask for the leaflet *Buyer Beware* for current restrictions.

DIPLOMATIC REPRESENTATIVES IN AFRICA

United States of America

Botswana: Tel: (267 31) 395-3982/3/4 Fax: (267 31) 395-6947
E-mail: consulargaboro@state.gov
United States Embassy, P.O. Box 90, Gaborone, Botswana

Burundi: Tel: (257) 223454 Fax: (257) 222926
United States Embassy, B.P. 1720, Ave. Des Etats-Unis, Bujumbura, Burundi

Congo: Tel: (243 88) 43608 Fax: (243 88) 41036
B.P. 697, 310 Ave. des Aviateurs, Kinshasa, Congo

Egypt: Tel: (202 2) 2797-3300 Fax: (202 2) 2797-3602
E-mail: CairoWebMaster@state.gov
United States Embassy Cairo, 8 Kamal El Din Salah Street, Garden City, Cairo, Egypt

Ethiopia: Tel: (251 11) 124-2424 Fax: (251 11) 124-2435
Email: pasaddis@state.gov
United States Embassy, Entoto Street, P.O. Box 1014, Addis Ababa, Ethiopia

Kenya: Tel: (254 20) 3636000 Fax: (254 20) 3633410
United States Embassy, United Nations Avenue
P.O. Box 606 Village Market Nairobi, Kenya 00621

Lesotho: Tel: (266 22) 312-666 Fax: (266 22) 310-116
Email: infomaseru@state.gov
United States Embassy, P.O. Box 333, Maseru 100, Lesotho

Madagascar: Tel: (261-20) 22 212-57, 212-73 209-56 Fax: (261-20) 22 345-39
United States Embassy, 14–16 Rue Raintovo, Antsahavola – Antananarivo 101, Madagascar

Malawi: Tel: (265) 773 166 Fax: (265) 770 471
United States Embassy, P.O. Box 30016, 16 Jomo Kenyatta Road, Lilongwe 3, Malawi

Mauritius: Tel: (230) 202-4400 Fax: (230) 208-9534
E-mail: usembass@intnet.mu
United States Embassy, Rogers Bldg., Fourth Floor, John Kennedy Ave., P.O. Box
544, Port Louis, Mauritius

Mozambique: Tel: (258-21) 49-27-97 Fax: (258-21) 49-01-14
United States Embassy, Avenida Kenneth Kaunda 193, Caixa Postal 783, Maputo,
Mozambique

Namibia: Tel: (264) 61 295 8500 Fax: (264) 61 295 8603
United States Embassy, Ausplan Bldg., 14 Lossen St., Private Bag 12029,
Windhoek, Namibia

Rwanda: Tel: (250) 505 601, 505 602, 505 603 / Ext 3315 Fax: (250) 507 143,
57 2128
E-mail: irckigali@state.gov
United States Embassy, Blvd. de la Révolution, B.P. 28, Kigali, Rwanda

Seychelles: Tel: (248) 22 22 56 Fax: (248) 22 51 59
E-mail: usoffice@seychelles.net
U.S. Consular Agency, Victoria House, 1st Floor, Room 112, P.O. Box 251,
Victoria, Seychelles

South Africa: Tel: (27 12) 431 4000 Fax: (27 12) 342 2299
United States Embassy, P.O. Box 9536, 877 Pretorius St., Pretoria, South Africa
Johannesburg Consulate: Tel: (27 11) 644 8000 Fax: (27 11) 646 6916
P.O. Box 1762, Houghton 2041, 1 River St, Killarney, Johannesburg, South Africa
Cape Town Consulate: Tel: (27 21) 702-7300 Fax: (27 21) 702-7493
PostNet Suite 50, Private Bag x26, Tokai 7966, 2 Reddam Ave, Westlake 7945,
South Africa

Swaziland: Tel: (268) 404-6441/5 Fax: (268) 404-5959
United States Embassy, 2350 Mbabane Place, P.O. Box 199, Mbabane, Swaziland

Tanzania: Tel: (255 22) 266 8001 / Ext 4122 Fax: (255 51) 266 8247
E-mail: DRSacs@state.gov
United States Embassy, 686 Old Bagamoyo Road, Msasani, P.O. Box 9123, Dar es
Salaam, Tanzania

Uganda: Tel: (256 41) 259 791 Fax: (256 41) 258 451
E-mail: Kampalauscitizen@state.gov.
United States Embassy, 1577 Gaba Road, Kansanga, P.O. Box 7007, Kampala,
Uganda

Zambia: Tel: (260 1) 250 955 Fax: (260 1) 252 225
Email: ConsularLusaka@state.gov
United States Embassy, Independence & United National Aves., P.O. Box 31617,
Lusaka, Zambia

Zimbabwe: Tel: (263 4) 250593/4 Fax: (263 4) 796488
Email: consularharare@state.gov
United States Embassy, 172 Herbert Chitepo Ave., P.O. Box 3340, Harare, Zimbabwe

Canada

Botswana: Tel: (267) 3904 411 Fax: (267) 3904 411
Consulate of Canada, Vision Hire Bldg, Queens Road, P.O. Box 882, Gaborone,
Botswana

Congo: Tel: (243) 89895 0310/0311/0312 Fax: (243) 81301 6515
Email: knsha@international.gc.ca
The Embassy of Canada, 17 Avenue Pumbu, Commune de la Gombe, (P.O. Box
8341) Kinshasa, Democratic Republic of Congo

Egypt: Tel: (20 2) 2791 8700 Fax: (20 2) 2791 8860
E-mail: cairo@international.gc.ca
The Embassy of Canada, 26 Kamel El Shenawy St., Garden City, P.O. Box 1667,
Cairo, Egypt

Ethiopia: Tel (251 11) 371 3022 Fax: (251 11) 371 3033
Email: addis@international.gc.ca
The Embassy of Canada, Old Airport Area, Nefas Silk Lafto Sub City, Kebele 04,
House No. 122, Addis Ababa, Ethiopia

Kenya: Tel: (254 20) 366 3000 Fax: (254 20) 366 3900
E-mail: nrobi@international.gc.ca
The High Commission of Canada, Limuru Road, Gigiri, P.O. Box 1013, 00621
Nairobi, Kenya

Madagascar: Tel: (261 20) 22 425 59 Fax: (261 20) 22 425 06
Email: consulat.canada@dts.mg
The Consulate of Canada, c/o Madagascar Minerals S.A., Villa 3H, Lot II-J-169,
Ivandry, Antananarivo, Madagascar

Mauritius: Tel: (230) 212-5500 Fax: (230) 208-3391
E-mail: canada@intnet.mu
The Consulate of Canada, 18 Jules Koenig Street, P.O. Box 209, Port Louis,
Mauritius

Mozambique: Tel: (258 21) 492 623 Fax: (258 21) 492 667
Email: mputo@international.gc.ca
The High Commission of Canada, Avenida Kenneth Kaunda, No. 1138, P.O. Box
1578, Maputo, Mozambique

Seychelles: Tel: (248) 225 225 Fax: (248) 225 127
The High Commission of Canada, 38 Mirambo St., Garden Ave., P.O. Box 1022,
Victoria, Mahe, Seychelles

South Africa: Tel: (27 12) 422 3000 Fax: (27 12) 422 3052
E-mail: pret@international.gc.ca
The High Commission of Canada, Private Bag X13, 1103 Arcadia St., Hatfield 0028, Pretoria, South Africa
Johannesburg: Tel: (27 11) 442 3130 Fax: (27 11) 442 3325
E-mail: jobrg@international.gc.ca
Canadian High Commission, P.O. Box 1394, Parklands, 2121 Johannesburg, South Africa

Tanzania: Tel: (255 22) 216 3300 Fax: (255 22) 211 6897
E-mail: dslam@international.gc.ca
The High Commission of Canada, 38 Mirambo St., P.O. Box 1022, Dar es Salaam, Tanzania

Uganda: Tel: (256 41) 258141 Fax: (256 41) 349484
E-mail: canada.consulate@utlonline.co.ug
The Consulate of Canada, IPS Building, Plot 14, Parliament Ave., P.O. Box 20115, Kampala, Uganda

Zambia: Tel: (260 1) 250 833 Fax: (260 1) 254 176
Email: Isaka@international.gc.ca
The High Commission of Canada, 5199 United Nations Ave., P.O. Box 31313, Lusaka, Zambia 10101

Zimbabwe: Tel: (263 4) 252181/5 Fax: (263 4) 252186
E-mail: hrare@international.gc.ca
The Embassy of Canada, 45 Baines Ave., P.O. Box 1430, Harare, Zimbabwe

United Kingdom

Botswana: Tel: (267) 3952841 Fax: (267) 3956105
E-mail: bhc@botsnet.bw
British High Commission, Private Bag 0023, Plot No. 1079-1084, Queens Road, Main Mall, Gaborone, Botswana

Burundi: Tel: (257) 22 246 478 Fax: (257) 22 246 479
Email: belo@cni.cbinf.com
British Liaison Office, Building Old East, Parcelle No. 1-2, Place de l'independence, Bujumbura, Burundi
Permanent staff in Kigali, Rwanda

Congo: Tel: (243 81) 715 0761 Fax: (243 81) 346 4291 E-mail: ambrit@ic.cd
British Embassy, 83 Avenue du Roi Baudouin, Kinshasa, Gombe, Congo

Ethiopia: Tel: (251 11) 661 2354 Fax: (251 11) 661 0588
Email: BritishEmbassy.AddisAbaba@fco.gov.uk
British Embassy, Comoros Street, P.O. Box 858, Addis Ababa, Ehtiopia

Kenya: Tel: (254 20) 284 4000 Fax: (254 20) 284 4033
British High Commission, Upper Hill Road, P.O. Box 30465, Nairobi, Kenya

Lesotho: Tel: (266 22) 313929 Fax: (266 22) 310254
E-mail: pmb@leo.co.ls
British Honorary Consul, Sentinel Park, United Nations Road, Maseru, Lesotho

Madagascar: Tel: (261 20) 24 521 80 Fax: (261 20) 24 263 29
E-mail: ricana@wanadoo.mg
British Honorary Consul, BP 12193, Ankorandrano, Antananarivo 101, Madagscar

Malawi: Tel: (265) 772400 Fax: (265) 772657
E-mail: bhclilongwe@fco.gov.uk
British High Commission, P.O. Box 30042, Lilongwe 3, Malawi

Mauritius: Tel: (230) 202 9400 Fax: (230) 202 9408
E-mail: bhc@bow.intnet.mu
British High Commission, Les Cascades Building, Edith Cavell Street, P.O. Box 1063, Port Louis, Mauritius

Mozambique: Tel: (258 21) 356000 Fax: (258 21) 356060
Email: bhc@consular@tvcabo.co.mz
British High Commission, Av Vladimir I Lenine 310, Caixa Postal 55, Maputo, Mozambique

Namibia: Tel: (264 61) 274800 Fax: (264 61) 228895
Email: general.windhoek@fco.gov.uk
British High Commission, 116 Robert Mugabe Ave., P.O. Box 22202, Windhoek, Namibia

Rwanda: Tel: (250) 584098 Fax: (250) 582044
Email: embassy.kigali@fco.gov.uk
British Embassy, Parcelle No. 1131, Boulevard de l'Umuganda, Kacyiru-Sud, BP 576, Kigali, Rwanda

Seychelles: Tel: (248) 283 666 Fax: (248) 283 657
E-mail: bhcvictoria@fco.gov.uk
British High Commission, Oliaji Trade Centre, Francis Rachel Street, P.O. Box 161, Victoria, Mahe, Seychelles

South Africa: Tel: (27 11) 327 0015 Fax: (27 21) 425 1427
Dunkeld Corner, 275 Jan Smuts Av., Dunkeld West 2196, Johannesburg 2001, South Africa
Cape Town: Tel: (27 21) 425 3670 Fax: (27 21) 425 1427
British Consulate General, 15th Floor, Southern Life Center, 8 Riebeek Street, Cape Town 8001 South Africa
British High Commission, 255 Hill St., Arcadia 0002, Pretoria, South Africa

Swaziland: Tel: (268) 551 6247 Fax: same
Email: nonbritcon@realnet.co.sz
British Honorary Consul, P.O. Box A41, Eveni, Mbabane, H103 Swaziland

Tanzania: Tel: (255 22) 211 0101 Fax: (255 22) 211 0102
Email: bhc.dar@fco.gov.uk
British High Commission, Umoja House, Garden Ave., P.O. Box 9200, Dar es Salaam, Tanzania

Uganda: Tel: (256 31) 2312000 or (256 41) 257304
Email: Consular.kampala@fco.gov.uk
British High Commission, 4 Windsor Loop, P.O. Box 7070, Kampala, Uganda

Zambia: Tel: (260 1) 251133 Fax: (260 1) 253798
Email: BHC-Lusaka@fco.gov.uk
British High Commission, 5210 Independence Ave., P.O. Box 50050, Lusaka, Zambia

Zimbabwe: Tel: (263 4) 772990 or 774700 Fax: (263 4) 774617
British Embassy, Corner House, Samora Machel Ave., Leopold Takawira St., P.O. Box 4490, Harare, Zimbabwe

DUTY-FREE ALLOWANCES

Contact the nearest tourist office or embassy for current, duty-free import allowances for the country(ies) that you intend to visit. The duty-free allowances vary; however, the following may be used as a general guideline: 1–2 liters (approximately 1–2 qt./33.8-67.4 fl. oz.) of spirits, one carton (200) of cigarettes or 100 cigars.

ELECTRICITY

Electric current is 220–240-volt AC 50 Hz. Adapters: Three-prong square or round plugs are most commonly used.

HEALTH

Malarial risk exists in all of the countries included in this guidebook (except for Lesotho and much of South Africa), so be sure to take your malaria pills (unless advised by your doctor not to take them), as prescribed before, during and after your trip. Contact your doctor, an immunologist or the Centers for Disease Control and Prevention in Atlanta (toll-free tel. 1-888-232-3228, fax 1-888-232-3299, web site: www.cdc.gov) for the best prophylaxis for your itinerary. Use an insect repellent. Wear long-sleeve shirts and slacks for further protection, especially at sunset and during the evening.

Bilharzia is a disease that infests most lakes and rivers on the continent but can be easily cured. Do not walk barefoot along the shore or wade or swim in a stream, river or lake unless you know for certain it is free of bilharzia. Bilharzia does not exist in salt water or in fast flowing rivers or along shorelines that have waves. A species of snail is involved in the reproductive cycle of bilharzia, and the snails are more often found near reeds and in slow-moving water. If you feel you may have contracted the disease, go to your doctor for a blood test. If diagnosed in its early stages, it is easily cured.

Wear a hat and bring sunblock to protect yourself from the tropical sun. Drink plenty of fluids and limit alcohol consumption at high altitudes.

In hot weather, do not drink alcohol and limit the consumption of coffee and tea unless you drink plenty of water.

For further information, obtain a copy of "Health Information for International Travel" from the U.S. Government Printing Office, Washington, DC 20402.

INOCULATIONS

See "Visa and Inoculations Requirements" on page 66.

INSURANCE

Travel insurance packages often include a combination of emergency evacuation, medical, baggage, and trip cancellation. I feel that it is imperative that all travelers to Africa cover themselves fully with an insurance package from a reputable provider. Many tour operators require at least emergency evacuation insurance as a requirement for joining a safari. The peace of mind afforded by such insurance far outweighs the cost. Ask your Africa travel specialist for information on relatively inexpensive group-rate insurance.

METRIC SYSTEM OF WEIGHTS AND MEASURES

The metric system is used in Africa. The U.S. equivalents are listed in the conversion chart below.

MEASUREMENT CONVERSIONS

1 inch	=	2.54 centimeters (cm)
1 foot	=	0.305 meter (m)
1 mile	=	1.60 kilometers (km)
1 square mile	=	2.59 square kilometers (km^2)
1 quart liquid	=	0.946 liter (l)
1 ounce	=	28 grams (g)
1 pound	=	0.454 kilogram (kg)
1 cm	=	0.39 inch (in.)
1 m	=	3.28 feet (ft.)
1 km	=	0.62 mile (mi.)
1 acre	=	0.4 hectares
1 km^2	=	0.3861 square mile (sq. mi.)
1 l	=	1.057 quarts (qt.)
1 g	=	0.035 ounce (oz.)
1 kg	=	2.2 pounds (lb.)

TEMPERATURE CONVERSIONS

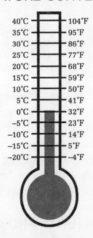

40°C	104°F
35°C	95°F
30°C	86°F
25°C	77°F
20°C	68°F
15°C	59°F
10°C	50°F
5°C	41°F
0°C	32°F
−5°C	23°F
−10°C	14°F
−15°C	5°F
−20°C	−4°F

TEMPERATURE CONVERSION FORMULAS
To convert degrees Centigrade into degrees Fahrenheit:
Multiply Centigrade by 1.8 and add 32.
To convert degrees Fahrenheit into degrees Centigrade:
Subtract 32 from Fahrenheit and divide by 1.8.

MONEY

One way to obtain additional funds is to have money sent by telegraph international money order (Western Union), telexed through a bank or sent via international courier (i.e., DHL). Do not count on finding ATM machines, except in South Africa and perhaps in some major cities in other countries. Traveler's checks are not widely accepted except at most airport banks.

SHOPPING

If you like bartering, bring clothing (new denims and T-shirts are great) or pens to trade for souvenirs. This works particularly well at roadside stands and in small villages in East and Central Africa, although the villagers are becoming more discerning in their tastes.

SOME SHOPPING IDEAS

Botswana: Baskets, wood carvings, pottery, tapestries and rugs. There are curio shops in many safari camps, hotels and lodges.

Burundi: Crafts available in numerous shops.

Congo, Democratic Republic of: Wood carvings, malachite, copper goods, semiprecious stones and baskets.

Kenya: Makonde and Akomba ebony wood carvings, soapstone carvings, colorful kangas and kikois (cloth wraps) and beaded belts. In Mombasa, Zanzibar chests, gold and silverwork, brasswork, Arab jewelry and antiques.

Lesotho: Basotho woven carpets are known worldwide, tapestry weaving and conical straw hats.

Malawi: Wood carvings, woven baskets.

Mauritius: Intricately detailed, handmade model sailing ships of camphor or teak; pareos (colorful light cotton wraps); knitwear, textiles, T-shirts, Mauritian dolls; tea; rum; and spices.

Namibia: Semiprecious stones and jewelry, karakul wool products, wood carvings, ostrich eggshell necklaces and beadwork.

Seychelles: Coco-de-mer nuts (may be purchased with a government permit that is not difficult to obtain), batik prints, spices for Creole cooking and locally produced jewelry, weaving and basketry.

South Africa: Diamonds, gold, wood carvings, dried flowers, wire art, wildlife paintings and sculpture, and wine.

Swaziland: Beautiful handwoven tapestries; baskets; earthenware and stoneware; and mouth-blown, handcrafted glass animals and tableware.

Tanzania: Makonde carvings, meerschaum pipes and tanzanite.

Uganda: Wood carvings.

Zambia: Wood carvings, statuettes, semiprecious stones and copper souvenirs.

Zimbabwe: Carvings of wood, stone and Zimbabwe's unique verdite; intricate baskets; wildlife paintings and sculpture; ceramic ware; and crocheted garments.

SHOPPING HOURS

Shops are usually open Monday-Friday from 8:00 or 9:00 a.m. until 5:00 to 6:00 p.m. and from 9:00 a.m. until 1:00 p.m. on Saturdays. Shops in the coastal cities of Kenya and Tanzania often close midday for siesta. Use the shopping hours given above as a general guideline; exact times can vary within the respective country.

THEFT

The number one rule in preventing theft on vacation is to leave all unnecessary valuables at home. What you must bring, lock in room safes or safety deposit boxes when not in use. Carry all valuables in your carry-on luggage — do not put any valuables in your checked luggage. Theft in Africa is generally no worse than in Europe or the United States, but consider leaving showy gold watches and jewelry at home. One difference is that Africans are poorer and may steal things that most American or European thieves would consider worthless. Be careful in all African cities (like most large cities in North America) and do not go walking around the streets at night.

TEMPERATURE AND RAINFALL

The temperature and rainfall charts on the following pages give average high and low temperatures and average rainfall for each month of the year for a number of locations. Keep in mind that these are average temperatures; you should expect variations of at least 7°F (5°C) from the averages listed in the charts. Also keep in mind that at higher altitudes you should expect cooler temperatures. This is why many parks and reserves in Africa can be warm during the day and cool to cold at night. The most common packing mistake safariers make is not bringing enough warm layers of clothing!

AVERAGE MONTHLY TEMPERATURES
MIN/MAX IN FAHRENHEIT

CITY	JAN	FEB	MAR	APR	MAY	JUN	JUL	AUG	SEP	OCT	NOV	DEC
EAST AFRICA												
Dar-Es-Salaam	77/88	76/87	76/89	74/87	72/85	68/85	66/84	66/84	68/84	68/86	73/87	76/88
Dodoma	66/86	66/85	64/84	64/84	62/83	57/82	57/79	57/81	59/85	63/88	64/89	65/88
Kigoma	67/81	68/82	68/82	67/82	68/83	67/82	63/83	65/85	67/86	69/85	68/81	67/80
Nairobi	55/78	56/80	58/78	58/76	56/74	54/70	51/70	52/71	53/76	55/77	56/74	55/75
Mombasa	75/88	76/88	77/89	76/87	75/84	74/83	71/81	71/81	72/83	74/85	75/86	76/87
Kampala	65/84	65/83	64/82	64/81	63/79	63/78	63/78	62/78	63/81	63/82	62/81	62/81
Kabale	49/76	50/76	50/75	51/74	51/73	50/73	48/75	49/75	50/76	51/75	50/73	50/73
Kigali	43/68	48/68	46/68	43/68	41/68	37/68	41/68	39/70	37/70	43/68	37/68	39/68
Bujumbura	66/83	66/83	66/83	66/83	66/83	65/85	64/85	65/87	67/89	68/87	67/83	67/83
SOUTHERN AFRICA												
Harare	61/79	61/79	59/79	56/79	50/75	45/71	45/71	47/75	54/80	58/84	60/82	61/79
Victoria Falls	65/85	64/85	62/85	57/84	49/81	43/76	42/77	47/82	55/89	62/91	64/90	64/86
Hwange	64/85	64/84	62/85	56/83	47/80	42/76	40/76	45/81	54/88	61/90	64/89	64/85
Kariba	71/88	71/88	69/88	65/87	58/84	53/80	52/79	57/84	67/91	74/95	74/93	72/89
Mana Pools	71/89	71/89	70/89	67/88	62/85	57/81	56/81	59/86	66/92	73/97	74/95	72/91
Bulawayo	61/82	61/81	60/80	57/80	50/75	46/70	46/71	49/75	55/82	59/86	61/85	61/83
Maun	66/90	66/88	64/88	57/88	48/82	43/77	43/77	48/82	55/91	64/95	66/93	66/90
Lusaka	63/78	63/79	62/79	59/79	55/78	50/73	49/73	53/77	59/84	64/88	64/85	63/81
S. Luangwa	68/90	68/88	66/90	64/90	66/88	54/86	52/84	54/86	59/95	68/104	72/99	72/91
Windhoek	63/86	63/84	59/81	55/77	48/72	45/68	45/68	46/73	54/79	57/84	61/84	63/88
Swakopmund	54/77	54/73	54/73	59/77	59/77	64/82	59/82	54/77	54/77	54/77	54/77	54/77
Johannesburg	59/79	57/77	55/75	52/72	46/66	41/61	41/61	45/66	48/72	54/75	55/77	57/77
Durban	70/82	70/82	68/82	63/79	55/75	50/73	50/73	54/73	59/73	63/75	64/77	68/81
Cape Town	61/79	59/79	57/77	54/73	50/68	46/64	45/63	45/64	46/66	50/70	55/75	59/77

AVERAGE MONTHLY TEMPERATURES
MIN/MAX IN CENTIGRADE

CITY	JAN	FEB	MAR	APR	MAY	JUN	JUL	AUG	SEP	OCT	NOV	DEC
EAST AFRICA												
Dar-es-Salaam	25/32	25/32	24/32	23/31	22/29	20/29	19/28	19/28	19/28	21/29	23/31	24/31
Dodoma	18/29	18/29	18/28	18/28	16/28	15/27	13/27	14/27	15/29	17/31	18/31	18/31
Kigoma	19/27	20/27	20/27	19/27	19/28	188/29	17/28	18/29	19/30	21/29	20/27	19/26
Nairobi	12/25	13/26	14/25	14/24	13/22	12/21	11/21	11/21	11/24	14/25	13/24	13/24
Mombasa	24/32	24/32	25/32	24/31	23/28	23/28	22/27	22/27	22/28	23/29	24/29	24/30
Kampala	18/28	18/28	18/27	18/26	25/17	26/18	26/18	26/17	27/17	27/17	27/17	27/17
Kabale	9/24	11/24	11/24	11/24	11/23	10/23	9/23	10/23	10/24	11/24	11/24	10/24
Kigali						No Numbers						
Bujumbura	19/28	19/28	19/28	19/28	19/28	18/29	18/29	18/31	19/32	20/31	19/29	19/29
SOUTHERN AFRICA												
Harare	17/27	17/27	15/27	13/27	10/24	8/22	7/22	8/24	12/27	14/29	16/28	16/27
Bulawayo	17/28	17/28	16/27	14/27	10/24	8/22	8/22	10/24	12/28	15/30	16/31	16/29
Victoria Falls	18/29	17/29	17/29	14/29	9/27	5/24	7/27	12/31	16/32	18/32	18/31	18/30
Hwange	18/29	18/29	17/29	14/29	9/27	5/24	5/24	7/27	12/31	16/32	16/32	18/30
Kariba	22/31	21/31	21/31	19/31	15/29	12/27	11/26	14/29	19/33	23/35	24/34	22/32
Mana Pools	22/32	21/32	21/32	20/31	17/29	14/27	13/27	15/30	19/34	23/36	23/35	22/33
Maun	19/32	19/31	18/31	14/31	9/28	6/25	6/25	9/28	13/33	18/35	19/34	19/34
Lusaka	17/26	17/26	17/26	15/26	13/25	10/23	10/23	12/25	15/30	18/31	18/30	18/30
S. Luangwa	20/32	20/31	19/32	18/32	19/31	12/30	11/29	12/30	15/35	20/40	22/37	22/33
Windhoek	17/30	17/29	15/27	13/25	9/22	7/20	7/20	8/23	12/26	14/29	16/29	17/31
Swakopmund	12/25	12/23	12/23	15/25	15/25	18/28	15/28	12/25	12/25	12/25	12/25	12/25
Johannesburg	15/26	14/25	13/24	11/22	8/19	5/16	5/16	7/19	9/22	12/24	13/25	14/25
Durban	21/28	21/28	20/28	17/26	13/24	10/23	10/23	12/23	15/23	17/24	18/25	20/27
Cape Town	16/26	15/26	14/25	12/23	10/20	8/18	7/17	7/18	8/19	10/21	13/24	15/25

AVERAGE MONTHLY RAINFALL IN INCHES

CITY	JAN	FEB	MAR	APR	MAY	JUN	JUL	AUG	SEP	OCT	NOV	DEC
EAST AFRICA												
Dar-es-Salaam	2.6	2.6	5.1	11.4	7.4	1.3	1.2	1.0	1.2	1.6	2.9	3.6
Dodoma	6.0	4.3	5.4	1.9	0.2	0	0	0	0	0.2	0.9	3.6
Kigoma	4.8	5.0	5.9	5.1	1.7	0.2	0.1	0.2	0.7	1.9	5.6	5.3
Nairobi	1.5	2.5	4.9	8.3	6.2	1.8	0.7	0.9	1.3	2.2	4.3	3.4
Mombasa	1.1	0.8	2.4	7.7	12.7	4.7	3.5	2.6	2.6	3.4	3.8	2.4
Kampala	1.8	2.4	5.1	6.9	5.8	2.9	1.8	3.4	3.6	3.8	4.8	3.9
Kabale	2.4	3.8	5.2	4.9	3.6	1.2	0.8	2.4	3.7	3.9	4.4	3.4
Kigali	3.5	3.5	4.1	6.5	4.9	1.0	.3	.8	2.4	3.9	3.9	3.5
Bujumbura	3.7	4.4	4.8	4.9	2.3	0.4	0.3	0.4	1.5	2.5	3.9	4.4
SOUTHERN AFRICA												
Harare	7.7	7.1	4.5	1.2	0.5	0.2	0	0.1	0.3	1.2	3.8	6.4
Bulawayo	5.6	4.4	3.3	0.8	0.4	0.1	0	0	0.2	0.8	3.3	4.9
Victoria Falls	6.6	5	2.8	1.0	0.1	0	0	0	0.7	1.1	2.5	6.8
Hwange	5.7	5.1	2.3	0.8	0.1	0	0	0	0.1	0.8	2.2	5.0
Kariba	7.5	6.2	4.4	1.2	0.2	0	0	0	0	0.7	2.9	6.9
Mana Pools	8.7	7.1	4.2	1.0	0.2	0	0	0	0	0.5	2.3	9.1
Maun	4.3	3.2	2.8	1.0	0.3	0.1	0	0	0	1.2	2.0	3.8
Lusaka	9.1	7.6	5.7	0.7	0.2	0	0	0	0	0.4	3.6	5.9
S. Luangwa	7.7	11.3	5.6	3.6	0	0	0	0	0	2.0	4.3	4.3
Windhoek	1.7	2.0	2.2	1.1	0.2	0.1	0.1	0.1	0.1	0.4	0.9	1.0
Swakopmund	0.5	0.5	0.5	0.4	0.4	0.4	0.3	0.4	0.4	0.6	0.6	0.4
Johannesburg	4.5	3.8	2.9	2.5	0.9	0.3	0.3	0.2	0.1	2.7	4.6	4.3
Durban	5.1	4.5	5.3	4.2	2.0	1.2	1.4	1.7	2.4	3.9	4.5	4.6
Cape Town	0.6	0.7	0.7	2.0	3.5	3.3	3.5	3.1	2.0	1.4	0.5	0.6

AVERAGE MONTHLY RAINFALL IN MILLIMETERS

CITY	JAN	FEB	MAR	APR	MAY	JUN	JUL	AUG	SEP	OCT	NOV	DEC
EAST AFRICA												
Dar-es-Salaam	66	66	130	292	188	33	33	26	31	42	74	91
Dodoma	152	110	138	49	5	0	0	0	0	5	24	92
Kigoma	123	128	150	130	44	5	3	5	19	28	143	135
Nairobi	39	65	125	211	158	47	15	24	32	53	110	87
Mombasa	25	19	65	197	320	120	90	65	65	87	98	62
Kampala	47	61	130	175	148	73	45	85	90	96	122	99
Kabale	58	97	130	125	92	28	20	58	98	99	110	87
Kigali	90	90	105	165	125	25	7	20	60	100	100	90
Bujumbura	95	110	121	125	56	11	5	11	37	65	100	115
SOUTHERN AFRICA												
Harare	196	179	118	28	14	3	0	3	5	28	97	163
Bulawayo	143	110	85	19	10	3	0	0	5	20	81	123
Victoria Falls	168	126	70	24	3	1	0	0	2	27	64	174
Hwange	145	129	57	20	3	0	0	0	2	21	56	127
Kariba	192	158	113	30	4	1	1	0	1	18	74	175
Mana Pools	221	181	107	26	4	0	0	0	1	13	59	231
Maun	110	80	70	25	7	3	0	0	0	30	50	95
Lusaka	232	192	144	18	3	0	0	0	0	11	92	150
S. Luangwa	195	287	141	91	0	0	0	0	0	50	108	110
Windhoek	43	53	56	28	5	3	3	3	3	10	23	26
Swakopmund	12	15	12	10	10	10	7	9	11	15	16	11
Johannesburg	112	96	74	61	23	8	8	5	3	69	117	109
Durban	130	114	135	107	54	31	36	43	61	99	114	117
Cape Town	15	18	18	50	90	85	90	80	50	36	13	15

TIME ZONES

EST = Eastern Standard Time (east coast of the United States)
GMT = Greenwich Mean Time (Greenwich, England)

EST + 3/GMT – 2
Cape Verde

EST + 4/GMT – 1
Guinea-Bissau

EST + 5/GMT
Algeria
Ascension
Burkina-Faso
The Gambia
Ghana
Guinea
Ivory Coast
Liberia
Mali
Mauritania
Morocco
St. Helena
São Tomé & Principe
Senegal
Sierra Leone
Togo
Tristan de Cunha

EST + 6/GMT + 1
Angola
Benin
Cameroon
Central African Republic
Chad
Congo
Democratic Republic
 of the Congo (western)
Equatorial Guinea
Gabon
Niger
Nigeria
Tunisia

EST + 7/GMT + 2
Botswana
Burundi
Democratic Republic of
 the Congo (eastern)
Egypt
Lesotho
Libya
Malawi

Mozambique
Namibia
Rwanda
South Africa
Sudan
Swaziland
Zambia
Zimbabwe

EST + 8/GMT + 3
Comoros
Djibouti
Eritrea
Ethiopia
Kenya
Madagascar
Somalia
Tanzania
Uganda

EST + 9/GMT + 4
Mauritius
Reunion
Seychelles

TIPPING

A 10% tip is recommended at restaurants for good service where a service charge is not included in the bill. For advice on what tips are appropriate for guides, safari camps and lodges, ask the Africa specialist booking your safari.

Visa and Inoculation Requirements

Travelers must obtain visas and have proof that they have received certain inoculations for entry into some African countries.

VISA REQUIREMENTS				INOCULATIONS
COUNTRY	U.S.	CANADA	U.K.	
Botswana	No	No	No	Yellow fever**
Egypt	Yes	Yes	Yes	Yellow fever**
Ethiopia	Yes	Yes	Yes	Yellow fever
Kenya***	Yes	Yes	Yes	Yellow fever**
Lesotho	No	No	No	Yellow fever**
Madagascar	Yes	Yes	Yes	Yellow fever**
Malawi	No	No	No	Yellow fever**
Mozambique	Yes	Yes	Yes	Yellow fever**
Namibia	No	No	No	Yellow fever**
Rwanda	No	No	No	Yellow fever
South Africa*	No	No	No	Yellow fever**
Swaziland	No	No	No	Yellow fever**
Tanzania***	Yes	Yes	Yes	Yellow fever
Zanzibar (Tanzania)				Yellow fever
Uganda	Yes	Yes	Yes	Yellow fever
Zambia***	Yes	Yes	Yes	Yellow fever**
Zimbabwe***	Yes	Yes	Yes	Yellow fever**

Notes:
1. Some optional vaccinations include: (a) hepatitis A, (b) hepatitis B, (c) typhoid, (d) tetanus, (e) meningitis, (f) oral polio.
2. Anti-malaria: It is not mandatory but is strongly urged. Anti-malaria is a tablet, not an inoculation. Malaria exists in almost all of the countries listed above.
3. Cholera: The cholera vaccination is not a guaranteed inoculation against infection, and most countries do not require a cholera vaccination for direct travel from the United States. Check with your local doctor and with embassies of the respective countries. Some require proof of a cholera vaccination even if you are arriving directly from the United States.
4. **Yellow fever: Only if arriving from infected area (i.e., Nigeria).
5. ***: Visa may be obtained on arrival by paying a visa fee.
6. Complete necessary visa forms and return with your valid passport (valid for at least six months after travel dates) to the embassy or consulate concerned or use a visa service.
7. *South Africa: Yellow fever vaccination is required if arriving from Kenya, Tanzania or Uganda. Visitors must have at least two consecutive blank pages in their passport.

Suggested Reading

GENERAL/WILDLIFE/AFRICA

Africa, John Reader, 2001 (USA: National Geographic)

Africa, Michael Poliza, 2006 (USA: teNeues Publishing Company)

Africa, A Continent Revealed, Rene Gordon, 1997 (U.K.: New Holland)

Africa, A Biography of the Continent, John Reader, 1998 (USA: Penguin)

Africa, An Artists Journal, Kim Donaldson, 2001 (U.K.: Pavilion; USA: Watson Guptil)

Africa in History, Basil Davidson, 2001 (U.K.: Phoenix Press)

Africa, Timeless Soul, Wilby, 1996 (U.K.: Pan MacMillian)

Africa, Biography of the Continent, John Reader, 1998 (U.K.: Penguin)

African Ceremonies, Carol Beckwith and Angela Fisher, 1999 (USA: Harry N. Abrams)

African Elephants, Daryl and Sharna Balfour, 1997 (South Africa: Struik)

African Folklore, Best of, A. Savoury, 1972 (South Africa: Struik)

African Game Trails, T. Roosevelt, 1983 (USA: St. Martins Press)

African Insect Life, A. Skaiffe, John Ledger and Anthony Barnister, revised 1997 (South Africa: Struik)

African Laughter, Doris Lessing, 1992 (U.K.: Flamingo)

African Magic, Heidi Holland, 2001 (U.K.: Viking/Allen Lane)

African Nights, K. Gallmann, 1995 (U.K.: Penguin Books)

African Predators, Gus Mills, 2001 (South Africa: Struik)

African Trilogy, P. Matthiessen, 2000 (U.K.: Harvill Press)

Africa's Big Five, William Taylor and Gerald Hinde, 2001 (South Africa: Struik)

Africa's Elephant, A Biography, Martin Meredith, 2001 (U.K.: Hodder & Stoughton)

Africa's Top Wildlife Countries, Mark Nolting, 2008 (USA: Global Travel)

Behaviour Guide to African Animals, Richard Estes, 1995 (South Africa: Russel Friedman Books; USA: University California Press)

Birds of Kenya & Tanzania, Zimmerman, Turner and Pearson, 1996 (U.K.: A & C Black)

Birds of the Indian Ocean Islands, I. Sinclair and O. Langrand, 1998 (South Africa: Struik)

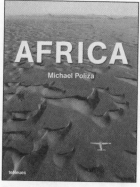

By Michael Poliza
ISBN: 978-3-8327-9127-8

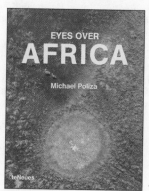

By Michael Poliza
ISBN: 978-3-8327-9209-1

Creatures of Habit, Peter Apps and Richard du Toit, 2000 (South Africa: Struik)

Elephant Memories, Cynthia Moss, 1999 (USA: Chicago University Press)

Elephants for Africa, Randall Moore, 2000 (South Africa: Abu Publications)

Eyes Over Africa, Michael Poliza, 2007 (USA: teNeues Publishing Company)

Field Guide to the Larger Mammals of Southern Africa, Chris and Tilde Stuart, 1996 (South Africa: Struik)

Field Guide to the Mammals of Southern Africa, Chris and Tilde Stuart, 1996 (South Africa: Struik)

Field Guide to the Reptiles of East Africa, S. Spawls, K. Howell, R. Drews and J. Ashe, 2002 (U.K.: Academic Press)

Gorilla: Struggle for Survival in the Virungas, Michael Nichols, 1989 (USA: Aperture Press)

Guide's Guide to Guiding, The, Garth Thompson, 2001 (South Africa: Russel Friedman Books)

I Dreamed of Africa, K. Gallman, 1991 (USA: Penguin Books)

Island Africa: The Evolution of Africa's Rare Animals and Plants, Jonathan Kingdon, 1990 (U.K.: William Collins)

The Kingdon Field Guide to African Mammals, Jonathan Kingdon, 1997 (U.K.: Academic Press)

Last Edens of Africa, Francois Odendaal, 1999 (South Africa: Southern Books)

Malaria , A Layman's Guide, Martine Maurel, 2001 (South Africa: Struik)

Mountain Gorillas–Biology, Conservation, and Coexistence, Gene Eckhart and Annette Lanjouw, 2008 (USA: University Press)

Night of the Lions, K. Gallman, 2000 (U.K.: Penguin Books)

North of South, Shiva Naipaul, 1994 (U.K.: Penguin)

Once We Were Hunters: A Journey with Africa's Indigenous People, P. Weinberg, 2001 (South Africa: David Philip)

Origins Reconsidered, R. E. Leakey and R. Lewin, 1992 (USA: Doubleday) (O/P)

Pyramids of Life, John Reader and Harvey Croze, 2000 (U.K.: Collins)

Roberts Birds of Southern Africa, Gordon Maclean, 1993 (South Africa: Voelcker Trust)

Running Wild, John McNutt and Lesley Boggs, 1996 (South Africa: Southern Book Publishers)

Safari Companion, A Guide to Watching African Mammals, Richard D. Estes, 2001 (South Africa: Russel Friedman Books; USA: Chelsea Green Publishing)

Scramble for Africa, 1876–1912, Pakenham, 1992 (USA: Avon Books; U.K.: Phoenix Press)

Smithers Mammals of Southern Africa, Peter Apps, 1996 (South Africa: Southern)

Southern, Central, and East African Mammals, A Photographic Guide Chris and Tilde Stuart, 2000 (South Africa: Struik)

The African Adventurers, Peter Capstick, 1992 (USA: St. Martins Press)

The Behavior Guide to African Mammals, Richard Despard Estes, 1991 (South Africa: Russel Friedman Books; USA: University of California Press)

The Blue Nile, Alan Moorehead, 1983 (U.K.: Penguin)

The End of the Game, Peter Beard, 1996 (USA: Chronicle Books; U.K.: Thames & Hudson)

The Great Migration, Harvey Croze, 1999 (U.K.: Harvill Press)

The Kingdon Field Guide to African Mammals, Jonathan Kingdon, 1997 (U.K.: Harcourt Brace)

The Tree Where Man Was Born, Peter Matthiessen, 1997 (USA: Dutton)

The White Nile, Alan Moorehead, 1973 (U.K.: Penguin)

Through a Window, J. Goodall, 2000 (U.K.: Phoenix Press)

Time With Leopards, Dale Hancock, 2000 (South Africa: Black Eagle Publications)
Vanishing Africa, Kate Klippensteen, 2002 (USA: Abbeville Press)
Whatever You Do, Don't Run, Chris Roche, 2006 (South Africa: Tafelberg Publishers)
When Elephants Weep, Emotional Lives of Animals, Jeffrey Masson, 1996 (U.K.: Vintage)
Wild Africa, Patrick Morris, et al., 2001 (U.K.: BBC Books)
Wildest Africa, Paul Tingay, 1999 (U.K.: New Holland)

SOUTHERN AFRICA

Complete Book of South African Birds, Peter Ginn, revised 1996 (South Africa: Struik)
Complete Book of South African Mammals, Gus Mills and Lex Hes, 1997 (South Africa: Struik)
Discovering Southern Africa, TV Bulpin, 2000 (South Africa: Tafelberg)
Field Guide to Mammals of Southern Africa, C. and T. Stuart, 1991 (South Africa: Struik)
Field Guide to Snakes and Reptiles of Southern Africa, Bill Branch, 1992 (South Africa: Struik)
Guide to Nests & Eggs of Southern African Birds, Warwick Tarboton, 2001 (South Africa: Struik)
I'd Rather Be On Safari, Gary Clark, 2001 (USA: Baranski)
Illustrated Guide to Game Parks and Nature Reserves of Southern Africa, 1999 (South Africa: Readers Digest)
In the Footsteps of Eve, Lee Berger, 2001 (USA: National Geographic*)*
Living Deserts of Southern Africa, Barry Lovegrove, 1993 (South Africa: Fernwood Press)
Long Walk to Freedom, Nelson Mandela, 1995 (U.K.: Abacus, Little Brown)
Lost World of the Kalahari, Laurens van der Post, 2001 (U.K.: Vintage)
Majestic Southern Africa, Land of Beauty and Splendour, Bulpin 1999 (South Africa: Readers Digest)
National Parks & Other Wild Places of Southern Africa, Nigel Dennis, 2000 (South Africa: Struik)
Newman's Birds of Southern Africa, Kenneth Newman, 2002 (South Africa: Struik)
Peoples of the South, Derek De La Harpe, 2001 (South Africa: Sunbird)
Raconteur Road, Shots into Africa, Obie Oberholzer, 2000 (South Africa: David Phillip Publishers)
Sasol Birds of Southern Africa, Ian Sinclair, 2002 (South Africa: Struik)
Smithers Mammals of Southern Africa: A Field Guide, R. H. N. Smithers, 1999 (South Africa: Struik)
Southern Africa Revealed, Elaine Hurford, 2000 (South Africa: Struik)
Southern African Trees: A Photographic Guide, Piet van Wyk, 1993 (South Africa: Struik)
Southern African Wildlife, Essential Illustrated Guide, 2002 (South Africa: Readers Digest)
Tracing the Rainbow, Art & Life in Southern Africa, Eisenhofer, 2001 (Germany: Arnoldsche)
Trees of Southern Africa, Keith Coates Palgrave, 1977 (South Africa: Struik)
Walk with a White Bushman, Laurens van der Post, 2002 (U.K.: Vintage)
Wildlife of Southern Africa: A Field Guide, V. Carruthers, 1997 (South Africa: Southern)
Zambezi River of the Gods, Jan and Fiona Teede, 1990 (South Africa: Russel Friedman Books)

BOTSWANA

Chobe, Africa's Untamed Wilderness, Balfour, 1999 (South Africa: Struik)
Common Birds of Botswana, Kenneth Newman, 1998 (South Africa: Southern)
Cry of the Kalahari, Mark and Delia Owens, 1984 (USA: Houghton Mifflin)
Hunting with Moon, The Lions of Savuti, Derek and Beverley Joubert, 1998 (USA: National Geographic)
Miracle Rivers, The Chobe & Okavango Rivers of Botswana, Pickford, 1999 (South Africa: Struik)
Okavango: Sea of Land, A. Bannister, 1996 (South Africa: Struik)
Okavango: Africa's Wetland Wilderness, A. Bailey, 2000 (South Africa: Struik)
Okavango: African's Last Eden, Frans Lanting, 1993 (USA: Chronicle U.S.)
Okavango: Jewel of the Kalahari, Karen Ross, 2003 (USA: Macmillan)
Panoramic Journey through Botswana, Alfred le Maitre, 2000 (South Africa: Struik)
Plants of the Okavango Delta, Karen and William Ellcry, 1997 (South Africa: Tsaro)
Prides: The Lions of Moremi, C. Harvey and P. Kat, 2000 (South Africa: Struik)
Running Wild, John McNutt and Lesley Boggs, 1996 (South Africa: Southern Book Publishers)
Shell Field Guide to the Common Trees of the Okavango Delta, Veronica Roodt, 1993 (Botswana: Shell)
Shell Field Guide to the Wildflowers of the Okavango Delta, Veronica Roodt, 1993 (Botswana: Shell)
The Africa Diaries, Derek and Beverley Joubert, 2000 (USA: National Geographic)
The Bushmen, P. Johnson, A. Bannister and A. Wallenburgh, 1999 (South Africa: Struik)
The Heart of the Hunter, Laurens Van der Post, 2002 (U.K.: Vintage)
The Kalahari: Survival in a Thirstland Wilderness, Joyce Knight, 1999 (South Africa: Struik)
The Lions and Elephants of the Chobe, Bruce Aitken, 1986 (South Africa: Stramill)
This is Botswana, Peter Joyce, 2000 (South Africa: Struik)
Wildlife of the Okavango: Common Animals and Plants, D. Butchart, 2000 (South Africa: Struik)

ZAMBIA and ZIMBABWE

African Laughter, Doris Lessing, 1992 (U.K.: Harper Collins)
Bitter Harvest, Ian Smith, 2001 (U.K.: Collins)
Don't Lets Go the Dogs Tonight, An African Childhood, Fuller, 2001 (USA: Random House)
Eye of the Elephant, Mark and Delia Owens, 1992 (USA: Houghton Mifflin)
Hwange, Retreat of the Elephants, Nick Greaves, 1996 (South Africa: Struik)
Kakuli, Norman Carr, 1995 (U.K.: Corporate Brochure Company) (O/P)
Luangwa, Zambias Treasure, Mike Coppinger, 2000 (South Africa: Inyathi Publishers)
Mukiwa, Peter Godwin, 1996 (U.K.: Picador)
The Leopard Hunts in Darkness (and other series), Wilbur Smith, 1992 (U.K.: MacMillan)
The Spirit of the Zambezi, Jeff and Veronica Stutchbury, 1991 (U.K.: Corporate Brochure Company)
This is Zimbabwe, Gerald Cubitt and Peter Joyce, 1992 (South Africa: Struik)
Zambezi — A Journey of a River, Michael Main, 1990 (South Africa: Southern Book Publishers) (O/P)
Zambezi — The River of the Gods, Jan and Fiona Teede, 1991 (U.K.: Andre Deutsch)

Zambezi, L. Watermeyer, J. Dabbs and Y. Christian, 1988 (Zimbabwe: Albida Samara
   Pvt. Ltd.)
Zambia Landscapes, David Rodgers, 2001 (South Africa: Struik)
Zambia Tapestries, David Rodgers, 2001 (South Africa: Struik)

MALAWI

Malawi, Lake of Stars, Vera Garland, 1998 (Malawi: Central Africana)

NAMIBIA

Desert Adventure, Paul Augustinus, 1997 (South Africa: Acorn Books)
Desertscapes of Namibia, Jean Du Plessis, 2002 (South Africa: Struik)
Etosha, A Visual Souvenir, Daryl and Sharna Balfour, 1998 (South Africa: Struik)
*Heat, Dust and Dreams, Exploration People & Environment Kaokoland &
   Damaraland,* Rice, 2001 (South Africa: Struik)
Himba — Nomads of Namibia, Margaret Jacobsen, 1991 (South Africa: Struik)
Namibia African Adventurers Guide, W. and S. Olivier, 1999 (South Africa: New
   Holland)
Namibia, Africa's Harsh Paradise, A. Bannister and P. Johnson, 1978 (South Africa:
   Struik)
Panoramic Journey through Namibia, Alfred le Maitre, 2000 (South Africa: Struik)
Sands of Silence, On Safari in Namibia, P. Capstick, 1991 (USA & U.K.:
   St. Martins Press)
Scenic Namibia, Thomas Dreschler, 2000 (South Africa: Tafelberg)
Sheltering Desert, Henno Martin, 1996 (South Africa: Ad Donker)
Skeleton Coast, a Journey through the Namib Desert, Benedict Allen, 1997 (U.K.: BBC)
Skeleton Coast, Amy Schoeman, 1999 (South Africa: Southern Book Publishers)
This is Namibia, Gerald Cubitt and Peter Joyce, 2000 (U.K. & South Africa:
   New Holland)

SOUTH AFRICA

Cape Floral Kingdom, Colin Paterson-Jones, 2000 (South Africa: Struik)
History of South Africa, Frank Welsh, Revised and Updated 2000 (U.K.: HarperCollins)
Kruger National Park, Wonders of an African Eden, Nigel Dennis, 1997 (USA: BHB
   International; South Africa and U.K.: New Holland)
Long Walk to Freedom, Nelson Mandela, 1995 (U.K.: Abacus, Little Brown)
Magnificent Natural Heritage of South Africa, Knobel, 1999 (South Africa: Sunbird.)
Magnificent South Africa, Hurford and Joyce, 1996 (South Africa: Struik)
My Traitor's Heart, Rian Malan, 2000 (USA: Moon Publications)
Presenting South Africa, Peter Joyce, 1999 (South Africa: Struik)
Rock Paintings of South Africa, Stephen Townley Bassett, 2002 (South Africa:
   David Philip)
Somewhere over the Rainbow, Travels in South Africa, Gavin Bell, 2001 (U.K.:
   Abacus, Little Brown)
The Covenant, James A. Michener, 1980 (USA: Random House)
The Heart of the Hunter (series), Laurens Van der Post, 1987 (U.K.: Vintage)
The Washing of the Spears: The Rise and Fall of the Zulu Nation, Donald R. Morris,
   1995 (U.K.: Pimlico)
This is South Africa, Peter Borchert, 2000 (South Africa: Struik)

Twentieth Century South Africa, William Beinart, 2002 (U.K.: Oxford University Press)
When the Lion Feeds (series), Wilbur Smith, 1986 (U.K.: MacMillan)
Wild South Africa, Lex Hes and Alan Mountain, 1998 (U.K.: New Holland)
Wildlife of the Cape Peninsula: Common Animals and Plants, D. Butchart, 2001 (South Africa: Struik)
Wildlife of the Lowveld: Common Animals and Plants, D. Butchart, 2001 (South Africa: Southern)
World That Made Mandela, L. Callinicos, 2001 (South Africa: STE Publishers)

EAST AFRICA

A Guide to the Seashores of Eastern Africa, M.D. Richmond (Ed.), 1997, (Sweden: Sida; Zanzibar: Sea Trust)
A Primates Memoir, Love, Death and Baboons in East Africa, Robert Sapolsky, 2001 (U.K.: Jonathan Cape)
Africa's Great Rift Valley, Nigel Pavitt, 2001 (USA: Harry N. Abrams)
African Trilogy, Peter Matthiessen, 1999 (U.K.: Harvill Press)
Among the Man-eaters, Stalking the Mysterious Lions of Tsavo, Philip Caputo, 2002 (USA: National Geographic)
Birds of Kenya & Tanzania, Zimmerman, Turner and Pearson, 1996 (U.K.: A & C Black; South Africa: Russel Friedman Books)
Field Guide to the Birds of East Africa, Terry Stevenson and John Fanshawe, 2002 (U.K.: Academic Press)
Field Guide to the Reptiles of East Africa, Stephen Spawls, 2002 (U.K.: Academic Press)
Guide to Mt. Kenya and Kilimanjaro, edited by Iain Allen, 1981 (Kenya: Mountain Club)
Helm Field Guide to Birds of Kenya and Tanzania, Dale Zimmerman and Donald A. Turner, 1999 (U.K.: Croom Helm)
Illustrated Checklist, Birds of East Africa, B. von Perlo, 1995 (U.K.: Collins)
In the Shadow of Kilimanjaro, Rick Ridgeway, 2000 (U.K.: Bloomsbury)
Pink Africa, Nigel Collar, 2000 (U.K.: Harvill Press)
Portraits in the Wild: Animal Behavior in East Africa, Second Edition, Cynthia Moss, 1982 (USA: University of Chicago Press) (O/P)
Safari Guide to Common Birds of East Africa, D. Hosking, 1996 (U.K.: Collins)
Safari Guide to Larger Mammals of East Africa, D. Hosking, 1996 (U.K.: Collins).
White Hunters, Golden Age of African Safaris, Brian Herne, 1999 (USA: Henry Holt)

KENYA

Big Cat Diary, Brian Jackson and Jonathan Scott, 1996 (U.K.: BBC)
Birds of Kenya & Tanzania, Zimmerman, Turner and Pearson, 1996 (U.K.: A & C Black; South Africa: Russel Friedman Books)
Born Free Trilogy, Joy Adamson, 2000 (U.K.: Macmillan)
Elephant Memories, Portraits in the Wild, Cynthia Moss, 1999 (USA: Chicago University Press)
F/G Birds of Kenya & Northern Tanzania, Dale A. Zimmerman, Donald A. Turner and David J. Pearson, 1999 (U.K.: A & C Black; South Africa: Russel Friedman Books)
Flame Trees of Thika: Memories of an African Childhood, Elspeth Huxley, 1998 (U.K.: Pimlico)
I Dreamed of Africa, Kuki Gallman, 1991 (U.K.: Penguin)
Illustrated Checklist Birds of East Africa, B. von Perlo, 1995 (U.K.: Collins).

Journey Through Kenya, M. Amin, D. Willetts and B. Tetley, 1982 (U.K.: Camerapix)
Kenya Pioneers, Errol Trzebinski, 1991 (U.K.: Mandarin)
Kenya the Beautiful, Brett Michaèl, 1997 (USA: BHB International; South Africa: Struik)
Kingdom of Lions, Jonathan Scott, 1992 (U.K.: Kyle Cathie; South Africa: Russel Friedman Books).
Out in the Midday Sun, Elspeth Huxley, 2000 (U.K.: Pimlico)
Out of Africa, Isak Dinesen, 1989 (U.K.: Penguin Books)
Samburu, Nigel Pavitt, 2002 (U.K.: Kyle Kathie)
The Great Safari — The Lives of George and Joy Adamson, William Morrow, 1993 (USA: Adrian House) (O/P)
The Ukimwe Road: From Kenya to Zimbabwe, Dervla Murphy, 1995 (U.K.: Flamingo)
Wildlife Wars, Battle to Save Africa's Elephants, Richard Leakey, 2001 (U.K.: Macmillan)
Vanishing Africa, The Samburu of Kenya, Kate Klippensteen, 2002 (USA: Abbeville Press)

TANZANIA

Cheetahs of the Serengeti Plains, TM Caro, 1994 (USA: University Chicago Press)
Golden Shadows, Flying Hooves, George B. Schaller, 1989 (USA: University of Chicago Press)
In the Dust of Kilimanjaro, David Western, 2000 (USA: Island Press)
Journal of Discovery of the Source of the Nile, John Hanning Speke, 1996 (USA: Dover Publications)
Kilimanjaro, A Journey to the roof of Africa, Audrey Salkeld, 2002 (USA: National Geographic)
Kilimanjaro: The White Roof of Africa, Harald Lange, 1985 (USA: Mountaineers Books) Large photo book (O/P)
Mara Serengeti, A Photographers Paradise, Jonathan Scott, 2000 (U.K.: Newpro U.K. Ltd)
Ngorongoro Great Game Park, Chris Stuart, 1995 (South Africa: Struik)
Serengeti Lions, Predator Prey Relationships, G. B. Schaller, 1976 (USA: University Chicago Press)
Serengeti: Natural Order on the African Plain, Mitsuaki Iwago, 1996 (USA: Chronicle Books)
Serengeti Shall Not Die, Bernard and Michael Grzimek, 1960 (U.K.: Hamish Hamilton)
Snows of Kilimanjaro, Ernest Hemingway, 1994 (U.K.: Arrow)
Tanzania, Portrait of a Nation, Paul Joynson-Hicks, 1998 (U.K.: Quiller Press)
The Chimpanzees of Gombe, Patterns of Behavior, Jane Goodall, 1986 (USA: Harvard University Press) Chimpanzee research.
Thorns to Kilimanjaro, Ian McCallum, 2000 (South Africa: David Philip Publishers)

RWANDA

Across the Red River, Rwanda, Burundi and the Heart of Darkness, Christian Jennings, 1999 (U.K.: Indigo Paperbacks)
Gorillas in the Mist, Dian Fossey, 2001 (U.K.: Phoenix Press)
In the Kingdom of Gorillas, Bill Weber and Amy Veder, 2002 (U.K.: Aurum Press)
Lake Regions of Central Africa, Richard Burton, 2001 (USA: Narrative Press)

UGANDA

Bonobo, The Forgotten Ape, Frans De Waal, 1997 (USA: University of California Press)
Ecology of an African Rain Forest, Thomas Struhsaker, 1998 (USA: University Florida Press)
Forest of Memories, Tales from the Heart of Africa, Donald McIntosh, 2001 (U.K.: Little Brown)
Guide to the Ruwenzori, H. A. Osmaston and D. Pasteur, 1972 (U.K.: West Col Productions)
Rwenzori Mountain National Park, Uganda, H. A. Osmaston and Joy Tukahirwa, 1999 (Uganda: Makerere University Press)
Uganda, Ian Leggett, 2001 (U.K.. Oxfam)
Uganda/Rwenzori, David Pluth, 1997 (Switzerland: Little Wolf)
Uganda: Pearl of Africa, Paul Joynson-Hicks, 1994 (U.K.: Quiller Press)

CONGO

Congo Journey, Redmond O'Henlon, 1996 (U.K.: Hamish Hamilton)
The Forest People, Colin Turnbull, 1994 (U.K.: Pocket Books) On pygmies of the Ituri Forest.
The Mountain People, Colin Turnbull, 1987 (U.K.: Pocket Books)
The Road from Leopold to Kabila, A Peoples History. Nsongola-Ntalaja, 2002 (U.K.: Zed Books)
Facing the Congo, Jeffrey Taylor, 2001 (U.K.: Little Brown)
Travels in the White Mans Grave, Memoirs from West & Central Africa. Donald McIntosh, 2001 (U.K.: Abacus)
In the Footsteps of Mr. Kurtz, Living on the Brink of Disaster in the Congo, Michaela Wrong, 2001 (U.K.: Fourth Estate)
King Leopold's Ghost, Story of Greed & Heroism in Colonial Africa, Adam Hochschild, 2000 (U.K.: Macmillan)

My African Safari Journal

On the following pages is a day-by-day account of my safari, with descriptions of the landscapes and weather, wildlife sightings, the way we traveled, the food we ate and the people we met.

Did you know? Mongooses use their lightning-fast reflexes to kill and avoid being bitten by venomous snakes such as cobras and adders.

_____

_____

_____

_____

_____

_____

_____

_____

_____

_____

_____

_____

_____

_____

_____

_____

_____

_____

_____

_____

_____

_____

_____

_____

_____

_____

Did you know? Male cheetah live in "coalitions" of two or more brothers which defend a territory and hunt cooperatively.

Did you know? Owls have soft, fringe-tipped feathers which allow them to swoop on prey silently.

_____

_____

_____

_____

_____

_____

_____

_____

_____

_____

_____

_____

_____

_____

_____

_____

_____

_____

_____

_____

_____

_____

_____

Did you know? Hyrax have padded hooves, and open-rooted "tusks"
which suggest a common ancestry with elephants.

_____

_____

_____

_____

_____

_____

_____

_____

_____

_____

_____

_____

_____

_____

_____

_____

_____

_____

_____

_____

_____

_____

_____

Did you know? Lions may mate as often as every 15 minutes during the female's three- to four-day oestrus cycle.

Did you know? Up to 50 percent of impala lambs are killed in the first two weeks of life, but since all females give birth in synchrony, predators are "swamped" with the overabundance.

Did you know? Robin-chats and morning-thrushes mimic dozens of other bird calls in order to impress potential mates with their repertoire.

_____

_____

_____

_____

_____

_____

_____

_____

_____

_____

_____

_____

_____

_____

_____

_____

_____

_____

_____

_____

_____

_____

_____

_____

_____

_____

_____

_____

Did you know? Lapwings will screech and stand their ground against advancing elephants or buffalo to prevent them from stepping on their eggs or young.

_____

_____

_____

_____

_____

_____

_____

_____

_____

_____

_____

_____

_____

_____

_____

_____

_____

_____

_____

_____

_____

_____

_____

_____

Did you know? A termite queen may lay over 5,000 eggs per day and live for over 15 years.

_____

_____

_____

_____

_____

_____

_____

_____

_____

_____

_____

_____

_____

_____

_____

_____

_____

_____

_____

_____

_____

_____

_____

Did you know? When winged termites take to the air upon emergence from their mounds, they are preyed upon by a great variety of creatures, including bats, toads, leopards, eagles and ants.

_____

_____

_____

_____

_____

_____

_____

_____

_____

_____

_____

_____

_____

_____

_____

_____

_____

_____

_____

_____

_____

_____

_____

_____

_____

_____

Did you know? There were 40,000 black rhino in Kenya in the 1970s, but less than 400 today — a situation mirrored in many other African countries.

Did you know? Rhino horn is made of keratin (like our own fingernails) but worth more than gold to Yemenese men who desire it for carved dagger handles.

_____

_____

_____

_____

_____

_____

_____

_____

_____

_____

_____

_____

_____

_____

_____

_____

_____

_____

_____

_____

_____

_____

_____

_____

_____

_____

Did you know? Zebra stallions look after up to six mares and their foals, typically following behind the group to ward off predators.

_____

_____

_____

_____

_____

_____

_____

_____

_____

_____

_____

_____

_____

_____

_____

_____

_____

_____

_____

_____

_____

_____

_____

_____

_____

_____

_____

Did you know? A pile of discarded crab shells at the water's edge indicates the favored feeding site of a giant kingfisher or otter.

_____

_____

_____

_____

_____

_____

_____

_____

_____

_____

_____

_____

_____

_____

_____

_____

_____

_____

_____

_____

_____

_____

_____

_____

_____

_____

Did you know? Birds sing most stridently at dawn, because the morning air is less dense and sound travels further.

Did you know? Elephants spend about 18 hours a day feeding, typically in three or four bouts.

Did you know? When out foraging in daylight, honey badgers are frequently accompanied by chanting goshawks which pounce on insects or rodents that escape the digging predator.

Did you know? Female hornbills are sealed into their cavity nest during the 30-day incubation period, relying on their mate to bring them food.

_____

_____

_____

_____

_____

_____

_____

_____

_____

_____

_____

_____

_____

_____

_____

_____

_____

_____

_____

_____

_____

_____

_____

_____

_____

_____

_____

_____

_____

Did you know? An oxpecker will consume up to 100 adult ticks per day, and thousands of tick larvae, ridding large herbivores of these parasites.

Did you know? The hyena-like aardwolf can consume over 250,000 termites in six hours of foraging.

....

_____

_____

_____

_____

_____

_____

_____

_____

_____

_____

_____

_____

_____

_____

_____

_____

_____

_____

_____

_____

_____

_____

_____

_____

_____

_____

_____

Did you know? Although lions regularly prey on warthog, and relish the meat, they will typically ignore the flesh of a bushpig.

Did you know? Spotted hyena clans are dominated and led by an alpha female, known as the matriarch.

_____

_____

_____

_____

_____

_____

_____

_____

_____

_____

_____

_____

_____

_____

_____

_____

_____

_____

_____

_____

_____

_____

_____

_____

_____

_____

_____

Did you know? Africa's "Big Five" are the elephant, buffalo, lion, leopard and rhino (black or white).

Did you know? Africa's so-called "Little Five" are the elephant-shrew, buffalo-weaver, antlion (an insect), leopard-tortoise and rhinoceros-beetle.

Did you know? The Egyptian vulture (which throws stones at ostrich eggs) and the green-backed heron (which floats food as fish bait) are among the very few bird species to use tools.

Did you know? Woodpeckers have a specially adapted skull to withstand constant battering and vibration as the bird knocks into wood.

Did you know? The quagga (a kind of zebra) and the bluebuck are the only two mammals to have gone extinct in Africa in the past 200 years.

Did you know? Elephants favor one or the other tusk, just as people are either left- or right-handed.

Did you know? A group of rhinos is called a "crash."

Did you know? The porcupine is Africa's longest-living rodent, capable of reaching 20 years.

Did you know? Englishman Tom Gullick has overtaken the late Phoebe Snetsinger of Missouri, USA, as the world's top bird lister; he has seen over 8,600 of the world's nearly 10,000 known bird species.

Did you know? The greatest number of bird species spotted in a 24-hour period is 342, achieved by Terry Stevenson, John Fanshawe and Andy Roberts in Kenya in 1986.

Did you know? Lions sleep or doze for up to twenty hours each day.

Did you know? Almost a quarter of the world's approximately 4,000 mammal species are bats.

Did you know? When threatened, pangolins roll themselves up into such a tight ball that even lions may find them impossible to unroll.

Did you know? The dwarf mongoose is the smallest carnivore in Africa, weighing just 10 ounces (300g) on average.

Did you know? Baboons are the only primates (other than humans) capable of surviving in desert environments.

Did you know? Verreaux's eagle is almost entirely dependent upon hyraxes for its prey, rarely catching and eating anything else.

Did you know? An estimated 5 billion birds migrate to Africa from Europe and Asia every year, most crossing the Mediterranean Sea at five key sites.

Did you know? The red-billed quelea is the most abundant bird on Earth with an estimated population of 1.5 billion breeding adults.

Did you know? No two giraffes have the same body pattern.

Did you know? Hippos do not have sweat glands but excrete an oily fluid which protects the skin against sunburn.

Did you know? Baby elephants have "milk tusks" which fall out when they are around one year old.

Did you know? A skeleton of a leopard was found at an altitude of 18,696 feet (5,700m) on Mount Kilimanjaro in 1926.

Did you know? The African wild dog has the largest litter size of all canines, with an average of 7 to 10, but as many as 19 pups.

_____

_____

_____

_____

_____

_____

_____

_____

_____

_____

_____

_____

_____

_____

_____

_____

_____

_____

_____

_____

_____

_____

_____

_____

_____

Did you know? The kori bustard is the world's heaviest bird, weighing up to 42 pounds (19kg).

_____

_____

_____

_____

_____

_____

_____

_____

_____

_____

_____

_____

_____

_____

_____

_____

_____

_____

_____

_____

_____

_____

_____

_____

_____

_____

_____

_____

Did you know? Nocturnal bushbabies mark their pathways along favored branches by urinating on their paws.

Did you know? Three million years ago the African savannas were home to many mammals which have since become extinct. Among these was a species of giant warthog (almost the size of a hippo) and a sabre-toothed cat larger than a lion.

Did you know? Colonies of ants live in the swollen thorn bases of some acacia trees which they defend from browsing animals by swarming over and biting their muzzles.

Did you know? Mongooses break open the eggs of ground-nesting birds by flicking them backwards, between their legs, against rocks. Once cracked, the small carnivores can feast on the nutritious albumen and yolk inside the eggs.

Did you know? The seeds of acacias and other leguminous trees germinate more easily if they have been eaten and expelled by a herbivore.

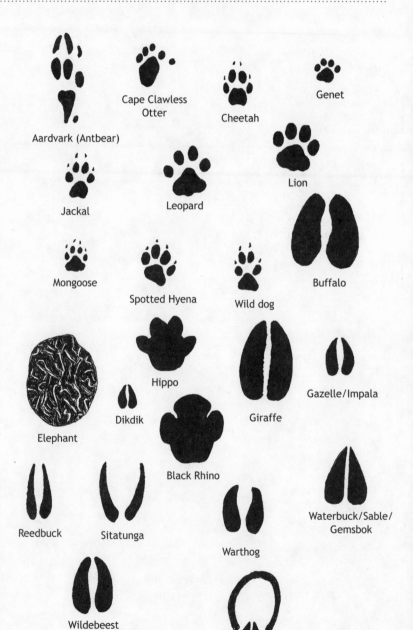

Aardvark (Antbear)

Cape Clawless Otter

Cheetah

Genet

Jackal

Leopard

Lion

Mongoose

Spotted Hyena

Wild dog

Buffalo

Hippo

Giraffe

Gazelle/Impala

Elephant

Dikdik

Black Rhino

Reedbuck

Sitatunga

Warthog

Waterbuck/Sable/ Gemsbok

Wildebeest

Zebra

IDENTIFICATION GUIDE, BEHAVIOR NOTES
AND CHECK BOXES OF SPECIES SEEN

African Mammals

√ mark off the species you see on your safari
in the check boxes

Mammal Watching

Africa is blessed with the greatest assemblage of large mammals of any region on Earth. But in addition to the spectacular and charismatic lion, giraffe, elephant and others, there are a host of smaller, but no less fascinating, mammals which make every safari a revelation.

Larger mammals are best watched from inside a safari vehicle, as the majority of animals in national parks regard this as nonthreatening. It is for this reason that your guide will typically advise you to remain seated when watching lion, cheetah and other species which have learned to avoid people and will usually panic and bolt when confronted with an upright human figure. Viewing from a "pop-top" roof is also nonthreatening to most mammals.

Finding mammals to watch and photograph is a combination of luck and awareness of a particular species' preferred habitat and habits. Skilled local trackers often display remarkable abilities to find and follow the footprints and other signs left by mammals, so it is wise to make use of their abilities where possible.

In national parks and other protected areas, larger mammals usually allow a close approach for photography as they are used to seeing safari vehicles. This is not the case in the more remote wilderness regions, where tracking on foot with an experienced guide is essential.

It is important to bear in mind that sensitivity is paramount with all wildlife watching to ensure that animals are not unduly disturbed, threatened or forced to behave in an unnatural way. Virtually every instance of a large mammal harming people is a result of a lack of respect in terms of allowing space for an animal to retreat. One of the most productive and exciting situations in which to watch mammals is at a waterhole. It is here that various species come together and where predators frequently lie in wait to ambush their prey.

Smaller, mostly nocturnal mammals pose a different challenge and it is often necessary to employ a wait-and-watch approach. Again, the expertise of a guide who may know the whereabouts of an active burrow or den site, might afford the chance to see fascinating creatures such as aardvark, honey badger or springhare. These and other denizens of the African night may also be encountered on wildlife reserve "night drives" when the sensitive use of a spotlight picks up their reflective eyes.

On the following pages, are illustrations and descriptive texts on the mammals which you are most likely to encounter on a safari in east, central and southern Africa, as well as some of the more interesting rarities. A check box next to each species allows you to mark those which you see on your safari. A comprehensive checklist may be found on pages 313–317.

Galagos (Bushbabies)

Related to the lemurs of Madagascar, Africa's smallest primates are arboreal and strictly nocturnal. Most species have loud calls, some resembling the wail of a human baby and this has given them their alternate name of "bushbaby." All galagos have exceptional eyesight and are able to see up to 100 feet (30m) using starlight alone. These agile primates have prodigious leaping abilities and can cover up to 6 feet (2m) in a single, elastic bound. Like most other primates, bushbabies are omnivorous, feeding on acacia gum, berries, insects and the eggs and nestlings of small birds. Galagos live in small family groups led by mature females, with territories being advertised by calling and scent marking — a process where individuals urinate on their hands and feet to leave distinctive odor trails on favored pathways. Night drives offer the best chance of seeing these interesting mammals, the eyes of which reflect strongly in spotlight.

There are around 20 species of galago, but with little overlap in range among members of the same genus, most parts of Africa have no more than two species in one locality. The similarly nocturnal but short-tailed potto is a strange and rarely-seen nocturnal primate of the Congo basin, the range of which extends into Uganda and western Kenya.

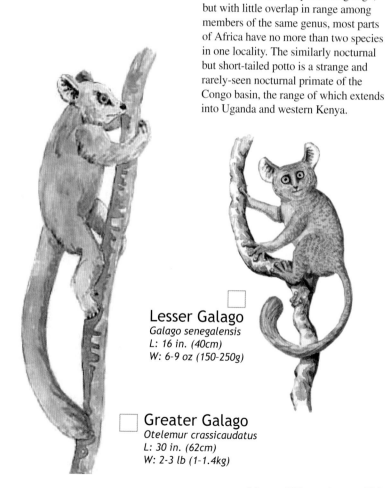

Lesser Galago
Galago senegalensis
L: 16 in. (40cm)
W: 6-9 oz (150-250g)

Greater Galago
Otelemur crassicaudatus
L: 30 in. (62cm)
W: 2-3 lb (1-1.4kg)

Baboons and Gelada

Baboons are terrestrial monkeys and among the most entertaining of African animals to watch, perhaps because they exhibit many behaviors rather similar to our own. Troops typically number between 20 and 80 individuals, although bigger aggregation of over 100 members are known. A troop consist of several kinship groups of adult females and their offspring, as well as a number of mature, sexually-active males. There is a strict hierarchy among the females and the males, with individual males generally having exclusive mating rights to certain kinship groups. Immature males are tolerated within the troop until they reach five years of age, after which they attempt to join neighboring troops.

Individual male baboons are formidable animals armed with large canine teeth, and fear only lions and large male leopards. When two or more male baboons are together, even these predators usually give them a wide berth. This partial immunity from predation has allowed baboons to develop a terrestrial lifestyle, although constant vigilance is required to keep the young out of danger. Baboons frequently forage alongside antelope as the acute hearing of these herbivores provides an early warning against predators. At night, baboons gather to roost in large trees along watercourses or on steep rock faces.

Like other primates, baboons are omnivorous. The troop forages in a loose group, digging up succulent roots, turning over rocks in search of insects and scorpions, gorging themselves on fruit and berries, or wading into shallow pools for water lily tubers. The newborn fawns of gazelle and antelope may be preyed upon by adult male baboons.

Olive Baboon
Papio anubis
L: 34-62 in. (85-150cm)
Wm: 46-96 lb (21-43kg)

Baboons can become a pest in agricultural areas as they raid orchards and feed on crops, so they are often heavily persecuted by farmers. They can even become a menace around safari lodges, where "baboon chasers" are sometimes employed to discourage them.

The number of baboon species is disputed, with some authors lumping the Guinea, chacma, olive and yellow baboons as a single species — the "savannah baboon."

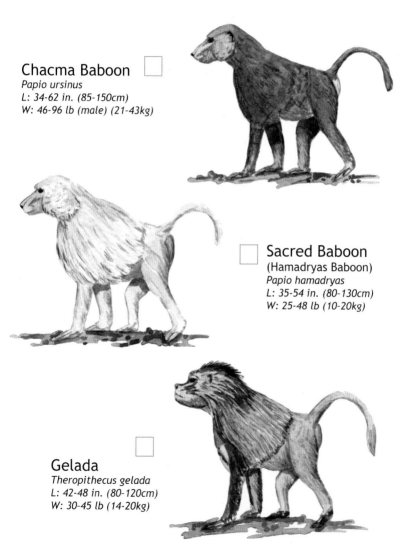

Chacma Baboon
Papio ursinus
L: 34-62 in. (85-150cm)
W: 46-96 lb (male) (21-43kg)

Sacred Baboon
(Hamadryas Baboon)
Papio hamadryas
L: 35-54 in. (80-130cm)
W: 25-48 lb (10-20kg)

Gelada
Theropithecus gelada
L: 42-48 in. (80-120cm)
W: 30-45 lb (14-20kg)

Monkeys

Monkeys occur throughout the wooded regions of Africa, with the greatest diversity of species living in the forests of central and eastern Africa. These primates are strictly arboreal and although some spend part of their time foraging on the ground, they quickly retreat into trees when disturbed.

Excluding baboons, featured on the previous pages, there are two primary groups of African monkeys — the geunons and the colobus.

The vervet monkey is the most widespread of the geunons, occuring in savannah woodland rather than forest. Vervets live in troops of between 8 and 50 individuals which comprise several family groups in a strict heirarchy. The offspring of high-ranking females are accorded a position in the troop just below their mothers and gain priority for food above adults of a lower-ranking family. One or more adult males — immigrants from other families — are key members of the troops. Young males transfer to other troops to prevent inbreeding with their siblings. Their diet consists of berries, seedpods, sap, flowers, insects, reptiles and nestling birds. Vervets quickly adapt to human settlements and learn to raid orchards and kitchens. Visitors to wildlife reserves should not feed monkeys as this encourages them to live on easy handouts and they rapidly become a real pest.

The forest-dwelling blue, Syke's and samango monkeys are closely related and regarded as a single, regionally variable, species by some authors. The samango and Sykes' occur on the eastern coastal lowlands, while the blue monkey occupies higher altitudes on northern Tanzania, Kenya and Ethiopia. The agile and attractive red-tailed monkey lives in lowland rainforest of the Congo basin, but extends east to Uganda and western Kenya. The relatively short-tailed Bale monkey is a vulnerable species of Ethiopia, while the golden, Le Hoest's and De Brazza monkeys are confined in East Africa to relict forests of the Rift Valley. The terrestrial, long-limbed patas monkey is primarily a species of the semiarid Sahel belt south of the Sahara, but small populations exist in northern Uganda, Kenya and Tanzania.

Colobus monkeys are entirely vegetarian and are unique among African primates in lacking a thumb. Their five forward-facing digits are unable to grasp moving objects such as live prey while their complex stomach can hold a third of their bodyweight in undigested leaves. With chemicals able to break down cellulose and detoxify plant compounds, colobus are browsers of the forest canopy. In East Africa, the black-and-white colobus has two distinct forms, with the short-coated subspecies (with white-tipped tail) in the lower altitudes surrounding Lake Victoria, and the longer-coated subspecies (with completely white tail) in high-altitude forests of Mount Kenya, Meru and Kilimanjaro. The smaller Zanzibar red colobus occurs only in the Jozani Forest of Zanzibar where it is readily observed although fewer than 1,500 survive.

Black-and-white Colobus
Colobus guereza
L: 50-60 in. (1.2-1.5m)
W: 14-32 lb (6.5-14kg)

Vervet Monkey
Cercopithecus aethiops
L: 40-75 in. (1-2m)
W: 9-16 lb (4-8kg)

Blue Monkey
Cercopithecus nictitans
L: 42-75 in.(1-2m)
W: 9-16 lb (4-8kg)

Mountain Gorilla

Mountain gorillas are among the world's most critically endangered mammals, with only around 600 surviving in two isolated populations: some 300 on the forested slopes of the Virunga volcanoes (shared by Rwanda, Uganda and the Democratic Republic of Congo) and a similar number in the Bwindi Impenetrable Forest of western Uganda. These are the only suitable habitats remaining for the species and since they occur at maximum density there is no realistic possibility of numbers increasing within this range. The priority for conservationists is therefore to safeguard the Virunga and Bwindi forests in perpetuity.

Gorillas live in troops led by a dominant adult male, whose massive size inspires respect and confidence among the family members. This so-called 'silverback' leads the family troop, deciding where to forage, rest and sleep within their home range.

Unlike the closely-related chimpanzee (and us humans, for that matter) the gorilla is entirely vegetarian, favoring a few selected leafy plants such as wild celery and bamboo shoots.

Over the past two decades, various mountain gorilla troops in the Virunga and Bwindi forests have been sensitively habituated to researchers, wildlife guards and small groups of ecotourists. Watching gorillas in their natural habitat is not only one of the most enthralling wildlife experiences imaginable, it is also a way of ensuring the conservation of gorilla habitat, as local communities and national governments derive tangible economic benefits from ecotourism.

Mountain Gorilla
Gorilla beringei
H: 5-6 ft (1.4-1.8m)
Wf: 187 lb (85kg)
Wm: 352 lb (160kg)

Chimpanzee

Chimpanzees are the closest relatives of humankind and geneticists have determined that our two species share 98% of their DNA. It is not surprising then, that these muscular primates display numerous behaviors which make them fascinating to watch. They have been the subject of intense study for over three decades at Gombe Stream in Tanzania, and primatologists have observed and monitored them at numerous other localities in central and eastern Africa.

Chimps live in communities which usually number up to ten but may be very much larger depending upon habitat and food resources. The communities are dominated by mature males which spend their whole life in an ancestral home range. Sexually mature females must move to neighboring troops. Infants are born after an eight-month pregnancy, weaned at five years and become sexually active at around eight, although they cannot conceive until the age of 12 or 13.

Forest of one kind or another is the habitat of chimpanzees and they may also be seen on the fringe of savannah in gallery or ravine forest. Like ourselves, they are omnivorous, feeding on fruit as well as insects (especially termites), birds, eggs and nestlings, small mammals and even monkeys, which are pursued and trapped in a carefully coordinated hunt. Social grooming is an important group behavior which maintains the hierarchy among adults. Facial expressions are as varied as our own, and over 30 recognizable sounds are made. Young chimps laugh, tickle each other and cry.

Chimpanzee
Pan troglodytes
H: 4-5 ft (90-160cm)
W: 66-120 lb (30-55kg)

Jackals

Close relatives of coyotes and foxes, jackals are intelligent and highly adaptable carnivores. In addition to carrion which is scavenged from kills made by larger predators or natural mortalities, rodents, reptiles, frogs, ground birds, beetles and other insects are all preyed upon. In parts of East Africa, golden jackals regularly capture and eat lesser flamingos. Jackals frequently follow hunting lion and cheetah, shadow spotted hyena clans, or rush to a site where vultures are descending from the sky. At the huge seal colonies on Namibia's coast, large numbers of black-backed jackals survive on natural mortalities and seal pups.

Jackals are a great advertisement for monogamy. Pairs stay together for life, share duties in raising litters of pups in underground dens, and put themselves at risk to defend one another. Pairs defend their territory rigorously against rivals of their own species. Both sexes are vociferous, maintaining contact and warding off rivals with howling cries and echoing calls.

In the Serengeti-Ngorongoro ecosystem, all three species of jackal may be seen together. In areas where humans have encroached into wild habitats, jackals are able to flourish by living on farmlands and the outskirts of cities.

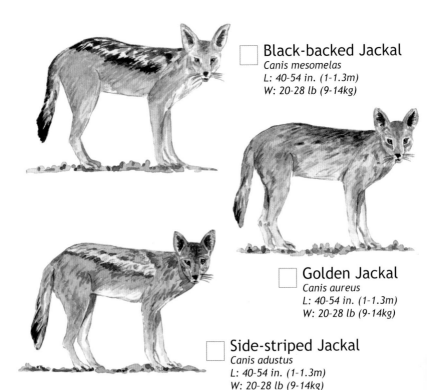

Black-backed Jackal
Canis mesomelas
L: 40-54 in. (1-1.3m)
W: 20-28 lb (9-14kg)

Golden Jackal
Canis aureus
L: 40-54 in. (1-1.3m)
W: 20-28 lb (9-14kg)

Side-striped Jackal
Canis adustus
L: 40-54 in. (1-1.3m)
W: 20-28 lb (9-14kg)

Foxes and Ethiopian Wolf

Both the bat-eared fox and Cape fox are small members of the canine family which prey largely upon insects although they will occasionally take small rodents and reptiles. They are most active after dark, but are frequently seen during the daytime in cooler weather.

The bat-eared fox occurs in two widely separated parts of Africa — the semiarid Kalahari-Karoo region of southern Africa, and the scrub-grasslands of East Africa. This endearing little fox uses its huge cup-shaped ears to detect the movements of termites and other subterranean insects which are then swiftly dug up with the front paws. Pairs raise litters of four to six pups which will remain with their parents for a year or more. These offspring sometimes help to raise their parent's next litter although they must eventually move on to establish their own territory. Leopards and large eagles are feared predators.

The shy Cape fox is found only in the southwestern part of the continent, where individuals and pairs may be encountered in the Kalahari, Karoo and Namib ecosystems.

The Ethiopian wolf is critically endangered and now confined to just a few localities in moorland on the high plateau of Ethiopia. Although related to the true wolf, it feeds largely on rodents. Packs consist of two or more adult females and up to five related males.

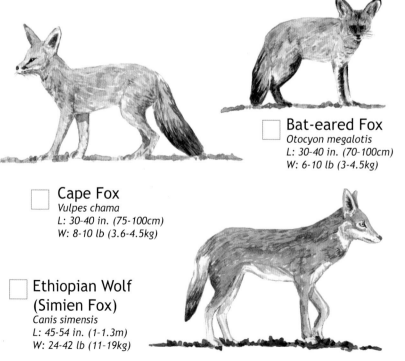

Bat-eared Fox
Otocyon megalotis
L: 30-40 in. (70-100cm)
W: 6-10 lb (3-4.5kg)

Cape Fox
Vulpes chama
L: 30-40 in. (75-100cm)
W: 8-10 lb (3.6-4.5kg)

Ethiopian Wolf
(Simien Fox)
Canis simensis
L: 45-54 in. (1-1.3m)
W: 24-42 lb (11-19kg)

African Wild Dog

This fascinating sociable carnivore lives in packs averaging ten adults and their offspring. The lineage of the pack is split along gender lines, with all females usually being related, and all males typically being siblings. An "alpha" female is the only pack member which gives birth, but all help to feed and safeguard her litter of pups. This dominant female seems to dictate pack movements and the selection of a den site.

Litters of up to 16 pups are born blind and helpless in an underground burrow, usually at the coldest time of the year (May to July in southern Africa). The pups spend the first three months within the den, but the timing is perfect, for when they are at their most demanding in terms of food provision, the invariably abundant Impala have dropped their lambs, which makes hunting easy for the adults.

Few predators are as efficient as the wild dog which enjoys a hunting success rate of around 80%, due to pack cooperation and individual stamina. Impala are the most frequent prey species over much of the dogs' range.

Northern Botswana, Zambia, Zimbabwe and southern Tanzania support the greatest number of wild dog, which is considered one of Africa's most threatened larger mammals with fewer than 5,000 individuals surviving. Good numbers also occur in South Africa's Kruger National Park and packs have been successfully introduced to other South African reserves. Direct persecution by stock farmers, wire snares, and diseases such as canine distemper and rabies threaten wild dogs throughout their range. Because feral dogs are often a significant problem outside of protected areas, some conservationists argue that renaming the species as the "painted dog" might help to eliminate confusion and unnecessary persecution of these endangered animals in rural districts adjacent to protected areas.

African Wild Dog
(Painted Dog/Cape Hunting Dog)
Lycaon pictus
L: 42-56 in. (1-1.4m)
W: 45-55 lb (20-25kg)

Spotted Hyena

Few animals have attracted such hatred and disparagement from humans as the spotted hyena, long regarded as a cowardly scavenger dependent upon the leftovers of lion. In reality, the spotted hyena is a efficient predator with highly advanced social behavior.

Spotted hyenas live in clans of up to 30 or 40 individuals, led by a dominant female known as the matriarch. Female hyenas remain in the clan of their birth but males leave the group by the age of three. A communal den, often an enlarged warthog burrow at the base of a termite mound, is the center of clan life, with pups of all ages socializing. Hyenas demarcate their territory by defecating repeatedly in particular places and the chalky, calcium-rich droppings persist for some time. Anal pasting and nocturnal vocalization are other means of territorial advertisement.

Spotted hyenas are most active after dark but are frequently encountered during the early morning and late afternoon. The hunting procedure of the clan is to run down prey until it becomes exhausted, usually selecting lame or young antelope and zebra. Much food is obtained by scavenging and they frequently rob cheetah and leopard of their prey. Powerful canines and molars allow hyenas to consume just about an entire animal, from hide and flesh, to hooves and bones.

Due to its ghostly whooping call and secretive nocturnal ways, the hyena is regarded as a witch or evil spirit in many African societies. For the Maasai, Karamajong and some other tribes, the hyena was (and still is in more remote locations) used as an "undertaker," consuming the body of the deceased and delivering a person's spirit to the afterlife.

Spotted Hyena
Crocuta crocuta
L: 5 ft (1.5m)
W: 88-176 lb (40-80kg)

Other Hyenas and Aardwolf

Somewhat smaller than the spotted hyena, and only rarely encountered, are the striped and brown hyenas. Both are almost entirely nocturnal, solitary, silent, shy and secretive. These animals are not as well studied as their spotted cousins and much still has to be learnt about their ecology.

The brown hyena occurs in desert and semiarid habitats from Namibia's Skeleton Coast, through the Kalahari, to the dry bushveld of South Africa. Carrion and wild melons make up the bulk of its diet, and it is an ineffective predator. The similarly-sized striped hyena is widespread from Tanzania north to the Horn of Africa, throughout the Sahara and east into Arabia and India. This secretive hyena may be seen on the fringes of Maasai villages where it scavenges on old animal hides and other scraps. Both brown and striped hyenas include ostrich eggs in their diet.

The much smaller aardwolf lacks powerful teeth and is a specialized termite-feeder. Individuals may be seen digging for and feasting on large numbers of these social insects after dark, sometimes following behind an aardvark (see page 152) which is able to excavate entire termite colonies.

Brown Hyena
Hyaena brunnea
L: 4-5 ft (1.2-1.5m)
W: 77-110 lb (35-50kg)

Aardwolf
Proteles cristata
L: 30-42 in. (80-90cm)
W: 18-26 lb (8-12kg)

Striped Hyena
Hyaena hyaena
L: 4-5 ft (1.2-1.5m)
W: 66-120 lb (35-50kg)

Smaller Cats

The African wild cat is the direct ancestor of the domestic cat and is virtually indistinguishable from a common house cat although it has rather long legs. This adaptable carnivore occurs throughout Africa where it is secretive and largely nocturnal. It is most often encountered during daytime in semiarid habitats such as the Kalahari and Etosha. Rodents and ground birds are favored prey.

The serval is at least twice the size of a wild cat and resembles a small cheetah. This long-limbed predator favors areas of tall grass, often close to water, in savannah and montane grasslands. Rodents are the main prey, but ground birds are often flushed and seized in flight as they take off. Serval appear to be less nocturnal in East Africa than in the southern part of the continent.

The caracal is about the same size as the serval but heavier in build and similar to a lynx (bobcat). It is powerful for its size, capturing hyrax, hares and guineafowl. The caracal occurs throughout Africa in desert, savannah, woodland and grassland, but it avoids closed-canopy forest. This is an adaptable carnivore able to flourish outside of protected areas where it may prey upon unguarded small livestock.

Not illustrated here are the tiny black-footed cat of the Karoo-Kalahari, and the golden cat of equatorial forest; these rare and elusive cats are seldom seen.

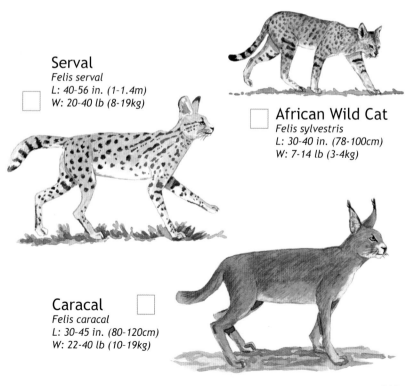

Serval
Felis serval
L: 40-56 in. (1-1.4m)
W: 20-40 lb (8-19kg)

African Wild Cat
Felis sylvestris
L: 30-40 in. (78-100cm)
W: 7-14 lb (3-4kg)

Caracal
Felis caracal
L: 30-45 in. (80-120cm)
W: 22-40 lb (10-19kg)

Cheetah

Built for speed, the cheetah is the world's fastest land mammal and has been reliably clocked at over 60 miles per hour. These lithe cats favor open habitats where gazelle, medium-sized antelope and hares are among the principle prey. When hunting, the cheetah targets a particular individual and then stalks as close as possible before exploding in a sudden burst of speed. Using its tail as a rudder, the cheetah quickly gains ground on its quarry which it then attempts to trip from behind. Once the victim is grounded, the spotted cat pins it down to suffocate. Only around one-quarter of pursuits end successfully for the cheetah, however, and when prey is successfully captured, the hunter must feed quickly to avoid detection and possible displacement by vultures or more powerful predators.

Female cheetah are solitary and raise litters of two to four cubs every second year. It is no easy task for the mother to provide for her family and there is usually a high mortality of cubs. Unlike leopards, female cheetah do not have fixed territories and wander over an extensive area, often moving to avoid contact with lion prides. Male cheetah are territorial and occupy large areas in which they have mating opportunities with a number of females. The larger the coalition of males (they are often siblings) the longer their tenure in an area of prime habitat.

Cheetah are readily distinguished from similarly-sized leopards by their proportionately longer legs, single coin-like spots, and distinctive black "tear marks" running from the eyes to the mouth. Cheetah cubs are covered in long grayish hair on their backs which may aid them in camouflage.

Cheetah
Acinonyx jubatus
L: 4.6-5.8 ft (1.5-1.8m)
W: 80-140 lb (35-65kg)

Leopard

The leopard is the most adaptable of Africa's large predators and is able to survive in virtually any habitat, being at home in forest, savannah, desert or mountain top. These secretive cats may be found in close proximity to human settlements, even on the outskirts of large cities.

Leopards are solitary and — in typical cat fashion — come together only to mate. Individuals live within home ranges in which they continually advertise their presence through calling and scent marking. All possible steps are taken to defend territories through scent, signs and signals rather than physical conflict. As a solitary hunter, a leopard cannot afford to become injured and must avoid confrontation. The size of a leopard's territory will depend upon the terrain and the density of available prey. Prime habitat often includes rocky outcrops or well-wooded drainage lines which provide ambush opportunities as well as den sites for cubs. One to three cubs are born blind and helpless and it is six weeks before they emerge from their den. Weaning takes place at about three months but it will be a year before they are able to fend for themselves. Female leopards range over smaller territories than males, and there is often overlap between mothers and their matured daughters.

Leopards are the ultimate opportunists, feeding on a wide range of prey from winged termites, rodents and stranded catfish, to grey duiker, warthog, bushbuck, impala and young zebra. Leopards are most active at night but are not strictly nocturnal and will readily slink down the trunk of a tree at midday to take advantage of a hunting opportunity.

Leopard
Panthera pardus
L: 4-4.5 ft (1.2-1.5m)
W: 62-142 lb (28-65kg)

Lion

The lion is the only truly social member of the cat family, with prides typically consisting of related females and their offspring. Male cubs are ejected from the pride when they approach maturity, whereas female cubs stay on as a second or third generation. Mothers help to raise one another's offspring, with litters often being synchronized. Prides are usually lorded over by adult males (normally two or three) which are often related (brothers). The males defend a territory larger in size than the home range of the lionesses and often rule over two or more prides.

Lions are the super predators of Africa. By and large, zebra, wildebeest and buffalo are the preferred prey, but this always depends upon the size of the pride, the terrain and the density of particular prey species. Only large prides will tackle buffalo, and — even then — males are often called upon to deliver the killing bite. Some prides specialize in certain species and develop effective hunting techniques for giraffe, warthog and others. One reason for living in a pride is not only to be tackling large prey but also to defend it. The spotted hyena is their main rival, and large clans of these tenacious carnivores are able to dispossess the big cats of their kills. Terrific battles may ensue between these competing predators, although the involvement of a big male lion invariably swings the balance. Since any predator has to avoid injury if it is to survive, lions will usually target the easiest available prey, preferring a limping zebra foal to a vigorous stallion. A substantial part of any lion's diet comes from pirating prey from other carnivores (particularly cheetah) and from scavenging from natural mortalities.

The lion's historical range in Africa has contracted by about two-thirds, and they are now largely confined to the more extensive protected areas. A few prides have, however, been successfully reintroduced to newly-created conservation areas.

Lion
Panthera leo
L: 8-11 ft (2.4-3.5m)
Wm: 520 lb (240kg)
Wf: 300 lb (130kg)

Otters

Although familiar to most people, and with species in North America and Europe, otters are secretive and rarely seen. The most widespread species in Africa is the Cape clawless otter which occurs at low densities in highland streams, large rivers, lakes, man-made dams, and coastal estuaries. Pairs defend a fixed territory which is advertised with dung-middens and they raise pups in a waterside burrow. Crabs are the primary food for this otter, and an accumulation of crab shells at favored feeding sites is a tell-tale sign of their presence in an area. They are most active at dawn and dusk. The smaller and rarely-seen spotted-necked otter feeds mostly on fish and requires clear water in which to hunt.

Cape Clawless Otter
Aonyx capensis
L: 45-64 in. (1.1-1.5m)
W: 26-46 lb (12-20kg)

Seals

Seals are fish predators of cold seas, and huge numbers of Cape fur seals occur in the Atlantic Ocean which laps the coast of Namibia and South Africa. Colonies of up to 400,000 exist on the "west coast" and it is thought that their numbers may have increased due to manipulation of the marine food chain by commercial fishing enterprises. There is constant activity at seal colonies, much of it hostile as adults compete for space, and provision their young. The great white shark is the main predator of fur seals, while black-backed jackals and brown hyenas find much to eat around breeding colonies. There are altogether seven species of seal in the cool waters of South Africa and Namibia.

Cape Fur Seal
Arctocephalus pusillus
L: 5-8 ft (1.8-2.4m)
Wm: 400-770 lb (200-350kg)
Wf: 200-250 lb (90-115kg)

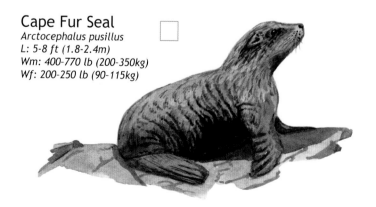

Mongooses

As small terrestrial carnivores related to weasels and polecats, mongooses are thought to be similar in design and ecology to the first mammalian carnivores which appeared on the scene around 60 million years ago when the era of dinosaurs was coming to an end.

There are over 20 species of mongoose in Africa. Most are opportunistic feeders, solitary, active after dark and poorly known, but the habits of several diurnal, group-living species are well known. Beetles, spiders, scorpions and lizards are among the favored prey of most mongooses, and many are known for their brave attacks on venomous snakes.

In savannah habitats the sociable banded mongoose and dwarf mongoose are frequently encountered, and often provide entertaining viewing as they interact with one another and forage for food. Both species commonly occupy termite mounds in which they tunnel nursery chambers, sleeping quarters and hideouts. The equally gregarious meerkat of the Kalahari and Karoo has been the subject of numerous documentary films which have highlighted the tight bonds between pack members. All for one, and one for all, seems to be the motto of group-living mongooses.

The solitary slender mongoose is active during the day and is often seen darting across vehicle tracks with its long black-tipped tail turned upwards. The much larger badger-sized white-tailed mongoose is strictly nocturnal, as is the Egyptian mongoose.

Banded Mongoose
Mungos mungo
L: 20-26 in. (50-65cm)
W: 2-4 lb (1-2kg)

Dwarf Mongoose
Helogale parvula
L: 12-16 in. (30-40cm)
W: 8-14 oz (225-400g)

Meerkat (Suricate)
Suricata suricata
L: 18-22 in. (45-55cm)
W: 1.4-2 lb (620-960g)

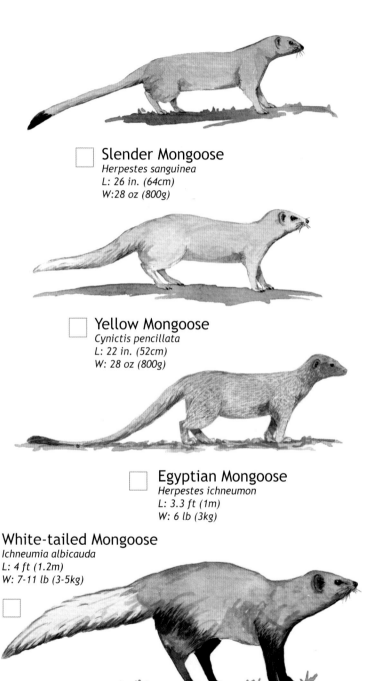

Slender Mongoose
Herpestes sanguinea
L: 26 in. (64cm)
W:28 oz (800g)

Yellow Mongoose
Cynictis pencillata
L: 22 in. (52cm)
W: 28 oz (800g)

Egyptian Mongoose
Herpestes ichneumon
L: 3.3 ft (1m)
W: 6 lb (3kg)

White-tailed Mongoose
Ichneumia albicauda
L: 4 ft (1.2m)
W: 7-11 lb (3-5kg)

Genets and Civets

Genets and civets belong to the viverrid family of small, strictly nocturnal carnivores with distinctive black-and-white-banded tails. All are solitary, with males and females coming together only briefly to mate.

There are at least eight species of genet in Africa, with the large-spotted (or blotched) genet being most common in the moister eastern half of the continent, and the small-spotted (or common) favoring the high plateau and dryer southwestern regions. Genets are agile climbers and live primarily arboreal lives, hunting for tree rats, roosting birds, geckos and insects. These slender, cat-sized predators are often located on safari night drives when their highly reflective eyes shine back at beams or spotlights. Genets may be residents or frequent visitors to the trees and roofs of safari camps.

The African civet is larger than any of the genets and rarely climbs into trees. This terrestrial, racoon-sized animal has a varied diet which includes berries and wild dates, as well as rodents and nestlings of ground birds. When alarmed or confronted, the civet raises the hair on its neck and back to appear much larger in size. Civets secrete copious amounts of sticky fluid to demarcate their territorial boundaries, and this "civetone" is harvested from captive animals (of a related Asian species) in the Far East.

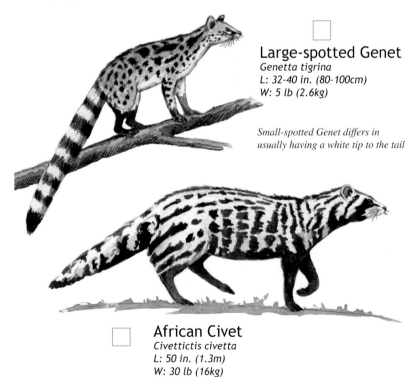

Large-spotted Genet
Genetta tigrina
L: 32-40 in. (80-100cm)
W: 5 lb (2.6kg)

Small-spotted Genet differs in usually having a white tip to the tail

African Civet
Civettictis civetta
L: 50 in. (1.3m)
W: 30 lb (16kg)

Honey Badger, Polecats and Weasels

These three small carnivores are primarily nocturnal and seldom seen, although the honey badger, or ratel, is often encountered in daylight hours in the Kalahari and Okavango during the dry winter season. All three belong to the mustelid family and are closely related to otters. They are mostly solitary with sexes living in distinct but overlapping territories, and coming together only to mate. Two to four pups are born in an underground burrow or den and typically accompany their mother for several months until they become independent. Invertebrates such as dung beetles and scorpions, as well as reptiles, small birds and rodents are among the preferred prey, but the honey badger in particular is a great opportunist and will scavenge from large carcasses and campsites.

Honey badgers are known to be incredibly pugnacious, and there are numerous observations of these muscular creatures standing their ground against leopards and even lions. Their powerful claws enable them to dig and climb with ease, so crocodile eggs and even vulture nestlings may feature in the diet from time to time. Honey and bee larvae are relished, and they may be led to active hives by a greater honeyguide (a rather drab-looking but vociferous bird — see page 207).

The skunk-like striped polecat and tiny striped weasel are shy and secretive so rarely encountered.

☐ **Honey Badger (Ratel)**
Mellivora capensis
L: 3.3 ft (1m)
W: 30 lb (14kg)

☐ **Striped Polecat (Zorilla)**
Ictonyx striatus
L: 24 in. (60cm)
W: 2.2 lb (1kg)

☐ **Striped Weasel**
Poecilogale albinucha
L: 20 in. (45cm)
W: 10 oz (280g)

Aardvark and Pangolin

The aardvark is an oddity among mammals, with no living relatives. This pig-like creature has a long truncated snout, donkey-like ears, and powerful bear-like paws, which are adaptations to locating and excavating termites and ants. Thousands of these social insects may be consumed in a single night of foraging. Interestingly, the aardvark rarely destroys an entire colony of termites, practicing a form of "sustainable harvesting" so not to deplete the food supply in its home range.

The aardvark plays an important ecological role for many other species, as its extensive underground burrows are occupied by foxes, large rodents, hyenas and others. Two birds, the South African shelduck and ant-eating chat, as well as various species of swallows, commonly nest in aardvark burrows. Unfortunately, this fascinating creature is both nocturnal and shy, so is seldom encountered. It is fairly common in some areas, however, as evidenced by the number of characteristic burrows and soil excavations.

The much smaller ground pangolin is primarily nocturnal, shy and increasingly rare. Individuals are killed for use by traditional healers and spiritualists, the scales being regarded as love charms among Zulu and other tribes. Like the aardvark, it is an "anteater" which has a specialized diet of ants and termites which are licked up with its long, sticky tongue. Although superficially similar to the ant-eating armadillos of America, the pangolins (there are three species in Africa) are not related but display traits of parallel evolution (a phenomenon whereby two unrelated families develop similar body forms for similar ecological niches).

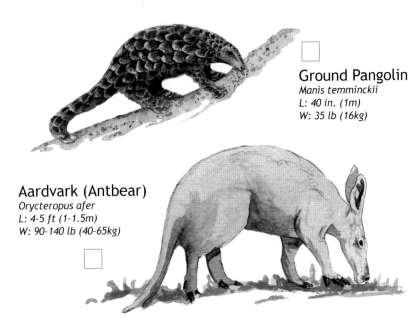

Ground Pangolin
Manis temminckii
L: 40 in. (1m)
W: 35 lb (16kg)

Aardvark (Antbear)
Orycteropus afer
L: 4-5 ft (1-1.5m)
W: 90-140 lb (40-65kg)

Hyraxes (Dassies)

Hyrax — or dassies as they are known in South Africa — resemble rabbits or rodents and were once commonly known as "rock rabbits." In fact, the hyraxes, of which there are 11 African species, are unique and fascinating creatures. With their rubbery-soled feet and dense coat of hair, hyrax are adapted for life among rocks. They are adept at bounding among boulders and able to withstand extremes of heat and cold. Families can typically be seen sunning themselves in the early morning and then retreating into shady crevices during the heat of the day. Hyrax obtain all their moisture requirements from their food and rarely drink.

The three family groups of hyrax — rock, bush and tree — are named after their preferred habitats. The diurnal rock hyraxes (five geographically separated species) live among boulder outcrops (kopjes), rocky cliffs and boulder-strewn slopes, often in the company of bush hyraxes (three geographically separated species). It takes a keen observer to tell the two species apart: the bush hyrax has a white eyebrow, whereas the rock hyrax is more uniformly colored. The tree hyrax (five species) are typically much darker with distinct facial markings, denser fur and a pale dorsal crest. All hyrax are noisy, but the tree hyrax is one of the most vociferous. The bizarre ratchet-like croaks and tormented screams of this nocturnal creature wake or disturb many a person out on safari!

Hyrax have many predators including Verreaux's eagle, leopard, caracal and African rock python. It is thought that hyrax and elephant may have evolved from a common ancestor in some distant era; the species share some interesting features including the arrangement of their toes — four front and three rear — which are equipped with hoof-like nails, and internal testicles. For such a small mammal, hyrax have an extraordinarily long gestation period of seven months.

Rock Hyrax
Procavia capensis
L: 16-22 in. (40-56cm)
W: 4-12 lb (1.8-5kg)

African Elephant

The African elephant is the largest of all land mammals and perhaps the continent's most charismatic animal. Visitors to wildlife reserves and wilderness areas are captivated by the power and grace of these magnificent animals, and by their apparent sensitivity and compassion.

Elephants may consume over 600 lbs (270kg) of leaves, grass, pods, bark and roots every day. Over half of the food eaten is poorly digested and deposited as fibrous dung within 24 hours. In this way, elephants break down plant material but also promote regeneration through seed dispersal, soil fertilization and the "opening up" of previously shaded areas to light. Along with the minuscule but equally impactful termites, elephants are the "landscape gardeners" of Africa. In fenced reserves elephant populations may threaten biodiversity due to their modification of habitats.

Elephants live in family groups led by a dominant female (the matriarch) which comprise related sisters, aunts and their offspring and have an intimate knowledge of a home range. Adult males, and "teenagers" of 12 and older, typically range in pairs, threesomes or groups of a dozen or more. Cows typically give birth to a single baby once every four or five years, and may live for up to 60 years. Mature males periodically enter a period of "musth" — a condition of high testosterone levels characterized by leaking temporal glands and dribbling urine — and then intimidate or fight with other bulls. Elephants in this condition should be treated with utmost caution by safari guides!

Only in recent years has it been discovered that elephants communicate with one another over long distances with subsonic "infra sound," growls, rumbles and squeaks too low in pitch for the human ear.

African Elephant
Loxodonta africana
L: 22-25 ft (6.8-7.5m); H: 8-13 ft (2.5-4m)
Wm: 11,000 lb (5,000kg); Wf: 6,600 lb (3,000kg)

Hippopotamus

The hippo once occupied almost every river system in Africa, from the southern Cape wetlands to the Nile Delta in Egypt, but due to hunting pressure it is now largely restricted to protected areas south of the Sahara. Hippos require deep water in which to submerge their bulky bodies and a supply of short grass on which to feed. Their skin lacks sweat glands, so hippo are prone to dehydration and they spend most of the day in water or mud, although they may bask in the sun for short periods. Hippos are extremely vocal when in water (but silent on land), as individuals grunt, honk and blow air from their nostrils. Calling seems to be contagious, and noisy bouts of honking and wheezing are made in response to disturbances, or when returning to the water after a night of feeding.

At sunset, hippo leave their aquatic refuge and wander down well-trod pathways to favored feeding grounds. Flat areas colonized by creeping grasses are favored, and a resident population maintains a lawn-like landscape. Individuals consume up to 130 lbs (60kg) of grass per night.

Hippos live in a hierarchical society in which individuals constantly display their status to one another. Adult females with their successive offspring form the foundation of social units called pods, and occupy a home range on a stretch of river, or lake. Mature males hold dominance in a restricted range but fierce and bloody clashes between rivals are commonplace. Hippo pods tend to be sedentary during the dry season but move far and wide when rain fills seasonal waterbodies.

Baby hippo are born in shallow water but are able to swim immediately and suckle while completely submerged. Youngsters are playful for the first year of life and weaned at around eight months.

Hippopotamus
Hippopotamus amphibius
L: 12 ft (3.5m); H: 5 ft (1.5m)
Wm: 7,000 lb (3,200kg)

White Rhinoceros

Second in size only to the African elephant, the white rhino is an animal of open country. In spite of its name, it does not differ from the black rhino in its skin color, and the names are misleading. Like its smaller cousin, the color of the white rhino's skin is determined by the soil of a particular region, as the animals roll in mud and dust. It is in the shape of the mouth that the two differ so markedly, and this also determines their diet. The broad, flat mouth of the white rhino is designed to crop big mouthfuls of grass.

Adult females live in overlapping home ranges and are often accompanied by their most recent offspring. They also tend to associate with other females and groups of a dozen or more may gather. Males are much less sociable and occupy well-patrolled territories with numerous conspicuous dung middens. Females and young add their own dung to a male's midden, but do not engage in the male's ritual of spreading and urine spraying. Rhino calves remain with their mother for two to three years, by which time she may be ready to deliver another calf. Interestingly, the juvenile white rhino always runs ahead of its mother, whereas the black rhino youngster runs ahead. This is thought to be a result of differing habitats, as the open country in which white rhinos live allows the juvenile to lead the way, while its mother wards off any threat from behind. Adult rhinos have no enemies other than man, but lion and spotted hyena may prey on calves.

White rhinoceros were close to extinction at the start of the 20th century due to excessive hunting. Only 30 or so individuals survived when South Africa's Umfolozi Game Reserve was created in 1897, but effective conservation allowed their population to recover strongly, especially since the 1960s when translocations to other protected areas were perfected. The northern race of the white rhino remains, however, on the brink of extinction.

White Rhinoceros
Ceratotherum simum
L: 12 ft (4m); H: 6 ft (1.7m)
Wm: 5,000 lb (2,300kg)

Black Rhinoceros

The black rhino has a hooked, prehensile upper lip, and carries its head high, in contrast to the drooping head of its grass-eating relative, the white rhino. A browser of herbs, low woody shrubs and tree foliage, the black rhino uses its pointed lip to grasp leaves and twigs, sometimes employing its horns to snap branches which are out of reach. Its wrinkled skin varies in color depending upon the tone of the mud in which it wallows to cool down or the dust it rolls in to combat ectoparasites. So it is, that black rhinos may be grey, rusty-red or even white!

Black rhino are reputed to be short tempered and readily charge as a first means of defense. Trackers require great skill and patience to approach these animals.

The preferred habitat of black rhino is the fringe of thickets and areas of dense woody growth, although individuals in Tanzania and Kenya may occupy more open habitats (such as the bowl of Ngorongoro Crater). They live in established territories but may share overlapping ranges and water holes without serious confrontation. Home ranges never extend more than 15 miles (24km) from a permanent supply of water and are crisscrossed by frequently used trails, marked by both sexes with dung middens. "Dunging" is a social behavior, and serves as a form of communication, such that a female on heat can be picked up by males.

Poaching has devastated the black rhino population, from an estimated 60,000 individuals in 1970 to less than 2,000 today, with just small, fragmented populations surviving in Tanzania, Kenya, Zimbabwe and Namibia. The situation is better in South Africa where effective conservation action and relocations have resulted in a secure and growing population.

Black Rhinoceros
Diceros bicornis
L: 10 ft (3m); H: 5 ft (1.5m)
Wm: 2,500 lb (1,200kg)

Warthog and Bushpig

The warthog is frequently regarded as the most comical of Africa's animals, due, no doubt to its bizarre, warty face and habit of running with its tail erect. Warthog are certainly entertaining animals to watch and important members of the herbivore community in savannah and open woodland. They feed on short green grass in the wet season and on succulent tubers and bulbs, which they uproot with their snouts, in the dry season. They often seek out the company of antelope, feeding in a relaxed manner while the taller and seemingly more nervous antelope are ever alert. Despite this clever association, warthog feature regularly in the diet of lion and leopard.

Few animals are as strictly diurnal as the warthog and it is practically unheard of to see one out and about after dark. When the sun sets all warthog reverse into one of several underground burrows in their home range. With tusks facing forward, a warthog in its burrow is safe from all except the most tenacious and desperately hungry of lions. Warthog give birth to two or three piglets which remain in the underground burrow for six weeks. It is common for two or more sows to stick together and for their piglets to assemble in "nursery groups." Despite being defended by their mothers, many piglets do not survive their first year as large cats, hyenas, jackals and large eagles relish them as prey.

The bushpig is the nocturnal equivalent of the warthog. Although it is widespread throughout forests and other well-wooded habitats it is rarely seen. It may become a pest to farmers in sugarcane fields outside protected areas. The giant forest hog is confined to equatorial forest.

Warthog
Phacochoerus africanus
L: 4 ft (1.2m); H: 25 in. (66cm)
W: 100-220 lb (45-100kg)

Bushpig
Potamochoerus larvatus
L: 4 ft (1.2m); H: 32 in.(80cm)
W: 120-250 lb (54-115kg)

Zebra

Few animals are as strongly synonymous with the African continent as zebras — the only wild members of the horse family south of the Sahara. There are three true species of zebra, the common and widely distributed plains zebra, the mountain zebra and Grevy's zebra.

Zebras are exclusive grazers, favoring short coarse grasses. They are particularly fond of freshly sprouted grass on recently burnt ground and will move large distances in search of this fodder. They are dependent on drinking water.

Zebra live in small family groups, usually consisting of between four and eight, led by a single dominant stallion. The adult mares in a group are usually related. Once they are able to fend for themselves, male offspring are evicted from the herd by their father — the stallion. Once the mares reach sexual maturity, they too leave the harem, being lured away by other stallions.

Zebras frequently associate with antelopes, gazelles, giraffe and even ostrich, benefiting from the different anti-predator senses and reactions of these animals. Zebra feature commonly in the diet of lion and spotted hyena, with youngsters being particularly susceptible. Stallions are vigorous in defense of their harem, and capable of inflicting life-threatening kicks to lion and other predators.

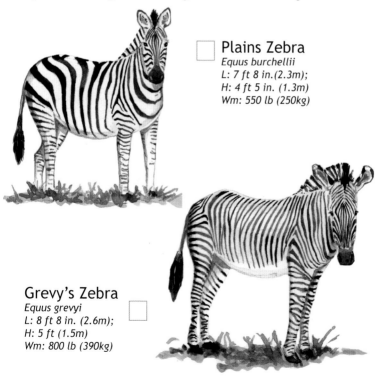

Plains Zebra
Equus burchellii
L: 7 ft 8 in.(2.3m);
H: 4 ft 5 in. (1.3m)
Wm: 550 lb (250kg)

Grevy's Zebra
Equus grevyi
L: 8 ft 8 in. (2.6m);
H: 5 ft (1.5m)
Wm: 800 lb (390kg)

Giraffe

The giraffe is the tallest member of the animal kingdom, with adults averaging a height of around five meters. Males can be told from females by the bald tops to their horns. The giraffe's unique form is the result of some remarkable adaptations and has enabled it to exploit a food niche not utilized by other herbivores — the foliage on the uppermost branches of trees.

Giraffe have an unusual social system in which females live apart from males in home ranges of about 10 square miles (25km²). The males may be solitary, but usually congregate in bachelor herds. Their large size is a deterrent to most predators, but lions are capable of toppling fully-grown adults and some prides actually select them as prey. A single calf is born and although mothers put up a stern defense against predators such as lion and spotted hyena, less than a quarter of young survive their first year.

Giraffe are selective browsers, favoring various species of *Acacia, Balanites, Commiphora* and *Ziziphus*, some of which have evolved chemical defenses and release unpalatable tannins when over-browsed. The thick blueish tongue is able to wrap around even the thorniest of twigs to remove nutritious foliage.

There are seven distinct forms of giraffe, each of which is regarded as a subspecies. The southern giraffe occupies the area south of the Zambezi, while the Maasai giraffe occurs in Tanzania and southern Kenya. Most distinctive of all, is the beautifully-patterned reticulated giraffe of the semiarid savannah of central and northern Kenya.

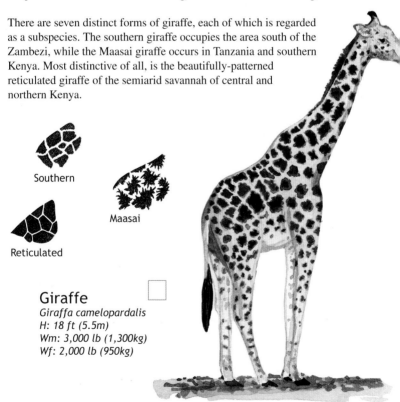

Southern

Maasai

Reticulated

Giraffe
Giraffa camelopardalis
H: 18 ft (5.5m)
Wm: 3,000 lb (1,300kg)
Wf: 2,000 lb (950kg)

African Buffalo

This massive relative of the domestic cow is regarded as one of Africa's "Big Five" due to its appeal as a trophy animal among hunters. Buffalo are completely dependent upon surface water, so are absent from arid and semiarid regions but are widespread and common in savannah, woodland and forest environments, although few now survive beyond the borders of protected areas. Buffalo are host to several diseases which may be lethal to domestic cattle and so have been eliminated from areas suitable for ranching.

Buffalo are gregarious animals with herds typically numbering several hundred, but sometimes over 1000. Several adult bulls, in prime breeding condition, accompany the herd which otherwise consists of cows, their calves and juveniles of both sexes. Old bulls, past their prime, keep each other company in bachelor groups. Their large size and gregarious nature make buffalo difficult quarry for predators but some lion prides actually specialize in hunting these big bovines. Older bulls are typically targeted by lions although it may take a pride several hours to corner, pin down and dispatch a belligerent buffalo. Calves may be preyed upon by clans of spotted hyena which will disturb a herd after dark to cause confusion and separate young from their mothers.

Buffalo are nonselective "bulk grazers" which favor taller grasses. By munching on these grasses and trampling rank grass underfoot, they open up areas for other more selective herbivores such as wildebeest and zebra. In common with many herbivores, buffalo herds move in response to rainfall and the resultant onset of nutritious grass growth. Herds often break up into smaller units during the wet season, but gather in large numbers again when seasonal rains come to an end.

☐ **African Buffalo**
Syncerus caffer
L: 10 ft (3m); H: 5 ft (1.5m)
Wm: 1,000-1,500 lb (500-700kg)

Wildebeests

There are two species of wildebeest, although the widespread common wildebeest is divided into four regional races (those in the Serengeti-Mara have a pale beard). The distinctive black wildebeest is restricted to the temperate highveld plateau of South Africa where it was hunted almost to extinction in the late 1800s. Today, all surviving animals are derived from captive-bred stock (a story similar to that of the North American bison, to which it bears some resemblance).

Common wildebeest are gregarious, forming herds of between ten and many thousands. The spectacular annual migration of wildebeest across the Serengeti is a well-known phenomenon and this seasonal movement in response to rainfall and resultant grass growth was probably shared by all populations of this unusual herbivore. Today, wildebeest over much of Africa have been hemmed into protected areas and are no longer able to follow traditional migration routes due to agricultural expansion, human settlements and fences. Only in the Serengeti-Mara ecosystem is such an extensive and vital migration still possible.

Short, nutritious grass is the required food of wildebeest. Optimum grazing conditions are created by a variety of factors including rain, fire, soil chemistry and grazing pressure from other herbivores such as buffalo. In higher rainfall areas, small herds may be sedentary, but the majority must move to rotate pasture. During the breeding season, male wildebeest occupy territories which — in extreme cases — may be no greater than the size an average suburban yard; the site is distinguished by the accumulation of droppings in a bare depression where the bull scrapes and rolls. Females synchronize the birth of their single calves at optimal grazing times and this also reduces the toll taken by lion, spotted hyena, cheetah and wild dog.

Common Wildebeest (Gnu)
Connochaetes taurinus
L: 7 ft (2m); H: 4 ft (1.3m)
W: 350-600 lb (160-270kg)

Black Wildebeest
Connochaetes gnou
L: 7 ft (2m); H: 3 ft (1m)
W: 240-250 lb (110-160kg)

Hartebeest, Topi and Tsessebe

This group of antelope all have high shoulders and long-snouted faces. This gives them a rather ungainly appearance, but this is deceptive for they are reputedly the fastest runners among antelope.

There are numerous regional races of these unusual antelope, with horn shape being the most variable and distinguishable trait. Hartebeest are exclusive grazers favoring narrow-bladed grasses. Open habitats of the fringe between grassy glades and wooded drainage lines seem to be preferred by all hartebeest.

Female hartebeest live in small herds although large aggregations may occur in some seasons. Adult males hold territories which are marked with extensive dung middens, and females that feed in these areas when they are in heat will be mated with by the territory holder. Fierce fights may ensue between rival bulls at this time.

The tsessebe of southern Africa and the topi of East Africa are regarded as two races of the same species, although the former is a more slender animal in both its body and horn shape. Male topi of the East African plains typically stand on termite mounds within their territories, while the females roam a home range in small herds.

In South Africa, two related hartebeest, the blesbok and bontebok differ only in the amount of white on their face, but wild populations were slaughtered to the point of extinction by Boer settlers and survive today only as commercially ranched livestock (although some have been introduced to protected areas).

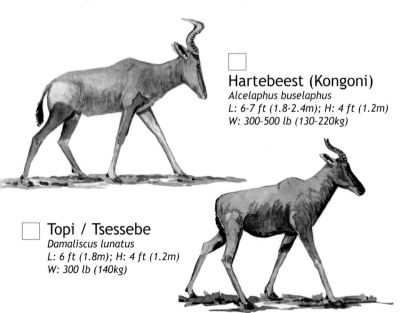

Hartebeest (Kongoni)
Alcelaphus buselaphus
L: 6-7 ft (1.8-2.4m); H: 4 ft (1.2m)
W: 300-500 lb (130-220kg)

Topi / Tsessebe
Damaliscus lunatus
L: 6 ft (1.8m); H: 4 ft (1.2m)
W: 300 lb (140kg)

Kudus and Nyala

A group of spiral-horned antelope, known as the tragelophines, occupy woodland and forest over much of Africa. They are alert and agile, and all have striped flanks to aid camouflage by breaking up their body outline in dense vegetation.

The greater kudu is a browser that favors dry woodland. Only males carry the spectacular corkscrew horns. Females and immatures live in small herds with mature males in tow during the dry season rut. Greater kudu are prodigious jumpers able to clear most fences with ease. The lesser kudu is a smaller, more slender antelope, favoring dryer semiarid savannah from northern Tanzania into the Horn of Africa.

Nyala occur in a limited range south of the Zambezi along Africa's eastern littoral, but are abundant in many Zululand reserves. The impressive horned males have dark shaggy coats, while the slender ewes are rusty red with distinctive white striping. The mountain nyala is a large antelope confined to the highlands of Ethiopia where it is common only in the Bale National Park.

Adapted for life in reedbeds and other aquatic habitats, the specialized sitatunga has elongated hooves. It is at home in Botswana's Okavango Delta, the western shores of Lake Victoria, northern Zambia and the Congo Basin.

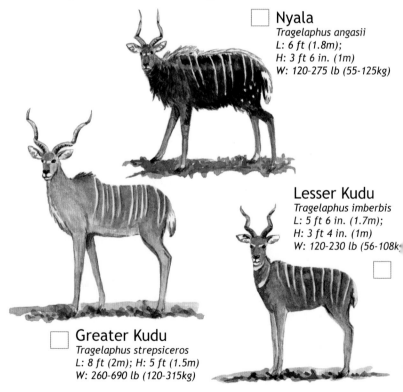

Nyala
Tragelaphus angasii
L: 6 ft (1.8m);
H: 3 ft 6 in. (1m)
W: 120-275 lb (55-125kg)

Lesser Kudu
Tragelaphus imberbis
L: 5 ft 6 in. (1.7m);
H: 3 ft 4 in. (1m)
W: 120-230 lb (56-108kg)

Greater Kudu
Tragelaphus strepsiceros
L: 8 ft (2m); H: 5 ft (1.5m)
W: 260-690 lb (120-315kg)

Impala, Bushbuck and Eland

The impala is both a grazer and a browser, occurring at very high densities in ideal habitat. Fringes or "ecotones" which provide a variety of grazing and browsing are favored, typically at the junction of savannah and woodland. Impala live in small to large herds which may be comprised of females and youngsters or "bachelors." Dominant males hold territories in which they attempt to keep a breeding herd, but the task of rounding up, mating and chasing challengers is exhausting and males seldom stay in command for more than two months.

The bushbuck is perhaps the most successful and widespread of all African antelope occurring in wooded habitats in the coastal forests of the southern Cape, the highlands of East Africa, the equatorial forests of the Congo basin and streamside thickets in dry savannah. Like the impala it eats both grass and foliage.

Largest of all antelope, the eland is able to survive in a variety of habitats from semidesert to subalpine grasslands of high mountains. Small herds are the typical social units, but males often live alone.

Bushbuck
Tragelaphus scriptus
L: 4 ft (1.2m); H: 30 in. (85cm)
W: 55-176 lb (25-80kg)

Impala
Aepyceros melampus
L: 4 ft 5 in. (1.3m);
H: 35 in. (90cm)
W: 88-165 lb (40-75kg)

Eland
Taurotragus oryx
L: 10 ft (4m); H: 5 ft (1.6m)
W: 700-2,000 lb (320-940kg)

Oryx

Known as the gemsbok in southern Africa, the oryx is a striking horse-like antelope with lance-shaped horns. The beisa (or fringe-eared) oryx is the East African counterpart. Oryx are powerfully built and both sexes possess horns although those of females are more slender.

These antelope can survive without drinking water as they are able to extract sufficient moisture from their diet (although they will drink readily when water is available) and have various morphological adaptations. In order to survive extreme ambient temperatures of up to 113° F (45° C), the oryx allows its own body temperature to rise accordingly and thus prevent the loss of moisture through perspiration. The antelope's hot blood is passed through a network of veins along its nasal passage before entering the brain in a system not unlike that of a car radiator.

Oryx are gregarious and typically form herds of up to 30 individuals. The herds comprise adult females and their young, as well as subadult males. Mature males occupy fixed territories through which female herds pass and provide mating opportunities. Rivalry between neighboring males, or wandering challengers, often leads to intense clashes which may result in snapped horns, serious injuries or even death.

Oryx feed primarily on grass, but will browse on shrubs and regularly eat succulent wild cucumbers and underground tubers, as well as acacia seed pods.

Oryx (Gemsbok)
Oryx gazella
L: 6 ft (1.6m); H: 4 ft 2 in. (1.3m
W: 260-460 lb (120-200kg)

Sable and Roan

The sable and roan antelope are large, horse-like antelope with conspicuous manes. They are closely related and favor areas of taller grassland on the fringes of broad-leaved woodland. Both species live in small herds consisting of numerous adult females, which have a hierarchy according to seniority, as well as subadults of both sexes. A single dominant bull accompanies the herd, and although he may wander off to feed alone, he is never far from his harem. At the end of their nine-month pregnancy, female roan and sable temporarily leave the herd to give birth to a single calf. The infant remains hidden in tall grass for its first week.

Sable are among the most strikingly colored of all antelope. The bulls are jet-black, while females and subadults have rich chestnut coats. The long curved horns are formidable weapons and bulls will ward off all predators except lion (although even these powerful cats treat adult sable with caution).

Roan antelope are widespread in woodlands south of the Sahara but are not common. They are selective grazers of particular species of medium-length grasses and appear more susceptible to drought and disease than most other antelope. With their long, tufted ears and robust corrugated horns, roan are among the most distinctive and attractive of antelope.

Roan
Hippotragus equinus
L: 8 ft (2.4m); H: 5 ft (1.5m)
W: 480-650 lb (220-280kg)

Sable
Hippotragus niger
L: 7 ft (2.1m); H: 5 ft (1.5m)
W: 450-580 lb (204-260kg)

Gazelles

Gazelles are the most widespread of all antelope, occurring not only throughout the drier parts of Africa, but also in the Middle East and across Asia to Siberia and China. All gazelles are gracefully built and characterized by pale, sandy-colored coats and corrugated, S-shaped horns.

The most remarkable aspect of gazelle biology is the ability of most species to flourish in arid areas devoid of surface water. Gazelles are able to extract the moisture they need from their food and reduce moisture loss by absorption of faeces and urine fluid. Most amazing, however, is the gazelle's ability to allow its body temperature to rise — by as much as 10 degrees — with the ambient temperature. This strategy is also employed by oryx and camel which, like gazelles, draw air through convoluted nasal passages in order to cool it down.

Gazelles are browsers of herbs, shrub foliage and seedpods, but also feed on fresh grass, so can switch diet according to environmental conditions. They are gregarious and exceptionally alert, relying on speed — as well as their choice of open country — to avoid predation. Cheetah are up to this challenge, however, and often target gazelles ahead of other prey.

The small, compact Thomson's gazelle is widespread in East Africa. Although it is more water dependent than other species, it is often the most abundant herbivore in open habitats. The larger Grant's gazelle prefers drier conditions although the two species may be seen side-by-side. A number of rare gazelle species which occur in and north of the Sahara are severely endangered and survive only in small pockets of suitable habitat.

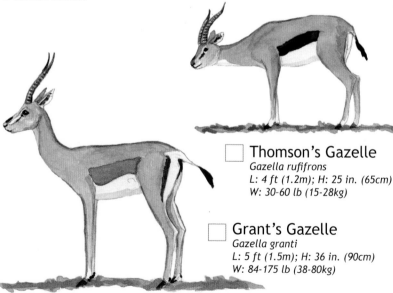

Thomson's Gazelle
Gazella rufifrons
L: 4 ft (1.2m); H: 25 in. (65cm)
W: 30-60 lb (15-28kg)

Grant's Gazelle
Gazella granti
L: 5 ft (1.5m); H: 36 in. (90cm)
W: 84-175 lb (38-80kg)

Springbok and Gerenuk

The springbok is the only gazelle that occurs in the dry southwestern corner of Africa, isolated from its relatives by the moist woodland belt of central Africa. It shares much in common with other gazelles although it has some strange anatomical differences such as hollow horn bases like those of goats.

Springbok are mixed feeders, taking mostly grass in summer and herb and shrub foliage in the dry winter months. The large velvety pods of the camelthorn acacia are a much favored food source in the Kalahari. The springbok's most remarkable behavior is "pronking" — its habit of springing up on its hooves. This begins as a rocking gait, progresses to a stot and then to full scale bouncing on stiff legs with the back arched. Once one animal in a herd begins to pronk the rest join in and create quite a spectacle; this behavior is thought to display fitness to potential predators. Less than 200 years ago, there were estimated to be many millions of springbok in the Karoo region of South Africa, but these herds were slaughtered by settlers. Good numbers still survive in the Kalahari and over much of Namibia.

The gerenuk is a gazelle with an elongated neck which allows it to reach foliage on the canopy of small trees out of reach to most other browsers. As if this physical advantage were not enough, the gerenuk also stands upright on its slender hind legs to give it even greater reach. By these means, this unique gazelle is able to occupy a distinctive niche. Gerenuk live in harem groups of 8 to 12, with one dominant male; they are distributed in semiarid acacia scrubland from northeastern Tanzania, through Kenya into the Horn of Africa.

Springbok
Antidorcas marsupialis
L: 4 ft (1.2m); H: 30 in. (80cm)
W: 100 lb (46kg)

Gerenuk
Litocranius walleri
L: 5 ft (1.5m); H: 4 ft (1.2m)
W: 64-110 lb (29-50kg)

Waterbuck and Reedbuck

Waterbuck are large, heavy-bodied antelope with noticeably long coats. The males have magnificent long sweeping horns, while the females are hornless. Two subspecies are recognized: the common waterbuck of southeastern Africa which has a broad white ring on its rump, and the darker-coated defassa waterbuck of East and western Africa, which has a large white patch under the tail. Unusual among antelope, waterbuck have a strong body scent.

Waterbuck are grazers and favor the wooded margins of rivers and wetlands, where family groups typically occupy the same home range for many years, sometimes for several generations. Waterbuck drink daily and are never found more than a few miles from water. They are commonly seen out in the open, either on floodplains or sandy riverbeds.

The southern and Bohor reedbucks occur in small groups of ewes and solitary males which attempt to keep the females under their influence, as their marshy home ranges shift with fluctuating conditions. A sharp whistle is the alarm call of reedbuck which count cheetah and leopard among their chief predators. The mountain reedbuck is adapted for life on grassy hillsides.

Common Waterbuck
Kobus ellipsiprymnus
L: 7 ft (2m); H: 4 ft (1.2m)
W: 350-570 lb (160-260kg)

Southern Reedbuck
Redunca arundinum
L: 5 ft 7 in. (1.6m);
H: 38 in. (96cm)
W: 86-170 lb (39-80kg)

Kob and Lechwe

These antelope favor seasonal marshlands which are very productive but unstable habitats. For much of the year, the marshlands are fertile lawns of high quality grazing, but at other times they are flooded or burnt so the antelope must move into fringing woodlands.

The kob is a large brick-red antelope divided into three races of which the Uganda kob occurs in East Africa. These robust antelope live in large aggregations on floodplains with distinct grazing and drinking areas. Adult males compete intensely for receptive females, with dozens converging in small "hubs" of just one acre which are littered with droppings and reek of urine-soaked soil.

Red lechwe are similar in appearance to kob but are more slender with longer horns in the males. They possess elongated hooves adapted for life in permanent wetlands with their sticky soils and so are able to spread themselves out into traditional herds. In this way, they avoid the intense social limitations of the kob in their seasonally shrinking habitats. The distinctive black lechwe occurs only in Zambia Bangweulu Swamps, while the Kafue lechwe is similarly restricted.

Puku are smaller than kob or lechwe and tolerant of seasonal fluctuations in habitat, being able to live in woodlands during the rainy season. They are common only in Zambia's Luangwa Valley but a small number survive along Botswana's Chobe River.

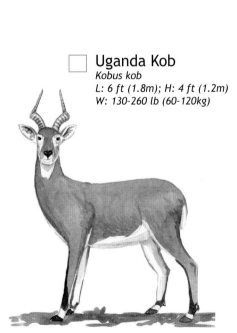

Uganda Kob
Kobus kob
L: 6 ft (1.8m); H: 4 ft (1.2m)
W: 130-260 lb (60-120kg)

Red Lechwe
Kobus leche
L: 6 ft (1.8m); H: 4 ft (1.2m)
W: 136-280 lb (62-128kg)

Duikers and Dikdik

All but one of Africa's 16 duiker species are denizens of closed forest. This exception is the grey duiker which is commonly encountered in savannah and open woodland. Duikers range in size from the tiny 9 lb (4kg) blue duiker to the 176 lb (80kg) yellow-backed duiker of equatorial rainforests.

The nature of their dense habitat, combined with their small size and secretive ways, make duiker among the least known of African mammals. To a greater or lesser extent duikers feed on fallen fruit, as well as fallen leaves, flowers, bark, gum and roots. Duikers are the only antelope to exhibit omnivorous tendencies and regularly feed upon insects, small vertebrates, eggs and even bird nestlings. Duikers are territorial and most species live in monogamous pairs. Both sexes are equipped with slit-shaped pre-orbital glands from which they excrete a strong-scented paste to be rubbed onto twigs and branches within the home range.

Most duikers snort and whistle, and traditional hunters frequently imitate the bleating call to lure them towards their nets, guns or clubs. Apart from man and his dogs, leopards and eagles are the most significant predators of duikers.

Dikdik are tiny, slender antelope with huge eyes and a distinctive trunk-like snout. They prefer semiarid savannah habitats dominated by acacia scrub and bush clumps, and have adaptations to allow them to survive in areas with no drinking water. In common with other miniature antelope, the dikdik is a browser rather than a grazer, and lives in monogamous pairs in a clearly defined home range.

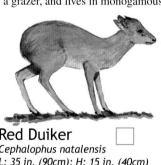

Blue Duiker
Cephalophus monticola
L: 25 in. (60cm); H: 14 in. (36cm)
W: 9 lb (4.2kg)

Red Duiker ☐
Cephalophus natalensis
L: 35 in. (90cm); H: 15 in. (40cm)
W: 25-30 lb (11-14kg)

☐

Grey Duiker
Sylvicapra grimmia
L: 45 in. (110cm);
H: 28 in. (70cm)
W: 33-50 lb (15-25kg)

Kirk's Dikdik ☐
Madoqua kirkii
L: 25 in. (70cm); H: 15 in. (38cm)
W: 8-16 lb (4-7kg)

Klipspringer, Steenbok and Oribi

The klipspringer is an extraordinary small antelope with many interesting physical adaptations to its preferred habitat of rocky outcrops and mountainsides. Most unusually, the klipspringer (this name means "rock jumper" in Afrikaans) has rubbery, cone-like hooves which cushion the stocky little antelope as it bounds among boulders. These small antelope are browsers of herbs and low shrubs.

Steenbok are small, brick-red antelope of open savannah habitats. Their large rounded ears with white linings are their most distinguishing feature, along with a black nose bridge, and slender, upright horns. Grass, leaves, seedpods and berries make up its diet.

The oribi has similar slender proportions to the steenbok but is a larger animal with conspicuous black gland spots beneath each ear. Open grassland is the favored habitat of oribi, from tropical palm savannah to temperate montane uplands. Oribi are primarily grazers of fresh grass but will also feed on leaves of herbs and shrubs.

Suni are tiny, secretive antelope of forests and thickets at the base of mountain ranges, and along the coast from Zululand to Kenya. They are extremely shy and seldom encountered. Other rarely-encountered miniature antelope not illustrated here are the Cape grysbok (which lives in fynbos shrubland of the southwestern Cape), and the Sharpe's grysbok (which favors mopane and brachystegia woodlands).

Steenbok
Raphicerus campestris
L: 35 in. (90cm);
H: 24 in. (60cm)
W: 20-25 lb (9-12kg)

Klipspringer
Oreotragus oreotragus
L: 35 in. (88cm);
H: 22 in. (56cm)
W: 20-35 lb (9-16kg)

Oribi
Ourebia ourebi
L: 44 in. (110cm);
H: 25 in. (62cm)
W: 23-36 lb (10-16kg)

Squirrels

Squirrels are rodents and, like their mouse and rat relatives, have prominent incisor teeth for gnawing at seeds, nuts and other plant material. All squirrels have long bushy tails and some are quite boldly patterned. They are active by day and are frequently encountered in savannah, forest and even in semideserts.

Bush squirrels frequent the branches of trees in savannah and woodland, and also spend a good deal of time on the ground foraging among fallen leaves and twigs. They often draw attention to themselves with their chirping alarm calls, accompanied by rapid flicking of their bushy tails. A variety of red squirrels occurs in coastal forest from Zululand north to Kenya, and in montane forest patches where sun squirrels are also resident.

Ground squirrels occur in the Kalahari and arid parts of Namibia, as well as the dry savannah of Tanzania, Kenya and Ethiopia. These are the largest of African squirrels and have the habit of using their raised tail as a shade umbrella in hot weather.

Ground Squirrel
Geosciurus inauris
L: 20 in. (50cm)
W: 36 oz (1kg)

Scrub Hare
Lepus saxatilis
L: 18 in. (45cm)
W: 3-6 lb (1-3kg)

Hares and Rabbits

Hares and rabbits are closely related and there is often no clear distinction between the various species. In general, rabbits are shorter-eared and burrow-living while hares have longer ears and find shelter above ground. African hares are primarily nocturnal and spend most of the day resting in tall grass or thickets. Hares are among the most frequently encountered mammals on safari night drives as they skip on and off vehicle tracks, confused — no doubt — by the spot lamps (good guides switch their motors and headlamps off momentarily to allow the hares to retreat). Cheetah sometimes flush and capture hares as they pace through grasslands, while eagle owls and small carnivores hunt them after dark. Rock hares (also known as rock rabbits) are attractive reddish-grey animals which live in hilly or mountainous habitats.

Porcupine, Springhare and other Rodents

Africa has a very diverse array of rodents, the largest of which is the impressive porcupine. This highly adaptable creature occurs in virtually every habitat type south of the Sahara, from the harsh Namib and Kalahari to lush montane forests. Family groups live in caves or burrows emerging after dark to feed on bark, roots and fallen berries, as well as in *shambas* (vegetable plots). Porcupines are also known to gnaw on bones for their high calcium content. When threatened, porcupines turn their back on their adversary and rattle their long quills. Lions or leopards may come away from a confrontation with a face full of quills.

The springhare is a bizarre kangaroo-like rodent of semiarid scrubland and dry savannah where it lives in colonies of ten individuals or more. A network of burrows is established by the colony in sandy terrain and the rodents emerge at dusk to feed on grass shoots and stems, as well as other herbage of low nutrient value. When seen after dark in a beam of a light, the reflective eyes bob up and down as the animals hop and spring about.

A great variety of mice, rats, gerbils, dormice, molerats and other rodents occur throughout Africa's varied habitats but most are nocturnal, shy and seldom seen. It is beyond the scope of this book to describe or illustrate these little creatures but it should not be forgotten that they play a vital role in ecosystems, as herbivores, seed dispersers and prey for a wide variety of small carnivores, owls, hawks and snakes.

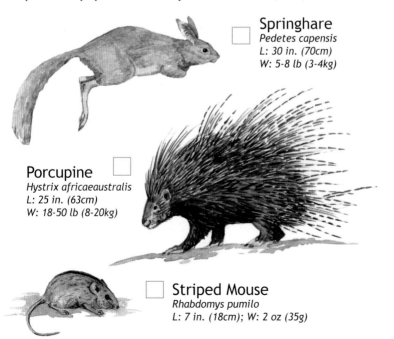

Springhare
Pedetes capensis
L: 30 in. (70cm)
W: 5-8 lb (3-4kg)

Porcupine
Hystrix africaeaustralis
L: 25 in. (63cm)
W: 18-50 lb (8-20kg)

Striped Mouse
Rhabdomys pumilo
L: 7 in. (18cm); W: 2 oz (35g)

Elephant Shrews and Hedgehog

With so many large and spectacular mammals to be seen in Africa, it is hardly surprising that many smaller creatures go largely unnoticed.

The elephant shrews (or sengis) are mouse-like animals with a long trunk-like snout which gives them a slightly elephantine appearance. Most species are active by day when they forage among rocks or along shaded pathways in a home range which has numerous shelters or burrows. They avoid exposed situations where they would be vulnerable to birds of prey. Ants, termites, earthworms and crickets are among the favored food items. For such tiny creatures, elephant shrews have a comparatively long gestation period and the newborn infants are well developed to minimize impacts of predation. There are three species of giant elephant shrew in East Africa. These much larger creatures are about the size of a domestic rabbit although slender with long legs, tail and snout. Terrestrial invertebrates are foraged for in the leaf litter of forests.

Hedgehogs are nocturnal insect-eaters well-known to many Europeans who see them in their gardens, woods and — all too often — as road casualties. The African species favor dry savannah or grassland habitats, feeding on worms, termites, beetles, fungi and fallen fruits. Hedgehogs characteristically roll themselves up into a ball when threatened, leaving would-be predators with nothing to attack but a spiny sphere of prickles.

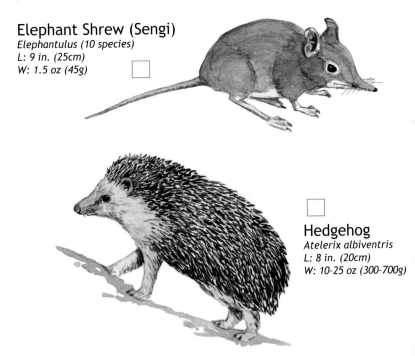

Elephant Shrew (Sengi)
Elephantulus (10 species)
L: 9 in. (25cm)
W: 1.5 oz (45g)

Hedgehog
Atelerix albiventris
L: 8 in. (20cm)
W: 10-25 oz (300-700g)

Bats

Bats are among the most misunderstood of all animals, with irrational fears pervading human folklore in many cultures, and an almost complete ignorance of the vital role that different species play in the control of insects and the life cycles of fruiting plants. There are almost 1,000 bat species, divided into two distinct groups — the insectivorous (micro) bats and fruit-eating (macro) bats.

Fruit bats are sometimes known as "flying foxes" on account of their dog-like snout, and the largest species may have a wingspan of one meter. Males have repetitive bell-like calls, and all chatter and squeak when feeding. In addition to feeding on figs and other fruit (and then dispersing the seeds), fruit bats relish nectar and pollinate the ornate flowers of sausage trees and baobabs.

Insect-eating bats (such as horseshoe bats) are characterized by small eyes, sharply pointed teeth, strangely shaped ears, and many also have bizarre nose structures. Seen up close, they appear rather frightening and this appearance has no doubt contributed to their unpopularity. It must be said, that vampire bats of tropical America do indeed suck the blood from sleeping mammals and may spread disease among livestock, but indiscriminate persecution of bats makes victims out of many harmless and ecologically useful species.

Able to find their way and hunt in complete darkness, micro bats use ultrasound (inaudible to the human ear) to navigate by echo-location. A call or chirp is made and "read" as it bounces back to the bat's sensitive ear receptors. This enables the bat to determine the precise distance between itself and a tree, rock, or other object and so avoid collision. Every species of bat has its own distinct call, and researchers determine their identity in this way. Small insectivorous bats are often seen hunting, or skimming rivers and pools, at dusk.

☐ Epauletted Fruit Bat
Epomophorus (6 species)
L: 6 in. (14cm)
W: 8 oz (200g)

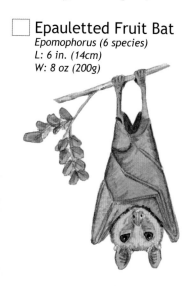

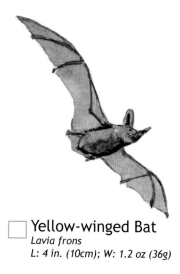

☐ Yellow-winged Bat
Lavia frons
L: 4 in. (10cm); W: 1.2 oz (36g)

Dolphins and Whales

Whales and dolphins live their lives largely unseen by humans, but whale watching has become a popular pastime around the world, and dolphins have long captured the human imagination. Africa has a diverse assemblage of whales and dolphins in its coastal waters. Collectively, whales, dolphins and porpoises are known as cetaceans.

The southern right whale is the most commonly observed species in South African waters, with popular viewing sites on the southern Cape coast. Females come close to shore from June to September when they give birth to their calves in sheltered bays. This whale is distinguished by the absence of a fin on its back, lack of throat grooves, and typically has crusty white barnacle growths on its head and body. Tiny crustaceans are the principal food. Humpback whales visit the east coast of Africa between May and September, when Antarctic waters are at their coldest. This whale is best known for its extraordinary repertoire of underwater calls which are often recorded as "whale song."

Bottle-nosed dolphins are highly intelligent cooperative hunters which follow the annual "sardine-run" — when huge shoals of these small fishes move between Plettenberg Bay and Durban on the South African coast, from June to August. These dolphins, along with sharks, seabirds and people feast on the bounty of sardines. Common dolphins can be seen just beyond the continental shelf on boat trips around the Cape Peninsula and all the way along the southern and east coast of Africa.

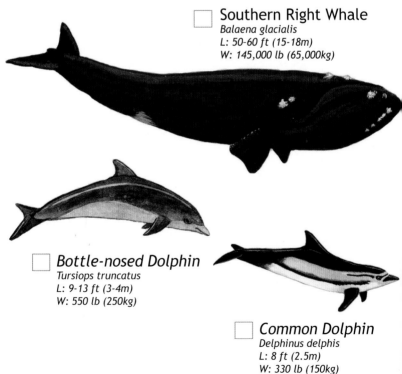

Southern Right Whale
Balaena glacialis
L: 50-60 ft (15-18m)
W: 145,000 lb (65,000kg)

Bottle-nosed Dolphin
Tursiops truncatus
L: 9-13 ft (3-4m)
W: 550 lb (250kg)

Common Dolphin
Delphinus delphis
L: 8 ft (2.5m)
W: 330 lb (150kg)

African Birds

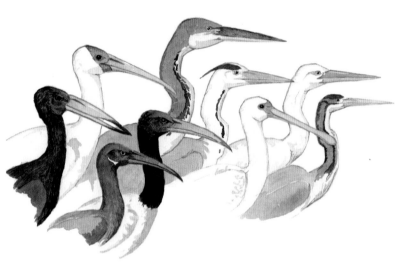

Over 2,300 species of birds have been recorded in Africa south of the Sahara, almost 25% of the world's nearly 10,000 species. There are 108 families of birds in Africa, and 17 of these are unique to the continent. Among the endemic families are turacos, mousebirds, sugarbirds and guineafowl, as well as the secretarybird, shoebill and hamerkop which are the sole representatives of their families.

Africa's birds, like those elsewhere, fall into three categories: residents, migrants and nomads (wanderers). Eurasian migrants visit Africa between September and April, while intra-African migrants move from the tropics to the subtropics.

Birds are most conspicuous in savannah habitats, and all of the large national parks and other protected areas support a diverse avifauna including eagles, storks, bee-eaters, hornbills, rollers and starlings. Forests are home to some spectacular birds but trogons and others are typically elusive and shy. Mountains, deserts and open grasslands are home to a lower diversity of birds but many interesting species live in these environments. Birds abound wherever there is water, so lakes, wetlands, rivers, estuaries and coastlines are excellent birdwatching habitats.

All but the most experienced birders are likely to become overwhelmed by the sheer diversity of African birds. The purpose of the following section is simply to introduce you to the main bird families, while illustrating a selection of the continent's more striking species. Knowing which family a bird belongs to is the first step of identification, with overall size, length of legs, and bill shape being vital factors. By flipping through the following pages you will familiarize yourself with Africa's bird families and soon recognize many of the species you'll encounter on safari. Your confidence will grow as you identify these species and a good safari guide will help you identify close relatives which will enable you to list them in the appropriate family boxes.

There are several comprehensive field guides which illustrate and describe in detail all the birds of eastern, southern and central Africa, as well as the Indian Ocean islands. These books are listed on pages 64–74 and are highly recommended for anyone wishing to have a detailed treatment of the birds in any particular region or country. Of particular importance when identifying birds beyond the family level, is noting plumage details, tail shape and the color of bill, legs and toes. The diagram below illustrates the important body parts. Another crucial factor in identifying many birds is voice, as many similar species have completely different calls or songs.

Identifying birds, or simply looking at or photographing them, will greatly enrich your African safari.

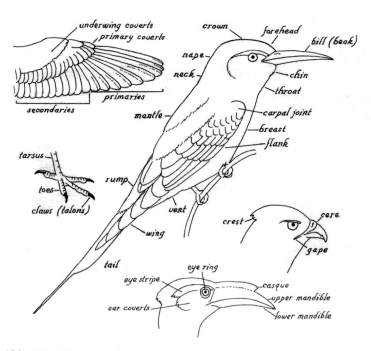

Pelicans, Cormorants and Darter

With their huge bills and flexible pouches, pelicans are unmistakable. They spend much of their time in the water, paddling with their big webbed feet, but also soar to great heights in thermals. The two species of African pelicans are gregarious and often fish in small flocks which cooperate to drive fish into shallow areas where they are scooped up. They are opportunistic and may scavenge fish from anglers.

Cormorants and darters are predominantly black or dark brown in color, with bills suitable for catching fish underwater. They are terrific divers but do not have waterproof plumage like ducks and grebes, so perch with wings outstretched to dry their oily feathers. Several African species frequent seashores, but the large white-breasted cormorant and slender reed cormorant can be seen in rivers and freshwater lakes. The African darter (anhinga) has long tail feathers and a dagger-shaped bill with which it spears fish. Darters swim low in the water with only their slender necks and heads protruding, and therefore have earned the nickname "snake birds."

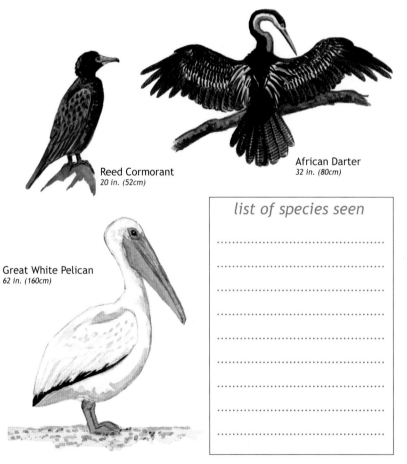

Reed Cormorant
20 in. (52cm)

African Darter
32 in. (80cm)

Great White Pelican
62 in. (160cm)

list of species seen

....

....

....

....

....

....

....

....

....

Herons, Egrets and Bitterns

These are medium-sized to large wading birds with long slender necks and legs, and dagger-like bills. All have a distinctive S-shaped neck which is tucked in when flying. Herons are generally larger than egrets, while the bitterns tend to be shorter legged than either. While herons and egrets forage openly on lakeshores, pools and floodplains, bitterns are much more secretive and keep largely to reedbeds. The nocturnal night herons roost in thickets or reeds during the day, emerging after dark to patrol the fringes of rivers and ponds. The goliath heron is the largest member of the family and occurs singly or in pairs; frogs, fish and even baby crocodiles feature in its diet. The grey heron is the most widespread of the larger herons, while the small green-backed heron is often encountered along quiet rivers and lake fringes. Egrets are often gregarious, particularly the cattle egret which often forages away from water in farmlands. In the past, many thousands of egrets were slaughtered for the plume trade, but most African species are common and many may have expanded in range and numbers due to the creation of artificial dams. Several heron species may join storks, ibises and cormorants to nest communally in "heronries."

Green-backed Heron
16 in. (42cm)

Cattle Egret
20 in. (52cm)

Goliath Heron
4 ft 8 in. (1.4m)

Grey Heron
3 ft (95cm)

list of species seen

....

....

....

....

....

....

....

....

....

....

....

....

....

....

Hamerkop, Shoebill and Grebes

There is no proven evolutionary link between the strange hamerkop and shoebill, but both resemble aberrant storks or herons, and share similar habits. They occur only in Africa. The hamerkop (named for its hammer-shaped head) is widespread throughout the continent where it frequents riversides and pools in search of frogs and toads. Pairs build a gigantic dome-shaped nest in the fork of a large tree, usually adding to the structure throughout the year. The enormous and bizarre shoebill is largely restricted to large papyrus swamps and reedbeds in Uganda and Zambia where it feeds mostly on lungfish and catfish. A sighting of the rare shoebill is a major highlight for many serious birders visiting Africa.

Grebes are small to medium-sized waterbirds, superficially similar to ducks and loons. Many have colorful head plumes and engage in elaborate courtship displays. They have pointed bills, fairly long necks and very short tails. The feet of grebes are set far back on the body which makes walking on land virtually impossible. The entirely aquatic grebes feed largely on fish captured by diving or '"up-ending." They fly only after dark, moving from one water body to another. The little grebe (dabchick) is the most common and widely distributed.

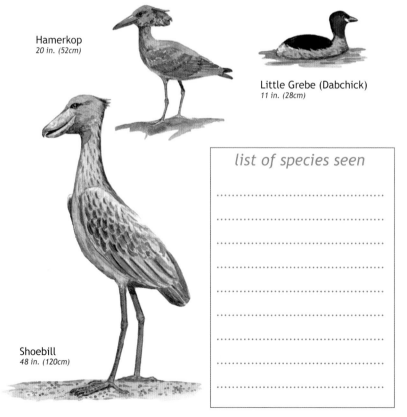

Hamerkop
20 in. (52cm)

Little Grebe (Dabchick)
11 in. (28cm)

Shoebill
48 in. (120cm)

list of species seen

....

....

....

....

....

....

....

....

....

Ibises and Spoonbills

Ibises and spoonbills are large wading birds with long necks and legs. Most favor shallow water and muddy shore habitats, but some ibises forage in grasslands or forest clearings. Ibises and spoonbills are gregarious often feeding, nesting or roosting in flocks, sometimes alongside herons, egrets and other birds. The widespread hadeda ibis often announces itself with a raucous call and this bird now occupies wooded suburbs of many African cities. The sacred ibis has adapted to scavenge from garbage dumps, while the glossy ibis is a bird of wetlands. The distinctive Southern bald ibis is found only in the montane grasslands of southern Africa. The African spoonbill uses its flattened bill to sweep small crustaceans off the substrate so they can be easily grasped.

African Spoonbill
3 ft (95cm)

Hadeda Ibis
2 ft 6 in. (76cm)

Sacred Ibis
2 ft 8 in. (80cm)

list of species seen

....
....
....
....
....
....
....
....
....
....
....
....
....
....

Storks

Storks are large, long-billed and long-legged birds with supreme soaring abilities. Although lacking talons and hooked bills of true raptors, storks are formidable predators which feed on a variety of living and dead animals. Some storks are specialized fish eaters and possess a unique trigger mechanism which allows them to snap their bill shut instantly. Of 19 stork species around the world, eight occur in Africa. The fabled European white stork is a nonbreeding migrant, although a small number are resident on the south-western Cape of South Africa. Like several other storks, they gather in large flocks often wheeling above in thermals as they move from one feeding area to another. The bald-headed marabou frequently attends carcasses with vultures and scavenges in and around cities such as Nairobi. The elegant saddle-billed stork is usually seen in pairs which forage along rivers and in wetlands. The African openbill and yellow-billed stork are gregarious and nest in large colonies. All storks lay two to four eggs in a large platform of sticks.

Marabou Stork
5 ft (1.5m)

Saddle-billed Stork
5 ft (1.5m)

list of species seen

....

....

....

....

....

....

....

....

....

....

....

....

....

....

Flamingos

Flamingos are unmistakable birds of shallow lakes and coastal lagoons. Their extraordinarily long neck and legs, and predominantly pink plumage prevent confusion with any other group of birds. The call of a flamingo is a goose-like honk.

Two of the world's five flamingo species occur in Africa, with the lesser flamingo numbering in the millions. Despite this large population size, the lesser flamingo has highly specific habitat requirements and is therefore vulnerable to population crashes. Large breeding colonies occur in East Africa's Rift Valley lakes (particularly Lake Natron) and at the Makgadikgadi Pans in northern Botswana.

The more widespread greater flamingo has less specific habitat requirements and feeds in deeper water than its smaller relative. Flamingos have a uniquely-shaped bill designed for filtering small organisms from the water. The greater flamingo feeds predominantly on tiny aquatic creatures while lesser flamingos favor blue-green algae.

Flamingo breeding activity is synchronized with rainfall. Huge flocks which are resident at a particular locality on one day may suddenly depart overnight to a favored breeding site which is usually a hot and inhospitable rain-filled lake. A single chalky-white egg is laid in a cone-shaped mud nest manufactured by the adults with their feet and bills.

Known predators of flamingos include African fish eagles and golden jackals, while marabou storks may raid nests for eggs and young.

Lesser Flamingo
3 ft (90cm)

list of species seen

....
....
....
....
....
....
....
....
....
....
....
....

Cranes

Grey Crowned Crane
3 ft 6 in. (1.1m)

Wattled Crane
4 ft (1.2m)

Cranes are long-legged birds of grasslands and wetlands, famous for the elaborate courtship "dances" performed by pairs. These graceful birds have inspired artists and conservationists around the word, but several species are now threatened due to habitat loss.

There are four crane species in Africa, with the grey crowned crane being the most widespread in savannah habitats of eastern and southern Africa. The large wattled crane is confined to permanent wetlands such as the Okavango Delta, while the blue crane is largely restricted to South Africa.

Cranes have a varied diet and feed by pecking on the ground or probing mud. Invertebrates, frogs, lizards, seeds and agricultural grain are all eaten. The famous "dances" of cranes involve synchronized bows, wing spreads and leaps, and pairs bond for life. Cranes have a haunting bugle-like call often uttered in flight. The nest is a platform of grass or reeds, often surrounded by a moat of water. Two young are usually raised.

list of species seen

....

....

....

....

....

....

....

....

....

....

....

Ducks and Geese

Across the world, ducks and geese are symbolic of wild places, even though a good number have adapted to man-made environments. Together with swans (of which there are no species in sub-Saharan Africa) ducks and geese are often referred to as "waterfowl" or "wildfowl" which indicates their age-old significance as a source of food and sport. There are over 150 species around the world, of which about 30 occur in Africa. All live in aquatic habitats where they feed on plant matter and invertebrates. Large clutches (up to 14 eggs in some species) are laid in a bowl among vegetation or in a tree cavity.

The Egyptian goose is perhaps the most widespread of African waterfowl, and these noisy birds are aggressive in defense of their territories and young. The white-faced whistling duck is one of two similar species which call with a sweet, high-pitched whistle when coming and going from feeding grounds or roost sites. The red-billed teal is one of several "typical" ducks which feed by dabbling at the water's edge or upending in deep water. The toy-like African pygmy-goose favors quiet inlets where water lilies abound.

list of species seen

Red-billed Teal
18 in. (45cm)

African
Pygmy-Goose
11 in. (30cm)

Egyptian Goose
28 in. (70cm)

Crakes, Rails, Gallinules, Moorhens, Coots and Finfoots

Collectively known as rallids, these are small to medium-sized birds with stubby tails and short rounded wings. Most are incredibly shy and typically solitary, although the gregarious coots do not follow this trend. All are omnivorous, feeding on insects, amphibians and a variety of plant material. Because they live in reedbeds and other dense habitats, rallids are vocal in advertisement of their territories. Among the species that are most often encountered, are the red-knobbed coot and common moorhen which may be abundant around dams, lakes and estuaries. The skittish black crake resides along rivers and pools and is the least timid of its family. With its bright red bill and frontal shield, the African purple swamphen (gallinule) is a spectacular bird. The tiny flufftails are the most elusive of all rallids.

The African finfoot is a shy and peculiar waterbird belonging to a separate family.

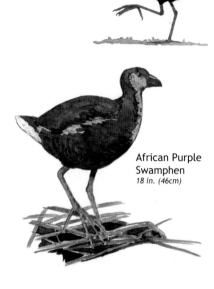

Black Crake
7 in. (18cm)

African Purple Swamphen
18 in. (46cm)

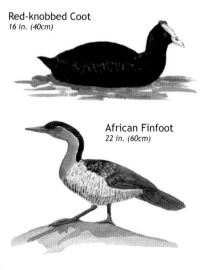

Red-knobbed Coot
16 in. (40cm)

African Finfoot
22 in. (60cm)

list of species seen

....
....
....
....
....
....
....
....
....
....

Bustards and Ostrich

These two bird families are not related, although they have similar lifestyles and occupy open landscapes, including deserts. Like ostriches, all bustards forage, roost and nest on the ground.

Bustards are medium to large-sized birds with distinctive calls and territorial displays. Their plumage is sandy-brown and most are well camouflaged. Males are larger, often with bold facial markings. Seeds, succulent plants and insects feature in the diet. The 40 lb (18kg) kori bustard is the world's heaviest flying bird.

The flightless ostrich is the world's largest bird, weighing up to 250 lbs (120kg) and its egg is the size of 24 chicken eggs. Ostrich have been domesticated in South Africa and Namibia (as well as in Texas and Australia). Wild ostriches are limited to large reserves and wilderness areas. Several females may lay their eggs in a single ground "nest."

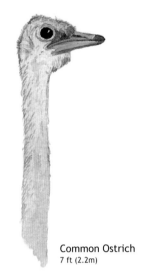

Common Ostrich
7 ft (2.2m)

Red-crested Korhaan
20 in. (50cm)

Kori Bustard
4 ft 2 in. (1.3m)

list of species seen

....
....
....
....
....
....
....
....
....
....
....
....
....
....

Guineafowl, Francolins and Spurfowl

These ground-dwelling birds are close relatives of partridges, pheasants and turkeys. They are collectively known as "game birds" due their popularity in human cuisine and sport hunting. Most African species are drably colored to blend in with their savannah and grassland habitats, but all are highly vocal. They have short rounded wings which allow for rapid but brief flight, and they often burst from cover in a flurry. All have strong legs, well developed for scraping for seeds and bulbs in hard soil. In several species the adult males have sharp rear-facing spurs above the hind toe (as in the domestic chicken) which are used in territorial fights. Most francolins and spurfowl live in pairs or small coveys, but the guineafowl are gregarious and may live in flocks of 100 or more. The helmeted guineafowl is widespread and often abundant in savannah and grassland, while the spectacular vulturine guineafowl lives in semiarid scrublands of East Africa. The much shyer crested guineafowl is a bird of coastal and evergreen forest. Quails (of which there are three African species) are miniature partridges, while the superficially similar buttonquails are thought to be more closely related to coursers (page 199).

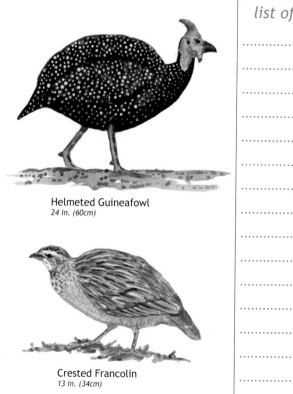

Helmeted Guineafowl
24 in. (60cm)

Crested Francolin
13 in. (34cm)

list of species seen

....
....
....
....
....
....
....
....
....
....
....
....
....
....
....

Vultures

Vultures are the undertakers of the African savannah, feeding primarily on the carcasses of large mammals, including the remains of carnivore kills. These big birds are superbly equipped for a scavenging lifestyle, as they soar to great heights in order to scan the countryside below. When one beady-eyed vulture spots a meal, it attracts many others as it descends rapidly to the scene. A squabble invariably ensues among feeding vultures as individuals feed voraciously. The white-backed vulture is usually the most numerous species, while the massive lappet-faced vulture is the most dominant. The uncommon white-headed vulture is often the first to locate a carcass, but it just as often pirates a smaller meal from an eagle or stork. The hooded vulture has a varied diet which includes termites and lion droppings, while the Egyptian vulture is known to throw small rocks at ostrich eggs in order to open and eat them.

White-backed Vulture
3 ft 2 in. (95cm)

list of species seen

....
....
....
....
....
....
....
....
....
....
....
....
....
....
....

Lappet-faced Vulture
4 ft (1.2m)

White-headed Vulture
2 ft 7 in. (84cm)

Eagles

Africa is home to a variety of impressive eagles, some no bigger than a hawk, others massive. All are equipped with powerful talons and a strong hooked bill for grasping and tearing their prey. Eagles are masters of flight, soaring effortlessly on thermals or swooping at great speed. Pairs typically mate for life, nesting on or below a tree canopy, or on a precipitous cliff. Several similarly-plumaged brown eagles pose identification problems for beginners, while the immature plumages of many are similarly confusing. The African fish eagle is a conspicuous resident of waterways and lakes, where its piercing cry is an evocative sound. The almost tailless bateleur soars with hardly a wing beat above the savannah tree tops, while powerful martial and crowned eagles prey upon monitors, hyrax and even small antelope.

African Fish Eagle
2 ft 4 in. (70cm)

Verreaux's Eagle
2 ft 8 in. (88cm)

Bateleur
2 ft 1 in. (62cm)

Martial Eagle
2 ft 8 in. (85cm)

list of species seen

....
....
....
....
....
....
....
....
....
....
....
....
....
....
....

Hawks, Kites and Buzzards

A variety of sparrowhawks and goshawks (collectively known as accipiters), kites, and buzzards (mostly of the genus *Buteo*) can be found in most habitats, although many are unobtrusive or even secretive. Not so, the almost gull-like black-shouldered kite which is a common roadside bird, while the scavenging black and yellow-billed kites may be numerous around towns and villages. The little sparrowhawk and African goshawk are predators of birds, while the pale chanting goshawk and lizard buzzard prefer reptiles. The shikra (little banded goshawk) takes birds, lizards and squirrels. The specialized bat hawk preys almost exclusively on these winged mammals and is active only at dusk and dawn. The jackal and augur buzzards are birds of grassy mountains, where they may be joined by migratory common and steppe buzzards.

Augur Buzzard
20 in. (52cm)

Black-shouldered Kite
13 in. (32cm)

Shikra
12 in. (30cm)

list of species seen

....
....
....
....
....
....
....
....
....
....
....
....
....
....
....
....

Secretarybird, Osprey and Harriers

The unique secretarybird is a specialized bird of prey which hunts snakes, lizards and rodents in open savannah or grassland. Pairs of these elegant birds construct a large platform nest of sticks, usually on a flat-crowned tree. The fish-eating osprey is a non-breeding migrant to Africa, where it takes up residence on lake shores and coastal estuaries. Harriers are narrow-winged, long-tailed raptors of grasslands and wetlands where they glide in buoyant flight in search of their rodent and bird prey. Several species of Eurasian harriers visit African grasslands between October and March.

Secretarybird
4 ft 5 in. (1.4m)

Osprey
2 ft 1 in. (65cm)

Montagu's Harrier
18 in. (48cm)

list of species seen

....
....
....
....
....
....
....
....
....
....
....
....
....
....

Falcons and Kestrels

These small to mid-size birds of prey are characterized by long pointed wings. They are further distinguished from other raptors by the notch, or 'tooth' on the cutting edge of the upper bill. Most have dark moustacial stripes from the base of the eye to the throat. The lanner and peregrine falcons are bird hunters, stooping at great speed to knock down their prey in flight. The peregrine has been clocked at more than 100 mph (160km/hr) which makes it the fastest of all birds. Kestrels feed primarily on rodents or insects such as winged termites and locusts, and they often gather in large numbers when food is abundant. The lesser kestrel is one of several Eurasian species that are nonbreeding migrants to Africa. The pygmy falcon is hardly bigger than a shrike and feeds mostly on sand lizards. All falcons and kestrels nest either on a rocky ledge or in a cavity.

Lanner Falcon
16 in. (42cm)

Lesser Kestrel
12 in. (30cm)

Pygmy Falcon
7 in. (18cm)

list of species seen

....
....
....
....
....
....
....
....
....
....
....
....
....
....
....

Lapwings and Plovers

These are small to medium-sized birds with slender legs, of open habitats such as short grasslands, farmlands and the shores of lakes, rivers and sea. Africa has 18 resident species and several seasonal migrants from Eurasia. The plumage of most species is brown, grey or black, with paler underparts and variable amounts of white on the wings; some have bold head or chest patterns. They are usually seen in pairs or small groups, quietly running off when approached or — if nesting — putting on a noisy distraction display. Two to four camouflaged eggs are laid on the ground in a shallow scrape. Pairs of blacksmith lapwings have been observed defending their eggs or nestlings from trampling by elephant and buffalo, by calling raucously and constantly flying into the face of the large mammals! Invertebrates such as worms, insects and crustaceans are the main food of lapwings and plovers.

Crowned Lapwing
12 in. (30cm)

White-fronted Plover
6 in. (16cm)

Three-banded Plover
7 in. (18cm)

Blacksmith Lapwing
12 in. (30cm)

list of species seen

....
....
....
....
....
....
....
....
....
....
....
....
....
....
....
....
....

Waders (shorebirds)

This is a group of small to mid-sized birds which includes sandpipers, godwits, snipes and curlews.

These waders have sensitive bill tips and probe mud or sand for their invertebrate prey. The length of neck, bill and legs is extremely variable as each species exploits a particular food source in a particular niche. With the exception of the African snipe, all species seen in Africa are nonbreeding migrants from the Arctic circle or temperate parts of Eurasia. They are present in greatest numbers between September and March, but some individuals remain in Africa throughout the year. Waders typically gather in mixed-species flocks on tidal mudflats, along beaches and on lake shores. Seeing large flocks of sandpipers rise, circle and land on a lake shore can be truly spectacular sight.

Wood Sandpiper
9 in. (21cm)

Greenshank
13 in. (32cm)

Common Sandpiper
8 in. (19cm)

list of species seen

....
....
....
....
....
....
....
....
....
....
....
....
....
....
....

Jacanas, Stilt, Avocet, Oystercatchers, Thick-knees, Coursers and Pratincoles

This diverse group of birds are related to lapwings and waders, but several species have a specialized anatomy. The African jacana has extraordinary long toes and claws which allows it to spread its body weight and walk on floating plants. These jacanas are also remarkable in having a polyandrous mating system in which females mate with several males which then attend to all parental duties. The black-winged stilt is aptly named with its very thin legs and bill, while the equally skinny pied avocet has a sharply up-curved bill. Oystercatchers are birds of rocky coastlines where they pry open mussels, oysters and other bivalves with their chisel-shaped bills. Thick-knees are nocturnal, large-eyed birds of open country and shorelines where their drab plumage affords superb camouflage. Coursers are also birds of the night with camouflaged plumage, and many species are attracted to recently burned or overgrazed grasslands where they feed and raise young. The short-legged pratincoles have pointed wings and forked tails. These gregarious birds are conspicuous in flight above grasslands, croplands and marshes.

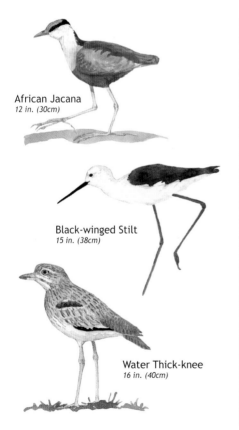

African Jacana
12 in. (30cm)

Black-winged Stilt
15 in. (38cm)

Water Thick-knee
16 in. (40cm)

list of species seen

....
....
....
....
....
....
....
....
....
....
....
....
....
....
....

Sandgrouse

Sandgrouse are plump, pigeon-like birds which feed exclusively on the ground. Their intricately-patterned plumage affords excellent camouflage in their preferred habitats of desert, scrubland and semiarid savannah. With a diet consisting largely of dry seeds, sandgrouse must drink daily and large numbers typically congregate at favored waterholes. Different species have particular drinking times, with the double-banded sandgrouse quenching their thirst at dusk or after dark and the yellow-throated sandgrouse drinking only in the morning. In a unique anatomical adaptation, male sandgrouse have absorbent breast feathers which enable them to carry water droplets back to their nestlings which may be many miles away. Sandgrouse fly rapidly and call in flight, often giving their presence away from a distance. Falcons are among the chief predators of sandgrouse, often waiting at favored drinking sites to ambush their quarry.

Namaqua Sandgrouse
10 in. (25cm)

Double-banded Sandgrouse
9 in. (21cm)

Yellow-throated Sandgrouse
12 in. (30cm)

list of species seen

....
....
....
....
....
....
....
....
....
....
....
....
....
....

Doves and Pigeons

Doves and pigeons are familiar birds across the world. The rock dove is resident in many large cities and domesticated hybrids are kept as racing pigeons. Doves are generally smaller than pigeons, but there are no distinct physical differences. There are over 30 species of pigeon and dove in Africa where they occur in all habitats from semidesert to tropical rainforest. The African mourning dove is one of several similar ring necked doves, while the emerald-spotted wood dove is a common but inconspicuous bird of savannah where its mournful call is repeated throughout the day. Most doves feed exclusively on seeds but some larger pigeons favor berries. The African green pigeon relishes ripe figs and may spend hours gorging itself in a single tree.

African Green Pigeon
11 in. (28cm)

Emerald-spotted Wood Dove
7 in. (18cm)

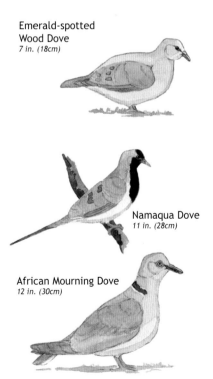

Namaqua Dove
11 in. (28cm)

African Mourning Dove
12 in. (30cm)

list of species seen

....
....
....
....
....
....
....
....
....
....
....
....
....
....
....
....
....

Gulls, Terns and Skimmers

These are predominantly white birds when adult, although most have a different nonbreeding plumage which makes identification tricky. Immatures have plumage in shades of brown and grey. Gulls and terns are agile in flight with long wings that extend beyond the tail when the bird is at rest. The greatest diversity occurs along seashores, but some species favor inland lakes of fresh water. The grey-headed gull is resident around many of Africa's lakes and, as a scavenger, also frequents garbage dumps. Terns are more slender than gulls and have longer pointed bills ideal for snapping up small fish from the surface of water. The whiskered, white-winged and Caspian terns frequent freshwater lakes, while the migratory gull-billed tern regularly visits Rift Valley lakes. The Arctic tern undergoes an extraordinary migration each year from its breeding grounds close to the north pole to the fringe of Antarctica, and numbers can be seen along the African coast. It is usual for several species of tern to mingle and roost together on isolated beaches. The African skimmer resides on larger rivers where it skims the water surface to capture small fish. This black and white bird has a unique bill with the lower mandible being longer than the upper. Like terns, skimmers lay their eggs in a shallow scrape on an exposed bed of sand.

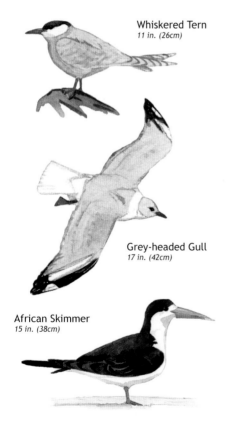

Whiskered Tern
11 in. (26cm)

Grey-headed Gull
17 in. (42cm)

African Skimmer
15 in. (38cm)

list of species seen

....
....
....
....
....
....
....
....
....
....
....
....
....
....
....

Parrots and Lovebirds

With just 20 species, half of which have very restricted distributions, Africa has a small variety of parrots in comparison to South America or Australia. Parrots are readily identified by their large head and strongly hooked bill. They are fast fliers, usually moving in a straight line and letting out a strong piercing call while on the move. African parrots are drably colored in comparison to their international relatives, although they display bright underwings and rumps in flight. The tiny lovebirds are more brightly plumaged in shades of lime green, yellow and red. Most lovebirds favor semiarid scrubland and savannah where they may go about in large flocks. All parrots are hole nesters, often in palm or baobab trees. The grey parrot is a popular cage bird due to its ability to mimic human voices, and large numbers are illegally trapped for the illegal pet trade.

Grey Parrot
12 in. (30cm)

Fischer's Lovebird
5 in. (13cm)

Brown (Meyer's) Parrot
10 in. (24cm)

list of species seen

....

....

....

....

....

....

....

....

....

....

....

....

....

....

Cuckoos and Coucals

Cuckoos are slender birds with long tails and pointed wings which give some species a hawk-like appearance. They have arched bills and feed predominantly on caterpillars. Most cuckoos are elusive and seldom seen, but they are among the most vociferous of all birds. Some have monotonous calls which may go for hours, and sometimes even on moonlit nights. True cuckoos are brood parasites which lay their eggs in the nest of a particular host species, which then carries out parental duties oblivious to the fact that it is not raising its own offspring. In most cases, the host's eggs or nestlings are evicted, but in others, the cuckoo chick is raised alongside its own nestlings. The diderick cuckoo parasitizes weavers and bishops, and is one of three small iridescent green cuckoos in Africa. The larger red-chested cuckoo is a noisy but secretive bird which parasitizes various robin-chats and thrushes. Most cuckoos are migratory, including the common cuckoo which journeys to Africa from European woodlands. The coucals are larger and bulkier than true cuckoos, and possess a deeper more powerful bill. The Senegal coucal is one of several species which favors the fringes of wetlands and proclaims its territory with a bubbling liquid call. Coucals raise their own young and do not parasitize the nests of other birds, but frequently include nestlings in their diet.

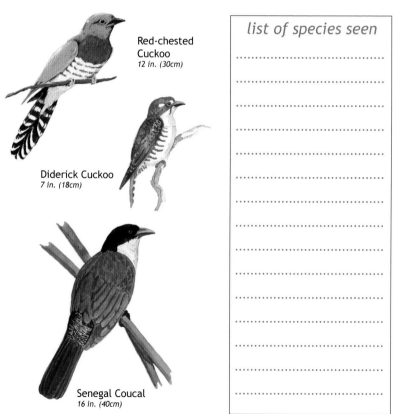

Red-chested
Cuckoo
12 in. (30cm)

Diderick Cuckoo
7 in. (18cm)

Senegal Coucal
16 in. (40cm)

list of species seen

....
....
....
....
....
....
....
....
....
....
....
....
....
....

Turacos

Turacos are a uniquely African bird family of 23 species, most of which are forest dwellers. Some are extremely beautiful with green or violet plumage with crimson wing feathers, while the savannah-dwellers (known as go-away birds) are predominantly grey in color. Turacos feed on berries and figs as well as flowers and leaf buds. Few birds have such harsh and unattractive calls, however, with croaks and barks being the most apt description for their vocal skills. The go-away birds of open acacia savannah derive their name from the rasping "go-way" cry which is sounded both as a contact call and a warning. This call is given whenever a human is seen and game hunters are often frustrated when their quarry reacts to this alarm call by fleeing. The grey go-away bird of Southern Africa and the bare-faced go-away bird of East Africa are among the most noticeable species on any safari. Less often seen are the richly-colored Ross's turaco of Ugandan and Kenyan forests, Knysna turaco of southern and eastern South Africa, and Ruspoli's turaco of Ethiopian juniper forests. The massive great blue turaco is a bird of the equatorial rainforest.

Grey Go-away Bird
19 in. (48cm)

Knysna Turaco
16 in. (40cm)

Ross's Turaco
21 in. (52cm)

list of species seen

....
....
....
....
....
....
....
....
....
....
....
....
....
....
....

Owls and Nightjars

Owls are the nocturnal equivalent of hawks, preying upon rodents, birds, geckos, frogs and insects. Since owls rely on their own acute hearing to hunt, silent flight is essential and so they have soft plumage with unique fuzzy feather edges. African owls range in size from the two-foot-tall Verreaux's eagle owl to the tiny pearl-spotted owlet and African scops owl. Among serious birders, the rare Pel's fishing owl is among Africa's most sought-after species. The barn owl is one of the world's mostly widely distributed birds, occurring on all continents. Nightjars are thought to be related to owls but these nocturnal insectivores are perhaps more similar to swifts (page 214). Many nightjars have melodic songs and they are most often seen resting on sandy vehicle tracks after dark.

Verreaux's (Giant) Eagle Owl
2 ft 2 in. (66cm)

Barn Owl
14 in. (35cm)

Pearl-spotted Owlet
7 in. (18cm)

Fiery-necked Nightjar
10 in. (24cm)

list of species seen

....
....
....
....
....
....
....
....
....
....
....
....
....
....

Hoopoes and Honeyguides

Hoopoes and wood-hoopoes are insectivorous birds with long, slender, curved bills. The African hoopoe forages on the ground but flies into trees when disturbed, often raising its ornate glove-shaped crest. Typical of its kind, the green wood-hoopoe is a gregarious, noisy bird which explores the bark of trees for beetle larvae and caterpillars. The common and Abyssinian scimitarbills go about in pairs but forage in the same manner as the larger wood-hoopoes. All hoopoes nest in tree cavities.

The unrelated honeyguides are drably colored birds, but all have distinctive calls. The greater honeyguide feeds on wax and bee larvae, sometimes leading humans to hives with its chattering call. Like cuckoos, honeyguides are brood parasites, laying their eggs in the nests of hoopoes, wood-hoopoes, barbets, bee-eaters and other hole nesters, which then raise the imposters as their own. All honeyguides have conspicuous white outer-tail feathers which are obvious in flight.

African Hoopoe
11 in. (26cm)

eater Honeyguide
(20cm)

Green Wood-Hoopoe
15 in. (36cm)

list of species seen

....
....
....
....
....
....
....
....
....
....
....
....
....
....
....
....
....

Hornbills

With their oversized, banana-shaped bills, hornbills are unmistakeable and these charismatic birds are also among the most interesting to observe. Although not brightly colored, many species have colorful bills or bare facial skin, and the males of some have a raised section on the upper mandible known as a casque. Most hornbills are omnivores, feeding on berries, figs and insects, although small rodents, lizards and nestling birds may also be taken. The massive southern ground hornbill regularly preys on large snakes. Hornbills appear to mate for life and have a unique breeding strategy in which the female is sealed into a nest cavity while incubating, receiving food from her mate. Once nestlings begin to grow feathers, the female emerges and joins her partner in feeding the brood.

Silvery-cheeked Hornbill
3 ft (1m)

Von der Decken's Hornbill
18 in. (46cm)

Southern Ground Hornbill
3 ft 4 in. (1.1m)

list of species seen

....
....
....
....
....
....
....
....
....
....
....
....
....
....

Woodpeckers and Barbets

Woodpeckers spend most of their time on the trunks of trees where they drill for beetle larvae and excavate nest holes. Several species feed mostly on ants. Most African woodpeckers are rather similar in appearance with greenish backs and barred or streaked underparts. Males often have bright red caps or moustache streaks. The strong tail feathers are used as a brace, while the two-forward, two-backward toe arrangement helps them grip branches. The ground woodpecker of southern Africa nests in sand banks and feeds in grasslands.

Barbets have some similarities to woodpeckers including the toe arrangement and ability to excavate their own nests in tree branches (although some favor sand banks or termite mounds). They have stout bills and feed primarily on berries and figs. Most barbets have strange trilling or rattling calls, often made in duet by a pair. The tinkerbirds are diminutive barbets with monotonous calls.

Bearded Woodpecker
9 in. (22cm)

Spot-flanked Barbet
5 in. (14cm)

Crested Barbet
9 in. (22cm)

Double-toothed Barbet
10 in. (24cm)

list of species seen

....
....
....
....
....
....
....
....
....
....
....
....
....
....
....

Rollers and Bee-eaters

Rollers are brightly colored birds with rather large heads and strong curved bills. With its spectacular cobalt blue wings, the lilac-breasted roller is one of the first bird species to be noticed on safari, especially as it flies across roads or sits on prominent perches. Rollers feed on large insects, scorpions and small reptiles. Their name comes from a tumbling courtship or territorial display flight in which birds "roll" through the air. Bee-eaters are slender, brilliantly-colored birds with thin, down-curved bills. As their name suggests they feed on bees as well as dragonflies and other winged insects. Most bee-eaters are gregarious when breeding at sandbank colonies, or when feeding, and many species are associated with water.

Lilac-breasted Roller
12 in. + 4 in. tail (32cm)

Little Bee-eater
6 in. (16cm)

Southern
Carmine Bee-eater
12 in. + 4 in. tail (32cm)

Broad-billed Roller
10 in. (26cm)

list of species seen

....
....
....
....
....
....
....
....
....
....
....
....
....
....
....

Kingfishers

Kingfishers are thickset birds with short tails, tiny feet and large heads with long straight bills. Of 17 species in Africa, seven live up to their name and feed primarily on fish, but the others are "dryland" kingfishers which prey upon lizards, beetles and other large insects. Kingfishers excavate nesting burrows in sandbanks, or commandeer tree holes made by woodpeckers. The giant kingfisher is the largest member of the family, while the minute African pygmy kingfisher is one of the smallest. The pied and malachite kingfisher are common along many African waterways, while the noisy and demonstrative woodland kingfisher is typical of the dry-land group.

Woodland Kingfisher
9 in. (22cm)

Giant Kingfisher
16 in. (42cm)

Pied Kingfisher
9 in. (24cm)

Malachite Kingfisher
5 in. (13cm)

list of species seen

....
....
....
....
....
....
....
....
....
....
....
....
....
....
....
....
....
....

Mousebirds, Trogons and Broadbills

Mousebirds are a uniquely African bird family with six species distributed in open savannah and woodland habitats. Their name comes from their predominantly grey color, long tail and habit of creeping around in bushes like mice. Mousebirds feed on small berries including those of mistletoe, as well as figs. Most are gregarious and call when in rapid flight.

Trogon diversity is greatest in southeast Asia and tropical America, and Africa has just three species. The beautiful narina trogon is a bird of the evergreen forest where it feeds on katydids, cicadas and other large insects. Trogons have deep hooting calls and nest in holes.

Broadbills are also better represented in Asia, and all but one of the four African species is dressed in sombre plumage. The dumpy African broadbill lives in forest and thickets where it draws attention to itself with a strange whirring call and acrobatic display.

Narina Trogon
12 in. (32cm)

African Broadbill
5 in. (13cm)

Blue-naped Mousebird
13 in. (34cm)

list of species seen

....
....
....
....
....
....
....
....
....
....

Larks, Longclaws, Pipits and Wagtails

Although larks are very similar in appearance to pipits they are not in fact related, whereas the longclaws and wagtails belong to the same family as pipits. All are birds of open country, especially grasslands, although the wagtails live along rivers and shorelines. The identification of most larks and pipits is a challenge even to experienced birders, but the longclaws have bright throat patches of yellow, orange or pink. Many larks have sweet melodious voices which aid identification, and the rufous-naped lark is one of the most widespread and conspicuous. Some larks feed primarily on seeds, but many are insectivorous like the pipits. All nest on the ground beneath grass tufts or among rocks.

Rufous-naped Lark
7 in. (18cm)

African Pied Wagtail
8 in. (20cm)

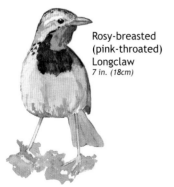

Rosy-breasted (pink-throated) Longclaw
7 in. (18cm)

list of species seen

....
....
....
....
....
....
....
....
....
....
....
....
....
....
....

Swifts and Swallows

Swifts and swallows are similar in appearance but are not closely related. Both families are adapted to feed in flight, taking minute winged insects. The most noticeable difference between swifts and swallows, is that the former have narrower wings which give them a sickle-shaped appearance, while swallows have broader wings and frequently manoeuvre their tail feathers in flight.

Swifts have tiny feet which do not allow them to perch on branches or wires, although they can cling strongly to rock walls. Interestingly, the closest relatives of swifts are the New World hummingbirds (a family absent in Africa). Swifts are typically black or dark brown in color, with white markings in some species. Tail shape is an important clue to the identification of species. The African palm swift nests in the crown of tall palms, while the little swift builds its nest on cliff overhangs, tall buildings or beneath bridges.

Swallows and martins come to the ground to collect mud for their cup-shaped nests. Many swallows are dark blue on the back with elongated tail streamers, while martins tend to be brown or blue with square tails. The barn swallow visits Africa from its European breeding grounds between October and April.

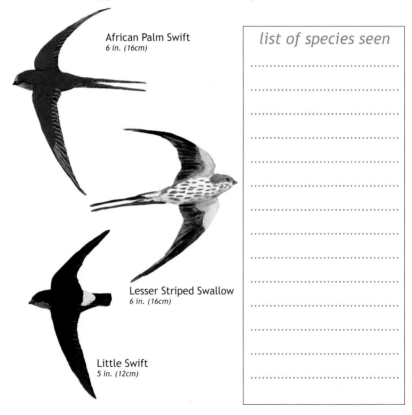

African Palm Swift
6 in. (16cm)

Lesser Striped Swallow
6 in. (16cm)

Little Swift
5 in. (12cm)

list of species seen

....

....

....

....

....

....

....

....

....

....

....

....

....

....

Bulbuls, Babblers and Nicators

Bulbuls (including brownbuls and greenbuls) are medium-sized birds lacking bright coloration. The forest-dwelling species are known as greenbuls and are extremely difficult to tell apart. The dark-capped bulbul and its close relatives are birds of open country and frequently visit gardens and picnic sites where they are conspicuous and noisy. Without exception, the greenbuls are skulking birds of forest interiors or canopies where they rarely present a clear view of themselves and are best identified by their call. Most bulbuls and greenbuls tend to go about in pairs, although groups may gather at abundant food sources. Small berries and insects feature in the diet.

Babblers (and chatterers) are aptly named for their insistent calls. These medium-sized birds live in family groups in which all members raise the young and defend a fixed territory. Babblers are devoid of bright colors although some are boldly patterned in black and white. The rufous chatterer and arrow-marked babbler are among the most conspicuous members of this family.

Nicators have some physical similarities to bushshrikes, but they are thought to be more closely related to bulbuls. The Eastern nicator is an extremely shy and skulking bird with an explosive liquid call.

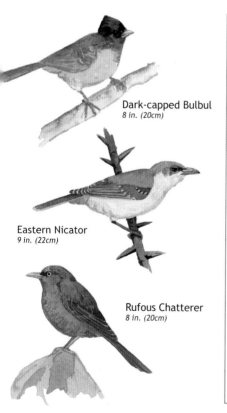

Dark-capped Bulbul
8 in. (20cm)

Eastern Nicator
9 in. (22cm)

Rufous Chatterer
8 in. (20cm)

list of species seen

....

....

....

....

....

....

....

....

....

....

....

....

....

....

Thrushes, Robins, Chats and Wheatear

This is a group of small to medium-sized birds, several with bright or distinct coloration. Numerous species have fine voices, and some are accomplished mimics of other birds. All have sharp, slender bills and forage mostly on the ground where they feed on earthworms and insects. Pairs form strong bonds and defend small territories with their strident calls.

Thrushes are plump birds with sombre plumage, usually seen flicking through dead leaves or hopping on lawns for their food. Rock thrushes are birds of mountainous country where they often perch conspicuously on boulders. Robin chats have orange underparts with bold head patterns, and favor dense cover of forests, thickets and gardens. Scrub robins are birds of dry savannah where they retreat into thickets when disturbed. Chats and wheatears are birds of open country including grasslands and deserts. Palm thrushes (also known as morning thrushes), stonechats, akalats and alethes also belong to this family of birds.

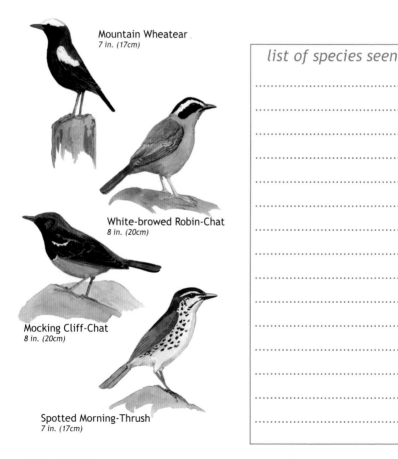

Mountain Wheatear
7 in. (17cm)

White-browed Robin-Chat
8 in. (20cm)

Mocking Cliff-Chat
8 in. (20cm)

Spotted Morning-Thrush
7 in. (17cm)

list of species seen

....
....
....
....
....
....
....
....
....
....
....
....
....
....

Warblers

This group of small to tiny birds includes many cryptic and furtive species, although many have loud and distinctive calls. Because most are difficult to differentiate, they are often ignored by all but the most serious of birdwatchers. All warblers are insectivorous and forage alone or in pairs. Some are nonbreeding migrants from Eurasia.

Warblers fall into various groups. The reed warblers are mostly brown and rarely emerge from reedbeds where they sing stridently. Tree warblers are brown or olive green and flit within leafy canopies. Apalisis are boldly marked with long tails and many have a dark band below the throat. Crombecs have slender curved bills and virtually no tail. The greenish-colored camaropteras have loud bleating calls and inhabit the densest thickets. Prinias are not shy and quickly investigate any disturbance by calling loudly and flicking their long tails. Cisticolas are tan or sand colored and the 50 or so African species show few distinguishing features. Cisticolas occupy grassland, marshland or savannah where species can be told apart by their habitat preference, call and back patterns.

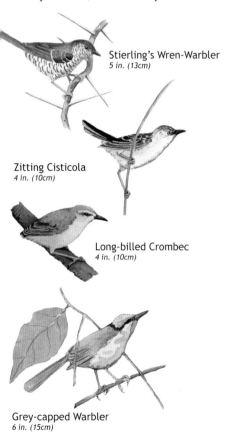

Stierling's Wren-Warbler
5 in. (13cm)

Zitting Cisticola
4 in. (10cm)

Long-billed Crombec
4 in. (10cm)

Grey-capped Warbler
6 in. (15cm)

list of species seen

....
....
....
....
....
....
....
....
....
....
....
....
....
....

Flycatchers and Batises

Flycatchers are small to medium-sized birds which fall into two main groups: the true flyatchers and the monarchs. The batises and wattle-eyes may actually be more closely related to shrikes (page 220) but this relationship is under taxonomic review. Nevertheless, all these birds have broad flat bills with bristles around their mouths which allow them to snap up insects in flight. The African paradise-flycatcher is one of the monarchs and the long-tailed males are among the most eye-catching of birds. All monarchs have broad tails which they regularly fan out. True flycatchers such as the ashy, spotted, silverbird and white-eyed slaty flycatcher, hawk insects from a perch to which they return with their food. Like others of its kind, the chin-spot batis feeds by searching the undersides of leaves for insects and their larvae. Wattle-eyes keep to dense cover, where they forage in the manner of batises, and several species are restricted to equatorial rainforest. All flycatchers build open cup-shaped nests, which — in the case of monarchs and batises — are miniature works of art bound together with spiders' web and decorated with lichen or moss. The Southern and Northern black flycatchers are easily confused with drongos, but lack the red eyes and hooked bills of these birds (page 219).

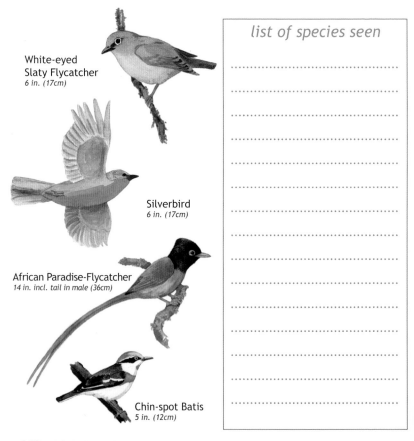

White-eyed
Slaty Flycatcher
6 in. (17cm)

Silverbird
6 in. (17cm)

African Paradise-Flycatcher
14 in. incl. tail in male (36cm)

Chin-spot Batis
5 in. (12cm)

list of species seen

....
....
....
....
....
....
....
....
....
....
....
....
....
....

Drongos, Orioles, Cuckooshrikes and Tits

Drongos, orioles and cuckooshrikes are medium-sized birds with sharp, slender bills used mostly for capturing insects. Drongos have hooked tips to their bills, and mouth bristles like flycatchers, which are used to hawk insects in flight. The cuckooshrikes are unobtrusive birds which search foliage and bark for their prey. The predominantly yellow orioles have a more varied diet which includes berries and nectar as well as caterpillars and insects. All of these birds build neat cup-shaped nests, bound with web and camouflaged with lichen or bark strips. The fork-tailed drongo is a conspicuous bird as it perches openly and frequently accompanies giraffe and other large mammals which disturb insects when they feed. Drongos are noteworthy for their bold attacks on large birds of prey, their aggressive mobbing of owls, and their ability to mimic calls of other birds. The African golden oriole has a beautiful liquid call typical of its family. Like the cuckooshrikes, orioles forage mostly in tree canopies and often go unseen.

Tits (same family as the American chickadees) are small, restless birds which forage among leaves and bark. They have short but strong bills which they use to pull insect larvae from seedpods and bark. Tits are mostly grey or black, have unmusical rasping calls and nest in tree cavities.

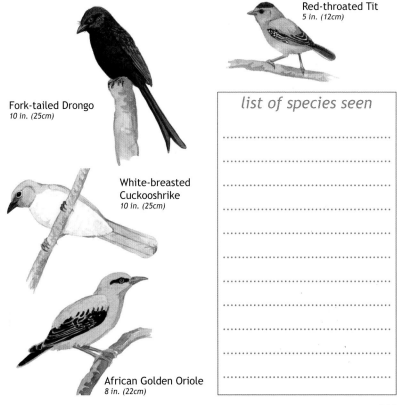

Red-throated Tit
5 in. (12cm)

Fork-tailed Drongo
10 in. (25cm)

White-breasted
Cuckooshrike
10 in. (25cm)

African Golden Oriole
8 in. (22cm)

list of species seen

....

....

....

....

....

....

....

....

....

....

Shrikes, Bushshrikes and Helmetshrikes

Shrikes and bushshrikes are mid-sized, predatory birds with hooked bills. The true shrikes are mostly grey or black in color and perch upright on perches in open habitats where they pounce on large insects, lizards and small rodents. Some, such as the common fiscal, spike excess prey onto thorns or barbed wire, to feed on later. The bushshrikes (including the boubous, tchagras and puffbacks) are secretive skulkers of thickets or tree canopies where pairs keep in contact with distinctive calls, often made in duet. The grey-headed bushshrike is the largest member of this tribe and frequently preys upon chameleons and small snakes. Most shrikes and bushshrikes eat nestling birds when the opportunity presents itself, and some prey upon waxbills and other small birds. The helmetshikes are similar in appearance to bushshrikes, but have flatter bills and are not as rapacious. Typical of its family, the white-crested helmetshrike goes about in family groups of up to 12, with all members helping to raise and feed the young in a classic example of "cooperative breeding." The magpie shrike and grey-backed fiscal also breed as family groups rather than in pairs, with previous offspring assisting in nesting duties. All shrikes, bushshrikes and helmetshrikes build cup-shaped nests which are usually camouflaged with strips of bark or lichen.

list of species seen

....

....

....

....

....

....

....

....

....

....

....

....

....

Magpie Shrike
20 in. incl.tail (50cm)

White-crested
Helmetshrike
8 in. (22cm)

Grey-headed
Bushshrike
11 in. (26cm)

Starlings, Oxpeckers and Crows

Starlings are medium-sized birds, many with glossy aqua-blue plumage and bright yellow or red eyes. All have slender bills for a mixed diet of insects and berries. Most are gregarious and gather in large flocks when not breeding. Wattled starlings breed in large colonies and — in the Serengeti — flocks follow the annual wildebeest migration to feed on insects disturbed by the herds. Oxpeckers are specialized starlings with deep, compressed bills which they use to comb ticks from the coats of large mammals. Flocks of these bright-billed birds accompany giraffe, buffalo and most antelope species in a truly commensual relationship, frequently taking to flight with alarm calls when people approach. Like true starlings, oxpeckers build bowl-shaped nests of straw and feathers inside tree cavities.

Crows and ravens (collectively known as corvids) are not closely related to starlings but have a similar anatomy and thus resemble oversized cousins. These familiar birds are predominantly black in color and all make a living as opportunists and scavengers. Crows and ravens are among the most intelligent of all birds and most adapt readily to human developments. All have harsh, croaking calls and build large stick nests in tall trees, cliff faces or man-made structures such as electricity pylons.

Greater Blue-eared Starling
7 in. (18cm)

Superb Starling
7 in. (18cm)

Red-billed Oxpecker
7 in. (18cm)

list of species seen

....

....

....

....

....

....

....

....

....

....

....

....

....

....

Sunbirds and White-eyes

Being specialized nectar feeders, sunbirds are the African equivalent of American hummingbirds, although they perch rather than hover while feeding. Like hummingbirds, they have long bills (and long tongues!) with which they sip nectar, and most species have a variety of specific plants which they favor (and inadvertently pollinate). The males of most sunbirds have iridescent plumage (another trait shared with hummingbirds) and aggressively chase rivals and competitors. That two unrelated bird families should be so similar in appearance and aspects of their behavior, is the result of convergent evolution, where species develop characteristics suited to a particular niche or lifestyle. The drably colored female sunbirds are confusingly similar and best identified by their bill shape, or — since they often forage in pairs or groups — by waiting for a male partner to appear. All make camouflaged purse-shaped nests suspended from plants. Sunbirds are sometimes erroneously called sugarbirds but this is in fact a unique family of two southern African nectivores, possibly related to Australian honeycreepers.

The white-eyes are tiny, green or yellow birds with a distinctive ring of white feathers around their eyes (not bare skin as it appears). They have slender sharp bills which they use to feed on aphids and other tiny insects as well as berries and nectar.

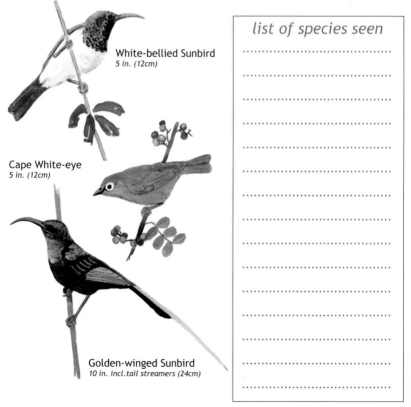

list of species seen

White-bellied Sunbird
5 in. (12cm)

Cape White-eye
5 in. (12cm)

Golden-winged Sunbird
10 in. incl. tail streamers (24cm)

Weavers, Queleas, Sparrows, Buntings, Seedeaters and Canaries

These small to medium-sized birds have compact bodies with short tails, and stout conical bills for cracking open seeds. They tend to be gregarious, and some species go about in great flocks. In the case of the red-billed quelea, these flocks are more aptly described as swarms and this is indeed the most numerous of Africa's birds. A quelea colony attracts hordes of predators from snakes and storks, to mongooses and monitors. Weavers are among the most conspicuous of Africa's birds, not only for their brilliant yellow plumage (mostly in males) but also for their neat and distinctive hanging nests. Each species has its own style of nest, some with lengthy entrance tubes. In the Kalahari, flocks of sociable weavers construct a massive multi-chambered nest resembling a haystack which is insulated to keep out heat and cold. Buffalo-weavers are bulkier than true weavers and most construct untidy twig nests. Sparrow-weavers build untidy nests suspended from the outermost branches of trees, sparrows are familiar to most people and some African species adapt to human settlements alongside the introduced (nonnative) house sparrow. Buntings are small seedeaters with black-and-white-striped heads. Seedeaters are drably colored canaries but like their predominantly yellow cousins, they are fine songsters.

Red-billed Quelea
5 in. (12cm)

Sociable Weaver
6 in. (15cm)

Village Weaver
6 in. (15cm)

White-headed Buffalo-Weaver
9 in. (24cm)

list of species seen

....
....
....
....
....
....
....
....
....
....
....
....
....
....
....

Bishops, Widowbirds and Whydahs

Bishops and widowbirds are close relatives of the weavers (page 223) but are featured separately here due to the elaborate and sometimes colorful breeding plumage of the males. The females are drab, sparrow-like birds, and the males lose their colors and plumes outside the breeding season when they too pose identification difficulties. All have conical bills and feed exclusively on seeds. Males are polygynous, mating with numerous females and leaving them to undertake all parental duties.

The whydahs are much smaller birds but, like the widowbirds, the males acquire long tail plumes during the breeding season. The females and nonbreeding males lack distinctive colors. Belonging to the estrilid family (opposite page) whydahs actually parasitize their relatives in the same manner as cuckoos, matching not only egg color but also the gape pattern of nestling waxbills. The male pinstriped whydah is an aggressive little bird, frequently having as many as six "wives" each of which will raise their own brood while he challenges rival males and courts other females. Male indigobirds (widowfinches) enjoy similar benefits, but are dressed only in black and lack decorative tail plumes.

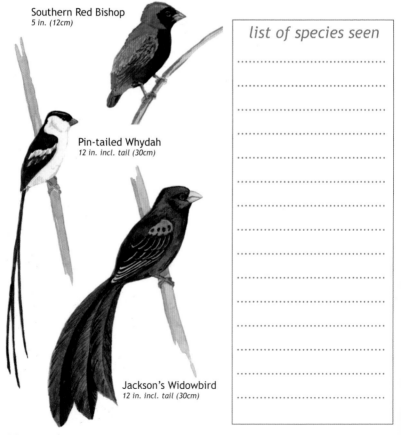

Southern Red Bishop
5 in. (12cm)

Pin-tailed Whydah
12 in. incl. tail (30cm)

Jackson's Widowbird
12 in. incl. tail (30cm)

list of species seen

....
....
....
....
....
....
....
....
....
....
....
....
....
....

Waxbills, Firefinches, Mannikins, Twinspots and other small finches

This group of small to tiny finches are collectively known as estrilids and most are brightly colored. All have small conical bills, ideal for feeding on grass seeds. Some go about in pairs while others are more gregarious and gather in flocks of a dozen or more. It is quite common for several species of waxbill, firefinch, pytilia and mannikin to feed together at an abundant seed supply. The mannikins (known as munias in Asia and Australia) are not to be confused with the berry-eating manakins (note different spelling) of tropical American forests. All estrilids build untidy nests made of fine grasses and lined with feathers, sometimes close to the nests of aggressive paper wasps which act as a deterrent to monkeys and other would-be nest robbers. Some commonly breed in the disused nests of weavers. Many waxbills are birds of semiarid scrublands, while twinspots and crimsonwings are residents of forests. Waxbills and firefinches are habitually parasitized by whydahs and indigobirds (previous page).

Red-billed Firefinch
4 in. (10cm)

Blue Waxbill/Cordonbleu
4 in. (11cm)

Violet-eared Waxbill
4 in. (11cm)

Peters' Twinspot
4 in. (11cm)

list of species seen

....
....
....
....
....
....
....
....
....
....
....
....
....
....

Penguins, Gannets and other seabirds

This is a mixed-bag of birds, placed together here at the end of the bird section since only a few travelers to Africa spend time birdwatching offshore. Penguins are associated with Antarctica and the cold sub-Antarctic waters of the Southern Ocean, so it comes as a surprise to many that the African penguin breeds close to Cape Town and can be seen on the Namibian and Garden Route coasts. Formerly known as the jackass penguin due to its hoarse braying call, this small penguin feeds primarily on pelagic fish caught beyond the continental shelf. The Cape gannet is a

African Penguin
2 ft (65cm)

gregarious bird which catches fish after a direct plunge into the sea. These predominantly white birds breed communally on offshore islands (also at Lambert's Bay on South Africa's west coast) before following the annual "sardine run" up the east coast of South Africa. A rich diversity of albatrosses, petrels, shearwaters, prions and storm-petrels visit the coast of Africa, particularly in the cold waters south of Cape Town. These birds are best seen on specialized offshore birding trips. Spectacular frigatebirds and tropicbirds, as well as boobies, fish in the warmer waters off the East African coast and are frequently encountered around Seychelles and other Indian Ocean islands.

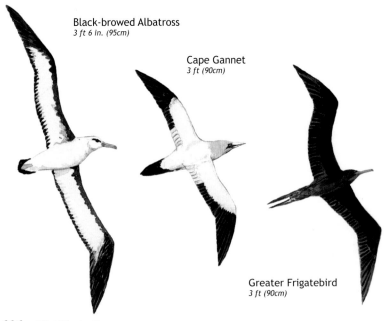

Black-browed Albatross
3 ft 6 in. (95cm)

Cape Gannet
3 ft (90cm)

Greater Frigatebird
3 ft (90cm)

AN INTRODUCTION TO

African Reptiles and Frogs

A wide variety of reptiles and amphibians occur in sub-Saharan Africa, but the great majority are secretive and seldom seen. Reptiles evolved earlier than birds or mammals, so that some of today's species — such as the crocodile and tortoise — have ancient lineages dating back to the Jurassic era when dinosaurs (reptiles themselves) ruled the planet.

Many people have a natural fear of snakes, and dislike all other reptiles, with the possible exception or tortoises and their relatives. Naturally, all reptiles play a vital role in various ecosystems, with snakes and lizards being among the most important predators of rodents and insects, respectively. Several snakes possess venom, which they use to immobilize their prey, and mambas, cobras and adders are among those which are potentially dangerous — even lethal — to people. For this reason, it is best to leave all snakes unmolested or boxed in, as they will rarely, if ever, strike if they have an escape route.

Only a few of the more conspicuous or interesting reptiles and frogs are featured on the following pages. You'll be likely to see crocodiles and terrapins near water, but snakes of any kind are rarely encountered. Lizards are divided into several families or groups, the most distinctive of which are featured here.

Frogs are fascinating creatures and are best looked for with a flashlight or spotlight after dark, particularly in wet weather. A chorus of calling frogs is an evocative and characteristic sound of the African night.

Nile Crocodile

This is the largest and most dangerous of African reptiles. Although stories relating to its size and ferocity are often exaggerated, the crocodile's awesome reputation as a powerful killer cannot be contested. Individuals over 10 feet (3m) in length are opportunistic feeders and include large mammals, including humans in their diet. Crocodiles display tender parental care, astonishing for a primeval reptile whose bodily form has remained unchanged for the past 100 million years. Female crocodiles bury their clutch of 50 or so white eggs in a shallow burrow close to water, and then rest nearby throughout the 90-day incubation period. Once the eggs hatch and the tiny, finger-sized young emerge, they begin yelping and the caring mother carefully takes each one into her mouth. Even unhatched eggs may be picked up and gently cracked to release the young. Packed into their mother's gular pouch, the youngsters are safe until she releases them at the water's edge.

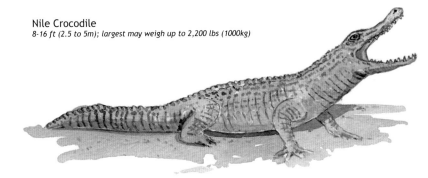

Nile Crocodile
8-16 ft (2.5 to 5m); largest may weigh up to 2,200 lbs (1000kg)

Young crocodiles are secretive and keep to the vegetated fringe of rivers and lakes, but adults bask openly on sandbanks. Fish form the main prey for all age classes, although babies start off with aquatic insects and frogs.

Feared and hated by rural people, and valued for their skins, crocodiles have been subjected to extreme hunting pressure throughout Africa. The oldest and largest specimens are to be found in protected areas, with the individuals in the Mara and Grumeti Rivers of the Serengeti-Mara being among the most impressive. Crocodiles are absent from lakes Naivasha, Nakuru, Natron and Manyara of the high central Rift Valley, but abundant in the western Rift lakes such as Albert, Edward and George, as well as the vast Lake Turkana which formerly held the densest population.

African Rock-Python

This is a huge, thick snake with a broad head and geometric skin pattern. Some individuals may reach a length of 16 feet (5m) when they are capable of capturing and swallowing large prey up to the size of adult Impala. Prey is killed by constriction, literally squeezed to death. Hyraxes in rocky outcrops, and canerats in marshes and sugarcane plantations are favored prey. These snakes are not poisonous but have long fangs capable of inflicting a severe ripping bite. Most active at dusk and after dark. Rock-pythons lay up to 50 eggs which hatch after 65 to 80 days. Females coil around the eggs to protect them, but the hatchlings must fend for themselves.

African Rock-Python
4-16 ft (up to 5m)

Nile Monitor

Nile Monitor
3-6 ft (1 to 2m)

This is a massive semiaquatic lizard which is most frequently seen on river banks and lake fringes. Adults are dark olive brown on the back, and paler below, while juveniles are boldly patterned in yellow and black. These powerful lizards feed on virtually anything they can overpower, as well as the eggs of crocodiles and birds. They will also scavenge from the carcasses of large mammals and fish. Females have the unique habit of laying their clutch of soft-shelled eggs in an active termite mound and then leaving the social insects to close up her diggings and so create ideal conditions for incubation. The similar rock monitor, is somewhat smaller and spends much of its time in trees.

Snakes

Africa has an extraordinary diversity of snakes, from tiny thread-like creatures which rarely come above ground, to the huge rock-python featured on page 229. All snakes are rather shy, however, and rarely encountered. This includes the venomous and potentially dangerous cobras, mambas and adders which will generally avoid humans unless cornered or aggravated in some way. All snakes are carnivorous, swallowing their prey whole and have unfused jaw bones and elastic skin.

Among the most commonly-seen snakes on safari are the various **tree snakes**, including the **boomslang** and well-camouflaged vine snake, which are frequently mobbed and harassed by noisy gangs of birds and so alert people to the presence of these nest robbers.

Adders and **vipers** can be rather slow moving and might be stumbled upon on rocky hillsides, scrub and desert. The puff adder is notoriously sluggish and sometimes suns itself on leafy pathways.

Most **cobras** are primarily nocturnal, feeding on toads and rodents. These dangerous snakes are best known for their expandible "hood," but this is only visible when agitated individuals flatten their neck prior to striking. Some species are able to spit venom with incredible accuracy into the eyes of an adversary. The legendary **black mamba** is diurnal and will not hesitate to strike if it has no escape route. Any bite by a cobra or mamba must be treated as a medical emergency.

The nocturnal **brown house-snake** frequently enters buildings to hunt rats and these harmless and useful reptiles should not be harmed. The **mole snake** seeks out rodents and moles in the subterranean burrows.

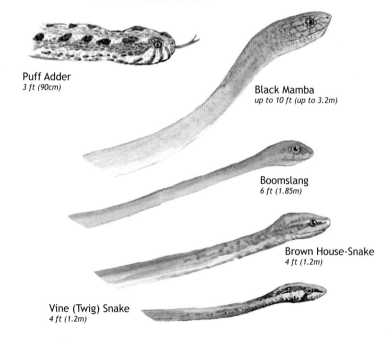

Puff Adder
3 ft (90cm)

Black Mamba
up to 10 ft (up to 3.2m)

Boomslang
6 ft (1.85m)

Brown House-Snake
4 ft (1.2m)

Vine (Twig) Snake
4 ft (1.2m)

Lizards

With the exception of geckos, all lizards are diurnal and many species are frequently encountered. Almost all lizards are insectivorous, although the larger monitors will take bigger vertebrate prey.

Agamas are squat lizards with large box-shaped heads. The males assume bright head and body colors during the breeding season, when they bob up and down on tree trunks or rocks. Females and nonbreeding males are cryptically camouflaged to match their favored terrain.

Skinks are slender, snake-like lizards with short legs; some are actually legless and live beneath the ground. Many species are quite tame and sun themselves in exposed positions, but they rapidly move to cover when threatened.

Geckos are mostly nocturnal and some species are familiar around lodges, hotels and homes where they capture moths and other insects attracted to lights. Dwarf geckos are diurnal and often seen on tree trunks and fallen logs. The dusk call of the barking gecko is a distinctive sound in the Namib and Kalahari.

Plated-lizards are denizens of large rock outcrops while **girdled-lizards** favor these and wooded habitats. **Sand-lizards** are often seen in arid and semiarid habitats. The **monitors** (also known as leguaans) can reach a great size and the Nile monitor is featured on page 229.

Chameleons are distinctive diurnal lizards which rely on their incredible camouflage and ability to change their skin color, in order to ambush insect prey and avoid predation. The widespread flap-necked chameleon may be encountered on night drives when roosting individuals show up whitish in spotlight beams.

Worm-lizards are rarely seen subterranean creatures.

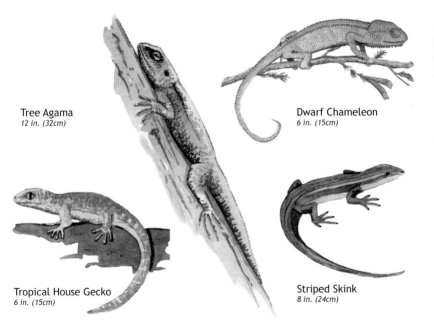

Tree Agama
12 in. (32cm)

Dwarf Chameleon
6 in. (15cm)

Tropical House Gecko
6 in. (15cm)

Striped Skink
8 in. (24cm)

Tortoises, Turtles and Terrapins

These reptiles are instantly recognizable by their shield-like shell. Fossils from ancient chelonians date back over 200 million years, revealing that tortoises and their relatives have been roaming our planet even before the rise of the dinosaurs. There are three main groups all of which have representatives in Africa.

Tortoises live on dry land, moving about on their club-like feet and retracting their heads into their shells when threatened. The large leopard tortoise is the most frequently encountered species and mature specimens may weigh over 44 pounds (20kg). Hinged tortoises have a shell which hinges backwards to protect their rear. A number of small tortoises including geometric tortoises and tent tortoises inhabit the dry parts of southern Africa.

Terrapins live in freshwater where they feed on aquatic plants, tadpoles, frogs and insects. Large individuals may ambush bigger prey such as doves which come to drink at waterholes. Some terrapins can be seen sunning themselves on the backs of hippos, and they may feed on ticks and other ectoparasites on large mammals.

Sea turtles spend their lives in the oceans where they feed largely on jellyfish. Females come ashore seasonally to lay their eggs in excavated nest burrows, and the tiny hatchlings must eventually traverse beaches to reach the sea. The huge leatherback turtle is a giant which can weigh up to 1760 pounds (800kg).

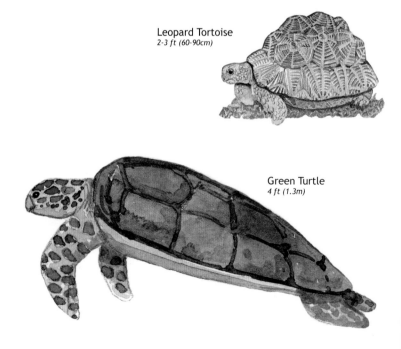

Leopard Tortoise
2-3 ft (60-90cm)

Green Turtle
4 ft (1.3m)

Frogs and Toads

Africa is home to a great variety of frogs and toads. Although all need water in which to breed, different species live in all kinds of environments including forest, savannah, grassland and even desert (where arid-adapted species emerge from burrows to reproduce rapidly in rain puddles). All are primarily nocturnal and more often heard than seen. Each species has a distinctive and often harsh call which is used to attract mates (and allows identification by people). At the onset of the rainy season, raucous symphonies of calling males can create a huge din in swamps and wetlands. In temperate southern Africa, many species hibernate during the dry winter months.

Frog numbers are thought to be declining all around the world. Their porous skins make them susceptible to chemical pollutants, but destruction of wetland habitats is perhaps the greatest factor. Changing climate and rainfall patterns, probably as a result of global warming, have a great impact on the breeding cycle of amphibians and may have resulted in the outbreak of chytrid fungus which is deadly to frogs and toads.

Toads are recognized by their warty skin and habit of moving freely on dry land. **Tree-frogs** have huge eyes and toes with sticky toe pads. **Reed-frogs** are tiny and often adorned in beautiful bright colors. **River-frogs** and **grass-frogs** fit the mould of the classic frog, with pointed snouts and long and muscular hind legs which allow them to leap great distances. **Bull-frogs** typically emerge only after rain when males aggressively defend territorial pools. The conspicuous **foam-nest frog** is able to sit exposed in full sunlight and builds an extraordinary white nest in which eggs develop into tadpoles.

Painted Reed-Frog
1 in. (3cm)

Foam-nest Frog
2 in. (6cm)

Guttural Toad
3 in. (9cm)

AN INTRODUCTION TO
African Insects

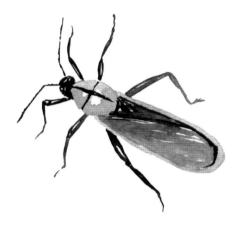

Insects are the most abundant of all life-forms, and the precise number of species is not much more than a guess. Southern Africa is thought to contain at least 80,000 insect species, and the continent as a whole may have four times this number. There may be as many as 30 million different insect species worldwide, although fewer than one million have been scientifically described.

A great many people see insects as little more than pests to be destroyed at any opportunity. While it is true that many insect species bring harm to mankind by attacking crops, gardens and wooden structures, and that flies, fleas and mosquitoes transmit diseases, the majority of insects are harmless. There are also a great many insects that perform valuable and even vital functions, including pollination, pest-control and waste disposal, upon which human societies are dependent.

While on safari you will encounter a host of colorful, unusual and fascinating insects. Learning a little about them can greatly enrich your experience and understanding of the ecosystems in which lions and elephants are just a part. Many insects are attracted to lights after dark, and you are sure to see many strange and fascinating creatures around your lodge and hotel accommodations. Biting insects such as mosquitoes can be inhibited by means of insect spray, or the burning of mosquito coils.

Insects are *arthropods* (which means "joint-footed") and thus related to spiders, scorpions, crabs, lobsters, millipedes and centipedes. All arthropods have external skeletons and have bodies divided into segments, but insects can be distinguished by their three-part bodies (head, thorax and abdomen) and three pairs of jointed legs; most insects have two pairs of wings. Caterpillars and grubs are the young (larval stage) of butterflies, moths, beetles and certain others, and do not resemble adults at all.

Butterflies and Moths

Colorful and active on bright sunny days, **butterflies** are often the first insects which attract the interest of people. Some African butterflies are extremely beautiful and make fine photographic subjects. Your guide may be able to help you identify some species, but good illustrated guide books are available.

Moths differ from butterflies in that most species are nocturnal (these too make ideal photographic subjects as they are drawn to lights around safari lodges and camps). Moths also tend to lay their wings flat when at rest, and usually have feathery rather than clubbed antennae (feelers). Most butterflies fold their wings vertically above their body and have clubbed antennae. All butterflies and moths lay eggs on particular "food plants" upon which their offspring will hatch and feed as developing caterpillars. Adult butterflies and moths feed on plant sap or nectar which they suck up with a long, tubular proboscis.

Dung-Beetles

There are more varieties of beetles than any other insect group, but it is the fascinating **dung-beetles** which are most likely to attract your attention on safari. Ranging in size from three inch "'monsters" to tiny, metallic green miniatures, dung-beetles are attracted to the fresh droppings of large mammals. The beetles are uniquely adapted to extract dung and roll it into a ball which is then pushed backwards to a burrow where it is either eaten or used as a fertile egg chamber. A pause at a rhino midden or clump of elephant droppings will provide you with a captivating experience as large and small dung-beetles jostle with one another for a share of the spoils.

Other conspicuous beetles include the horned **rhinoceros-beetles**, ground-hunting **tiger-beetles**, desert-dwelling **darkling-beetles** and the large and nocturnal **longicorn** (or longhorn) **beetles** with their extended antennae.

Termites

The conspicuous mounds made by termites are a distinctive feature of African savannahs and, though tiny and practically blind, these sociable insects play a major role in the functioning of ecosystems. Impressive towers of clay built by some termite species provide a home for a variety of other creatures and are often colonized by plants to create new habitats such as thickets.

Termites typically feed on dead plant material such as wood, bark and straw, being able to digest woody fibers with the help of bacteria that live in their stomachs. Acting as highly efficient decomposers, the termites return the plant nutrients to the soil through their faeces and saliva. Lacking pigment and a protective exoskeleton, termites operate mostly underground, but some species forage above ground after dark. In some parts of Africa, there may be as many as 10,000 termites to a square yard of soil surface, so it is not surprising that these insects also feature in the diet of numerous other species. Termites are often incorrectly referred to as "white ants" or "flying ants" although they are not closely related to ants at all. But, like ants, they live in well-ordered colonies with soldiers, workers and reproductives. A new colony begins when two winged alates, of opposite sexes, manage to avoid predation on their risky nuptial flight (birds, toads and bats consume most) and burrow into a suitable substrate. The offspring of this "royal pair" will then become the workers and soldiers required to build the mound.

Ants

Ants are considered to be the most advanced of social insects, with colonies containing a single queen and numbers of wingless workers and soldiers. Black or red are the typical colors of African ants. Most species create colonies underground, which may contain tens of thousands of members, but other species occur in smaller numbers in hollow twigs or acacia thorns. The round mud-ball nests of cocktail ants are conspicuous in some regions. Most ants are carnivorous, boldly attacking

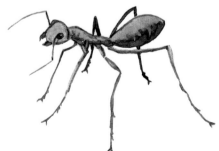

other insects or consuming dead animals of all kinds, but some feed on seeds, plant sap or "honeydew" secreted by aphids and sap-sucking bugs. Army ants form hunting parties which overpower and eat other insects; these formidable creatures are known as "siafu" in East Africa. Ants are not dangerous to humans although some can deliver a painful bite.

Wasps

Although some species are aggressive and capable of injecting venom, wasps are a fascinatingly diverse group of insects.

It is advisable to leave the large **paper-wasps** and **hornets** well alone, as these fearless creatures attack and sting in defense of their nests. Similar in shape, but not aggressive or venomous, are the **mason-** and **potter-wasps** which construct beautiful clay-pot egg chambers, or large many-celled dormitories.

The largest of wasps are the **spider-hunting wasps** which have the interesting but macabre habit of capturing spiders, injecting them with paralyzing venom, and then laying their eggs into the body of their victim. Once the wasp egg hatches, it will feed on the flesh of the paralyzed spider. Iridescent **cuckoo-wasps** are cleptoparasites which lay their eggs into the nests of other wasp species.

A great variety of tiny wasps lay their own eggs inside the eggs or larvae of other insects. In this way, these parasites control the numbers of their host insects some of which would otherwise assume plague proportions. The small and delicate **fig-wasps** perform a critical pollination function for fig trees, which — through their bounty of fruit — are a vital source of food for an entire web of wildlife.

Praying Mantids

Well-known for its unique body form and characteristic pose of upheld front limbs (which recalls somebody at prayer), the praying mantid (or mantis) is a carnivorous insect with a fascinating lifestyle. There are thought to be 200 to 300 species in sub-Saharan Africa. Mantids have distinctive triangular heads and long wings which fold flat over their abdomen. The head can be rotated with more flexibility than that of any other insect, while the front legs are equipped with hook-like spines on their inner surface, which hold prey securely. All mantids are extremely well camouflaged in colors which blend into their natural habitats. Most species

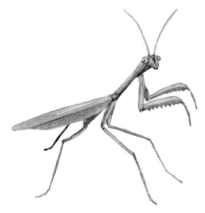

are plain green or brown, but some are ornately colored in shades of pink and yellow. The typical means of capturing prey is for the mantid to sit patiently and wait until a suitable insect or spider comes within range. Like many insects, mantids can often be seen around the artificial lights of buildings after dark. Although not designed for nocturnal activity (their highly evolved camouflage is an adaptation to hunting and a disguise during daylight), they prey on the dazed moths and other insects attracted to lights.

Dragonflies

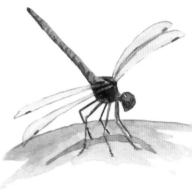

Due to their bright coloration and conspicuous behavior, dragonflies quickly attract attention. Six or more species might be seen at the waterside or in vegetation fringing marshes. Dragonflies and their damselfly relatives, belong to the insect order Odonata. They are most active in warm weather and the majority of adults die at the onset of winter. Their eggs and larvae, however, can withstand the cold and a new generation of adults emerge each year.

There are several distinctive groups of dragonflies. Massive **emperors** course low above the surface in pursuit of flies, bees and even smaller dragonflies. **Skimmers** and **dropwings** perch conspicuously on fringing grass or reeds, bursting out to chase rivals or capture prey. Impossibly brilliant **jewels** glitter alongside rapids, and delicate **sprites** dance above shallows. **Hawkers** rest among branches and often emerge at dusk to hunt. Many dragonfly species return to favored perches and make rewarding photographic subjects.

Antlions

As you look down at sand tracks or walk on pathways, one thing that you will notice are small but distinctive conical pitfall traps. These are made by the larvae of an insect known as an antlion. It is a flattened, nondescript creature apart from its large sickle-shaped mouthparts. As an ant or other small insect slips into the pitfall trap, so it is seized by the hidden antlion, to be dragged beneath the ground and consumed. After morphing into an adult, the antlion resembles a drab dragonfly although it has relatively poor, flapping flight and is active only after dark. Close relatives of the antlions are the lacewings, delicate pale green insects familiar to many people in North America.

AN INTRODUCTION TO

African Trees

There are so many different tree species in Africa, that it takes years of study and fieldwork to be able to identify the majority. In addition to leaf structure (*simple* or *compound* is the most basic division), it is often necessary to examine the growth form, bark texture, flower parts and fruit, in order to accurately identify a tree.

While on safari, it is nevertheless worthwhile to be able to recognize some of the more conspicuous and interesting trees. Thorn trees — or acacias — are often the most abundant trees in flat countryside, with many similar species occurring side-by-side. In hilly terrain, various species of bushwillow — or combretum — tend to dominate. Naturally, trees reach greater proportions when their roots are able to reach underground water supplies, and evergreen species often prevail along rivers and seasonal watercourses. In savannah and woodlands, many African trees shed their leaves in the dry winter months. Some species have beautiful yellow and amber foliage prior to shedding, although this is never as striking as the fall (autumn) shows in North America and Europe. In African forests, trees shed and replace their leaves throughout the year, so they are never devoid of green foliage.

Many African trees have spectacular colorful flowers, which attract pollinators and provide a rich nectar source for birds and insects. Trees of any one species flower simultaneously, putting on remarkable floral displays in savannah and other habitats. The seeds and pods of many species often take on distinctive shapes and forms, none more so than the extraordinary sausage tree featured on page 242.

Trees play a major role in African culture and livelihood, for they provide food in the way of berries, nuts and fruit, bark for medicine, as well as shelter and sometimes the main source of fuel. Certain large fig trees are regarded as sacred by the Maasai and others.

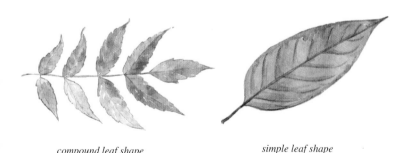

compound leaf shape   *simple leaf shape*

Acacias (Thorn Trees)

With their flat crowns, and spreading branches, acacias — such as the umbrella thorn — are the embodiment of Africa. Spaced out on the park-like savannah, with giraffe browsing on their foliage and wildebeest resting in their shade, they form the backdrop for many an African scene.

Acacias are typified by feathery, compound leaves, divided into numerous pairs of tiny leaflets. All African species have thorns, whether straight or hooked. Their foliage and pods are relished by all browsers. Although the often fierce thorns do act as a deterrent for some browsers, it is the colonies of cocktail ants which more aggressively defend these trees. By and large, ants are abundant in acacia trees where they are provided with sweet nectar in return for their vigorous defense; even large antelope such as greater kudu can tolerate biting ants only for a period of time before moving elsewhere.

Most acacias are tolerant of fire and have thick or corky bark to withstand heat. The hard seeds of these leguminous trees actually benefit from fire as the heat splits the outer covering and speeds up germination.

Acacia flowers are either bright yellow or cream in color, and maybe ball- or catkin-shaped depending upon the species. Bees and other insects are attracted in the thousands during the flowering period. Most thorn trees exude a sweet sticky gum from their bark and this is relished by bushbabies and people alike.

Smaller birds frequently build their nests in acacia trees and shrubs, as the thorns deter would-be predators of the eggs and nestlings. Large flat-topped thorn trees are favored sites for eagles, vultures and storks.

Among the more distinctive acacias are the **fever tree** (with its ghostly yellow trunk and stems), **camel thorn** (which grows in desert drainage lines), and the shapely **umbrella thorn** so beloved of photographers.

Umbrella Acacia

Palms

Africa does not have a great variety of palm trees, but these stately and instantly recognizable plants occur in many habitats, often near water.

Palms are distinctive in that almost all species have a single unbranched stem or trunk (the doum palm of east Africa is a notable exception). The large leathery leaves are either fan- or feather-shaped, and droop down in a spiral from the crown.

The **wild date palm** is widely distributed, occurring on stream and river banks and the fringes of Okavango islands. Baboons and civets relish the dates, while elephants strip the tough leaves. Tall fan (or lala) palms are a feature of the Okavango Delta, where elephants feed on the bell-shaped or spherical fruits; the seed is encased in an ivory-like kernel which may be carved into jewelry or ornaments. **Borassus palms** are the tallest of African palms and noted for their swollen trunks. The **raphia palm** of lagoon fringes has the longest leaves (up to 60 feet [18m]) of any plant. **Coconut palms** fringe beaches in Tanzania and Kenya, as well as Indian Ocean islands.

Borassus Palm

Euphorbias

Euphorbias are succulent plants armed with sharp spines. In shape and form many varieties strongly resemble cacti. The larger tree-like species are sometimes referred to as candelabras in view of their distinctive shape. All euphorbias contain a sticky, milky latex which can cause temporary blindness. Euphorbia flowers are small and inconspicuous but produce copious nectar and attract large numbers of bees and other insects, as well as birds. The only animal known to eat euphorbia stems is the black rhinoceros.

Euphorbia ingens

Baobab

These huge, broad-trunked trees are unmistakeable, particularly when they lose their leaves in the dry season. It is then that they suit their nickname of "upside-down tree" as their bare branches resemble roots. Baobabs are among the oldest of life-forms with some specimens aged at well over 1,000 years. The smooth bark and soft pulpy fiber is relished by elephants which may destroy even large specimens. The large showy white flowers open at night to be pollinated by fruit bats.

Adansonia digitata

Baobab seeds are surrounded by a white pulp within a large velvety pod. Mature baobabs typically have many holes and crevices which provide homes for bushbabies, owls and many other creatures. Large hollow specimens may even be used as rooms, or grain houses by rural people.

Sausage Tree

This is a large deciduous tree which favors riverside habitats. The extraordinary fruits of the sausage tree may grow up to 2 feet (60cm) in length, and hang in clusters from the outer branches. Baboons eat the pulp inside the sausage-shaped fruits, and so disperse the seeds. Interestingly, the sap from these fruits is used as a skin care product.

The sausage tree has spectacular burgundy flowers shaped like trumpets. Sunbirds visit these flowers for nectar during the day, while fruit bats and hawk moths feast at night. The short-lived flowers fall to the ground after pollination, leaving an extravagant wine-red carpet beneath the tree.

These trees often take on a wide-spreading shape which makes their broad branches ideal resting places for leopards.

Kigelia africana

Sycamore Fig

This is a distinctive tree of African riverbanks and watercourses, where its buttressed trunk and caramel-colored bark stand out. Like other members of the *Ficus* genus, its flowers are hidden within the figs, which only ripen when the flowers have been pollinated by a particular species of fig wasp. This unique mutual relationship between tree and tiny insect sets in motion a great food web, as the abundance of juicy figs are fed upon by all manner of creatures from fishes and duiker, to hornbills and green pigeons. Unlike most other tree species which flower and fruit in a particular season, figs produce their crop at random so that there is usually at least one productive tree in an area.

Ficus sycomorus

The majority of African fig trees fall into one of two categories: the rock splitters and the stranglers. The tenacious aerial roots of these trees enable them to get a hold in impossibly small cracks, or wrap themselves around, and ultimately squeeze to death, even the largest of host trees.

Aloes

Only a few aloe species assume the proportions of a tree, but several species stand as tall as man, and decorate hillsides and valleys with their distinctive form and bright flower heads. These are succulent plants able to withstand dry conditions. Many African species are grown in sub-tropical gardens around the world. *Aloe vera* is a north African species which is now widely cultivated for its medicinal value; the clear sap is a cure for skin rashes and blemishes.

Aloe spicata

Aloes carry hundreds of tubular flowers on candelabra-shaped stalks, attracting sunbirds and bees to their nectar.

Other distinctive African trees

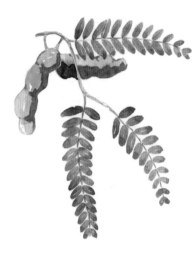

Tamarind *(Tamarindus indica)*

Pod Mahogany *(Afzelia quanzensis)*

Miombo (*Brachystegia* species)

Mopane *(Colophospermum mopane)*

Other distinctive African trees

Marula *(Sclerocarya birrea)*

Bushwillow (*Combretum* species)

Monkey Orange
(*Strychnos* species)

Sickle Bush
(Dichrostachys cinnerea)

Other distinctive African trees

Coral Tree (*Erythrina* species)

Jackalberry
(*Diospyros mespiliformis*)

Mangosteen (*Garcinia* species)

Cluster-leaf (*Terminalia* species)

Country and Wildlife Reserve Maps

EAST AFRICA

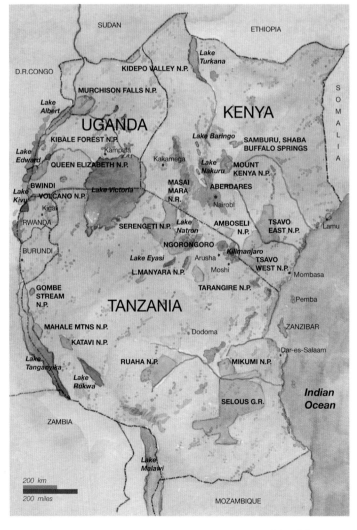

SUDAN

ETHIOPIA

Lake Turkana

D.R.CONGO

KIDEPO VALLEY N.P.

MURCHISON FALLS N.P.

Lake Albert

UGANDA

KENYA

S O M A L I A

KIBALE FOREST N.P.

Lake Baringo

SAMBURU, SHABA BUFFALO SPRINGS

Lake Edward

Kampala

Kakamega

QUEEN ELIZABETH N.P.

Lake Nakuru

MOUNT KENYA N.P.

BWINDI

Lake Kivu

VOLCANO N.P.

Lake Victoria

MASAI MARA N.R.

ABERDARES

Nairobi

Kigali

RWANDA

SERENGETI N.P.

Lake Natron

AMBOSELI N.P.

TSAVO EAST N.P.

Lamu

BURUNDI

NGORONGORO

Lake Eyasi

Arusha

Kilimanjaro

Moshi

TSAVO WEST N.P.

L.MANYARA N.P.

TARANGIRE N.P.

Mombasa

GOMBE STREAM N.P.

TANZANIA

Pemba

MAHALE MTNS N.P.

Dodoma

ZANZIBAR

KATAVI N.P.

Dar-es-Salaam

Lake Tanganyika

RUAHA N.P.

MIKUMI N.P.

Lake Rukwa

Indian Ocean

SELOUS G.R.

ZAMBIA

200 km

200 miles

Lake Malawi

MOZAMBIQUE

SOUTHERN AFRICA

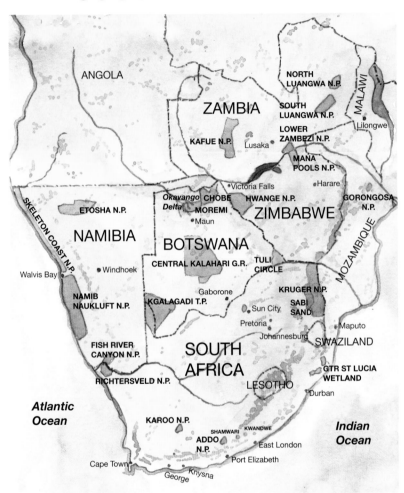

ANGOLA

ZAMBIA

NORTH LUANGWA N.P.

SOUTH LUANGWA N.P.

MALAWI

•Lilongwe

KAFUE N.P.

LOWER ZAMBEZI N.P.

Lusaka

MANA POOLS N.P.

•Victoria Falls

•Harare

SKELETON COAST N.P.

ETOSHA N.P.

Okavango Delta

CHOBE

HWANGE N.P.

GORONGOSA N.P.

MOREMI

ZIMBABWE

•Maun

NAMIBIA

BOTSWANA

MOZAMBIQUE

CENTRAL KALAHARI G.R.

TULI CIRCLE

Walvis Bay•

•Windhoek

NAMIB NAUKLUFT N.P.

Gaborone•

KRUGER N.P.

KGALAGADI T.P.

•Sun City

SABI SAND

Pretoria•

•Maputo

Johannesburg•

SWAZILAND

FISH RIVER CANYON N.P.

SOUTH AFRICA

GTR ST LUCIA WETLAND

RICHTERSVELD N.P.

LESOTHO

•Durban

Atlantic Ocean

KAROO N.P.

Indian Ocean

SHAMWARI KWANDWE

ADDO N.P.

•East London

Cape Town•

•Port Elizabeth

Knysna

•George

Botswana

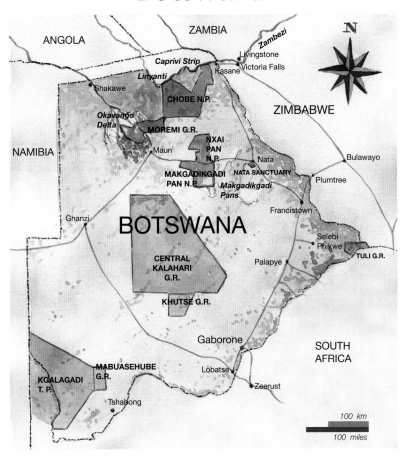

Botswana is dominated by the great Kalahari desert which is actually a varied landscape of grasslands, bush scrub and savannah. In the far northwest, the Okavango River spills out onto the deep Kalahari sands to create the magical Okavango Delta — one of the continent's great wilderness regions. At some 224,606 square miles (581,730km²) Botswana is about the size of Texas (or France). The average elevation is around 3,200 feet (1,000m) above sea level. Botswana's population numbers some 1.6 million, with the great majority living in the south-east, including the capital city of Gaborone. Setswana and English are the official languages. Currency is the Pula.

Chobe National Park

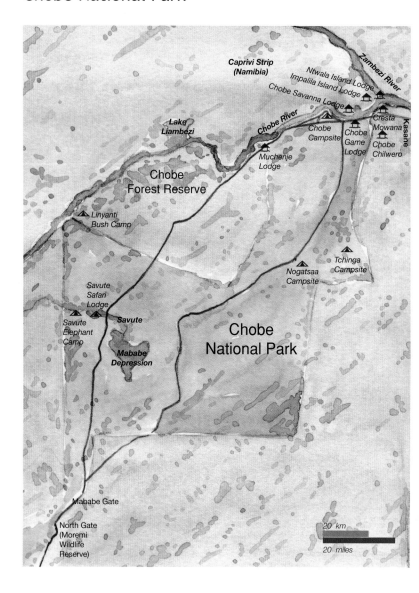

Caprivi Strip
(Namibia)

Zambezi River

Ntwala Island Lodge
Impalila Island Lodge
Chobe Savanna Lodge

Lake
Liambezi

Chobe River

Kasane

Cresta
Mowana

Chobe
Campsite

Chobe
Game
Lodge

Chobe
Chilwero

Muchenje
Lodge

Chobe
Forest Reserve

Linyanti
Bush Camp

Tchinga
Campsite

Nogatsaa
Campsite

Savute
Safari
Lodge

Savute
Elephant
Camp

Savute

Chobe
National Park

Mababe
Depression

Mababe Gate

North Gate
(Moremi
Wildlife
Reserve)

20 km

20 miles

Linyanti

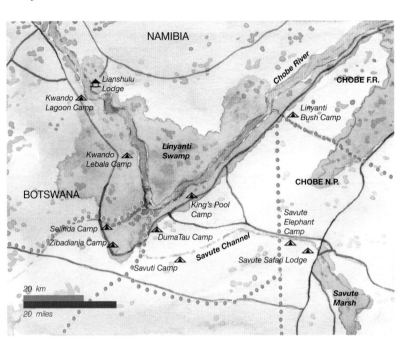

NAMIBIA

Chobe River

CHOBE F.R.

Lianshulu
Lodge

Kwando
Lagoon Camp

Linyanti
Bush Camp

Linyanti
Swamp

Kwando
Lebala Camp

CHOBE N.P.

BOTSWANA

King's Pool
Camp

Savute
Elephant
Camp

Selinda Camp

Zibadianja Camp

DumaTau Camp

Savute Channel

Savuti Camp

Savute Safari Lodge

20 km

20 miles

Savute
Marsh

African Wild Dog

Okavango Delta

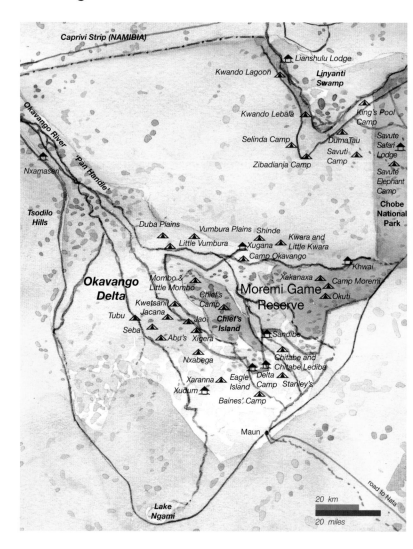

Caprivi Strip (NAMIBIA)

Lianshulu Lodge

Kwando Lagoon

Linyanti Swamp

King's Pool Camp

Kwando Lebala

Okavango River

Selinda Camp

DumaTau

Savute Safari Lodge

Savuti Camp

Zibadianja Camp

Nxamaseri

Pan Handle

Savute Elephant Camp

Chobe National Park

Tsodilo Hills

Duba Plains

Vumbura Plains   Shinde

Little Vumbura

Xugana

Kwara and Little Kwara

Camp Okavango

Khwai

Okavango Delta

Mombo & Little Mombo

Xakanaxa   Camp Moremi

Moremi Game Reserve

Okuti

Kwetsani   Chief's Camp

Jacana

Tubu

Jao   **Chief's Island**

Seba

Abu's   Xigera

Sandibe

Nxabega

Chitabe and Chitabe Lediba

Xaranna   Eagle Island

Delta Camp   Stanley's

Xudum

Baines' Camp

Maun

road to Nata

Lake Ngami

20 km

20 miles

Democratic Republic of Congo (East)

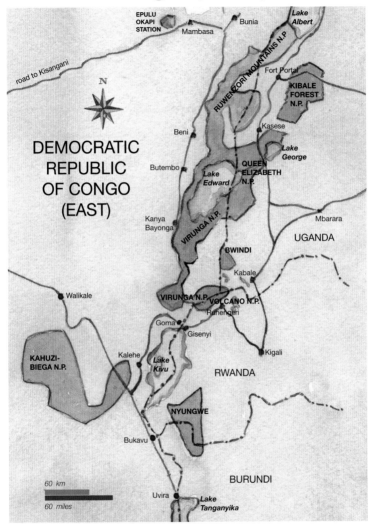

EPULU OKAPI STATION
Mambasa
Bunia
Lake Albert
road to Kisangani
RUWENZORI MOUNTAINS N.P
Fort Portal
KIBALE FOREST N.P.
N
Beni
Kasese
DEMOCRATIC REPUBLIC OF CONGO (EAST)
Butembo
Lake Edward
QUEEN ELIZABETH N.P.
Lake George
Kanya Bayonga
VIRUNGA N.P.
Mbarara
UGANDA
BWINDI
Kabale
Walikale
VIRUNGA N.P.
VOLCANO N.P.
Ruhengeri
Goma
Gisenyi
Kigali
KAHUZI-BIEGA N.P.
Kalehe
Lake Kivu
RWANDA
NYUNGWE
Bukavu
BURUNDI
60 km
60 miles
Uvira
Lake Tanganyika

D.R.Congo is the third largest country in Africa with a surface area of 905,567 square miles (2,345,410km²). Most of the country lies within the Congo Basin (the world's second largest rainforest after the Amazon) below 980 ft (300m). In the extreme east of the country the Albertine Rift gives rise to the Ruwenzori Mountains and the Virunga Volcano chain. As a former Belgian colony, French is the official language of D.R. Congo, although there are over 200 ethnic groups with their own language. The currency is the Franc Congolais.

Ethiopia

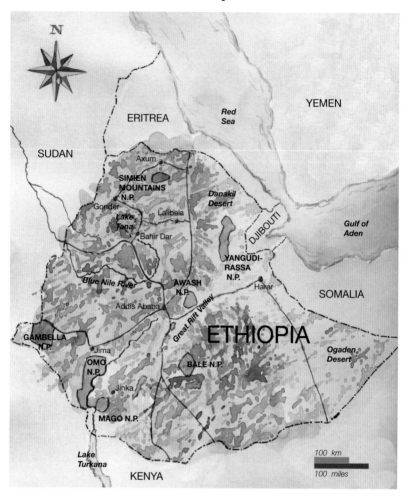

Ethiopia is a mountainous country situated in the Horn of Africa, covering some 435,070 square miles (1,127,127km^2) about twice the size of Texas. It has three distinct climate zones relative to topography. The highest peaks in the Simien mountains rise above 14,400 feet (4,400m), while those in the Bale mountains are just slightly lower. These cool temperate uplands are in stark contrast to the low-lying Danakil and Ogaden deserts which are among the hottest places on Earth. A number of endemic mammals, birds and other species are confined to Ethiopia. There are 84 indigenous languages, but English is widely used. Currency is the Birr.

Kenya

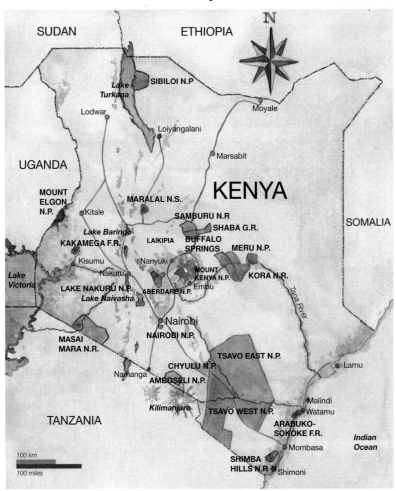

From the warm tropical waters of the Indian Ocean, to the icy heights of Mount Kenya at 17,058 feet (5,199m), this is truly "a world in one country." Desert and arid savannah prevails in the northern frontier and southeast, while remnant forests extend over the high country and wetter west. Covering 225,000 square miles (582,750km^2), Kenya is about the same size as Texas or France. The population numbers some 33 million, with over 2.5 million in the capital city of Nairobi. KiSwahili and English are the official languages. Currency is the Kenyan shilling.

Amboseli National Park

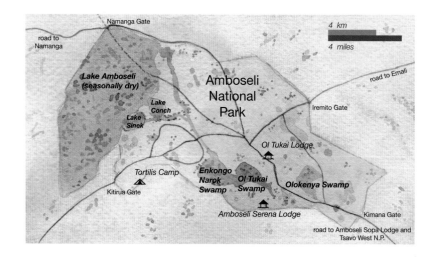

Laikipia

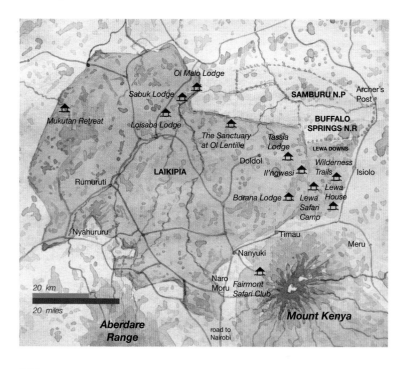

Masai Mara National Reserve

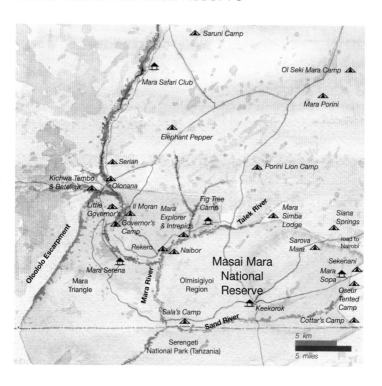

Samburu National Reserve — Buffalo Springs National Reserve

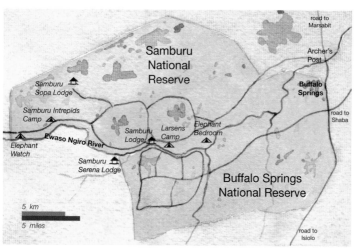

Tsavo National Park

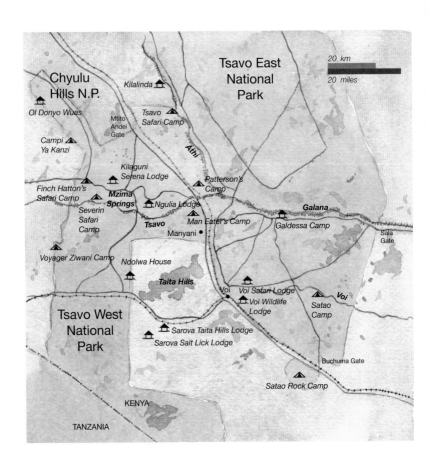

Chyulu
Hills N.P.

Ol Donyo Wuas

Campi
Ya Kanzi

Kilalinda

Mtito
Andei
Gate

Tsavo
Safari Camp

Tsavo East
National
Park

20 km

20 miles

Kilaguni
Serena Lodge

Finch Hatton's
Safari Camp

Mzima
Springs

Severin
Safari
Camp

Athi

Patterson's
Camp

Ngulia Lodge

Tsavo

Man Eater's Camp

Galana

Galdessa Camp

Sala
Gate

Voyager Ziwani Camp

Ndolwa House

Manyani

Taita Hills

Voi

Voi Safari Lodge

Voi Wildlife
Lodge

Voi

Satao
Camp

Tsavo West
National
Park

Sarova Taita Hills Lodge

Sarova Salt Lick Lodge

Buchuma Gate

Satao Rock Camp

KENYA

TANZANIA

Lesotho

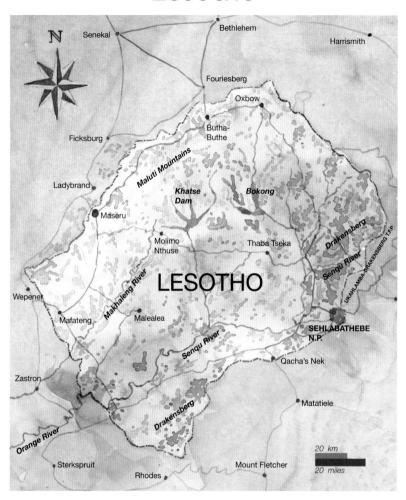

Lesotho is a small mountainous country, surrounded on all sides by South Africa. The landscape is spectacular with jagged peaks of the Maluti and Drakensberg mountains rising to over 11,200 feet (3,482m) and deep river valleys. Nowhere is the elevation below 5,000 feet (1,500m), ensuring that the climate is cool throughout the year, with snow being regular from May to August. With an area of some 11,720 square miles (30,355km^2) Lesotho is about the size of Maryland (or Belgium). An estimated 2.2 million people inhabit the cool grasslands, with many living in and around the capital city of Maseru. Sesotho and English are the languages. Currency is the Loti.

Malawi

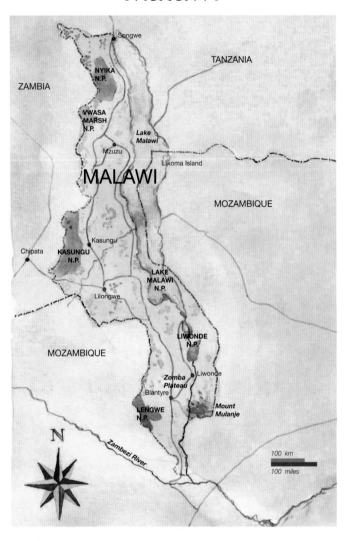

Known to many as the "Warm Heart of Africa" Malawi is a beautiful country dominated by the great lake of the same name. The altitude varies from 120 feet (37m) in the Shire Valley to 9,847 feet (3,002m) on the summit of Mount Mulanje. Brachystegia (miombo) woodland prevails over most of the country, with open grassland and moorland on higher ground. The population of Malawi is around 12 million, with about 500,000 in the capital of Lilongwe. The majority of the population are subsistence farmers. Chicewa and English are the official languages. Currency is the Malawian Kwacha.

Liwonde

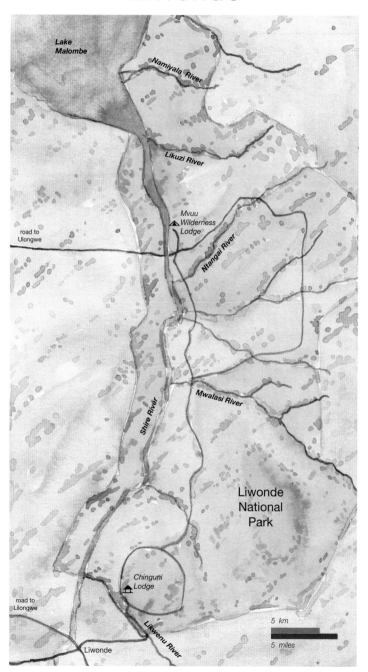

Lake
Malombe

Namiyala River

Likuzi River

Mvuu
Wilderness
Lodge

road to
Ulongwe

Ntangai River

Mwalasi River

Shire River

Liwonde
National
Park

Chinguni
Lodge

road to
Lilongwe

Likwenu River

Liwonde

5 km

5 miles

Mauritius

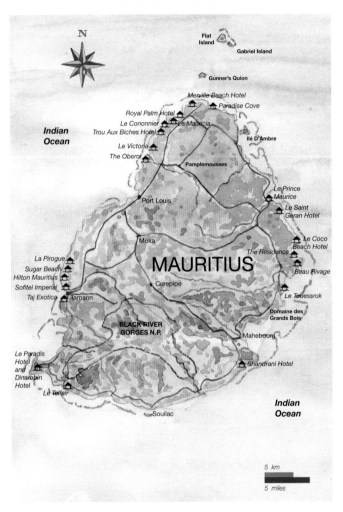

Mauritius is a volcanic island in the southwestern Indian Ocean, 520 miles (840km) east of Madagascar. The island extends over 720 square miles (1,865km²), which is about the size of Rhode Island (or Luxembourg). The terrain of Mauritius is hilly with some small but spectacular mountains, the highest of which rise to some 2,700 feet (824m). The 125 mile (200km) coastline is fringed by coral reef although much of this is not in a pristine state. The island was previously forested but — along with much of the native fauna — much of this has been lost to development. The dodo is the most famous victim of colonization by humans. The resident population is estimated at 1.2 million. Creole, French and English are predominate languages.

Mozambique

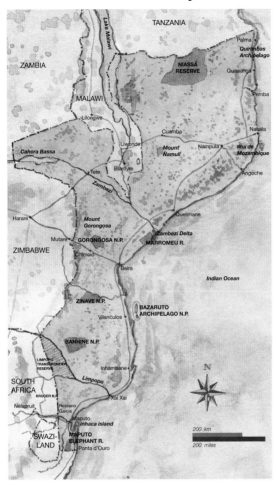

Mozambique is a huge country of about 308,640 square miles (799,380km²), which is larger than either Texas or France. Maputo is the capital city, and more than 80% of the population lives on or near the Indian Ocean. Much of the country is a low-lying coastal plain, drained by the Zambezi and Limpopo river systems. The climate is warm to hot, and frost free, with rainfall between October and March. Moist miombo woodland is the dominant habitat of the interior, with semiarid acacia and mopane woodland-savannah along the low-lying drainage systems. Much of the coastal vegetation has been replaced by sugarcane and other forms of agriculture, but the coast and offshore islands are spectacularly beautiful. A colony of Portugal until 1976, Portuguese is still widely spoken and forms a common language among the many ethnic groups. The currency is the meticais.

Namibia

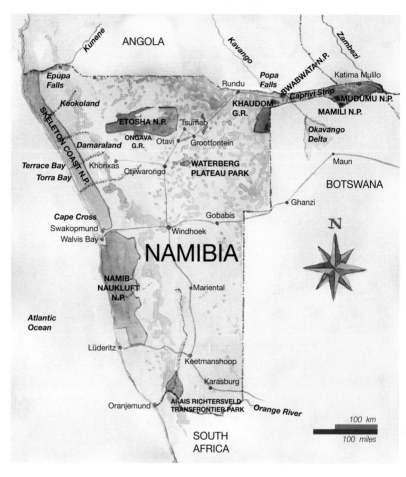

Namibia is one of Africa's driest countries, with the Namib and Kalahari deserts dominating the landscape. Elevation ranges from sea level on the Atlantic seaboard to some 5,410 feet (1,650m) at Windhoek on the central plateau. In the far north, the permanent water of the Kunene and Okavango Rivers allows for productive agriculture and it is here that most of the population live. Just over two million people inhabit the 318,250 square miles (824,268km²) of Namibia which is about the size of Texas and Oklahoma combined. Windhoek is the capital city. English is the official language. Currency is the Namibian Dollar.

Etosha National Park

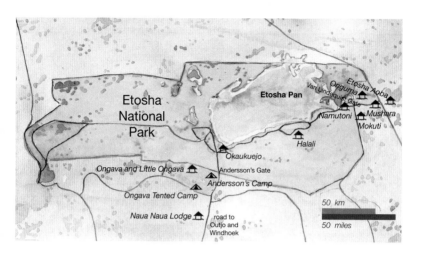

Etosha National Park

Etosha Pan

Onguma
Van Lindequist Gate
Etosha Aoba
Namutoni
Mushara
Mokuti
Halali
Okaukuejo
Ongava and Little Ongava
Andersson's Gate
Andersson's Camp
Ongava Tented Camp
Naua Naua Lodge
road to Outjo and Windhoek

50 km

50 miles

Lion

Namib-Naukluft Park

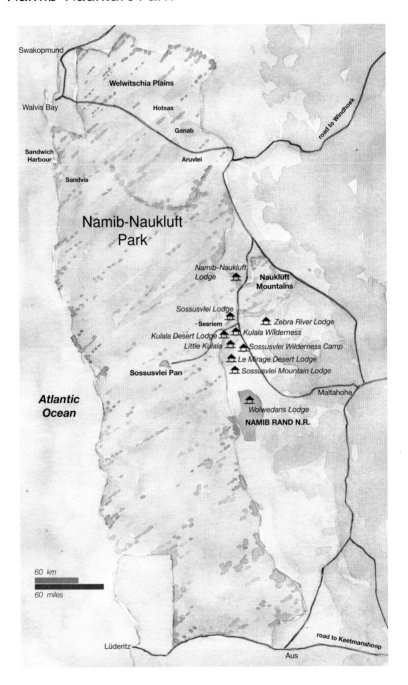

Swakopmund

Welwitschia Plains

Walvis Bay

Hotsas

Ganab

Sandwich
Harbour

Aruvlei

Sandvis

Namib-Naukluft Park

Naukluft Mountains

Namib-Naukluft Lodge

Sossusvlei Lodge

Sesriem

Zebra River Lodge

Kulala Desert Lodge   *Kulala Wilderness*

Little Kulala   *Sossusvlei Wilderness Camp*

Le Mirage Desert Lodge

Sossusvlei Mountain Lodge

Sossusvlei Pan

Atlantic Ocean

Maltahohe

Wolwedans Lodge

NAMIB RAND N.R.

road to Windhoek

60 km

60 miles

Lüderitz

Aus

road to Keetmanshoop

Rwanda and Burundi

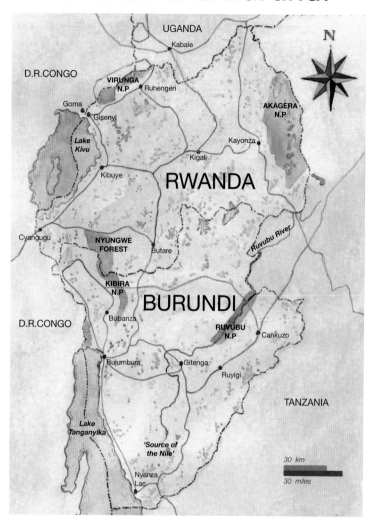

These two small countries are characterized by rolling hills and volcanic peaks, with altitude varying from 3,960 feet (1,207m) to 14,786 feet (4,500m) above sea level. Mount Karisimbi in northern Rwanda's Virunga range is the highest peak. Both countries are former Belgian colonies, previously united as Ruanda-Urundi. Although each country is only about 10,000 square miles (26,700km^2) they have a collective population of close to 20 million, making these fertile landscapes among the most densely populated in the world. Kinyarawanda is the predominant language in Rwanda, with Kirundi being spoken in Burundi; French is widely understood in both territories. Currency in both countries is the Franc.

Virunga Mountains

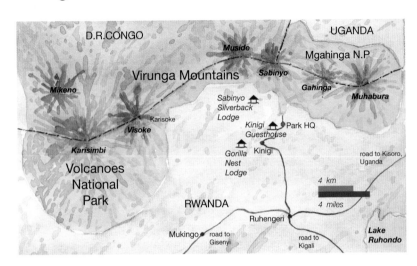

Mountain Gorilla

Seychelles

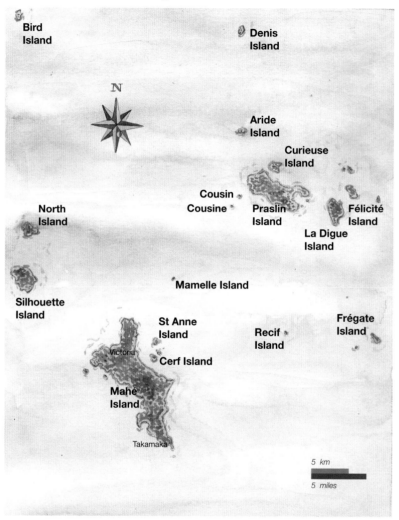

The Seychelles comprise 115 islands which cover a collective area of just 171 square miles (433km²) in the western Indian Ocean. Mahé, the largest of the islands is located 4 degrees south of the equator. The islands are made of either granite or coral, with the former having peaks rising up to 2,970 feet (905m). Most of the coraline or "outer" islands are just a few feet above sea level. Due to its geographic isolation, most of the flora and fauna is unique, but plants and animals introduced by man have greatly altered the landscape and endangered many species. The resident population is less than 100,000 with Creole, French and English widely spoken.

South Africa

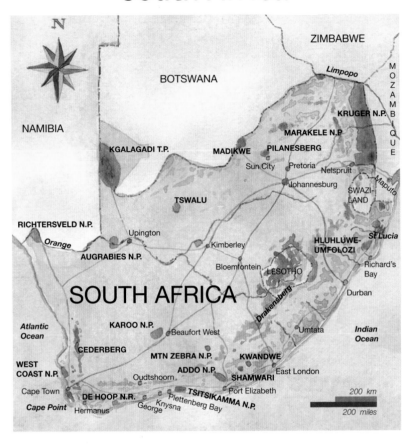

At the southern end of the continent, South Africa is an extremely diverse country with temperate highlands, subtropical savannah, alpine-like mountains, semi-desert and unique Mediterranean-like shrub lands known as "fynbos." Much of the country is a high plateau averaging some 4,800 feet (1,500m) above sea level, with the Drakensberg rising to 11,400 feet (3,450m). The country is flanked by the cool Atlantic and warm Indian Oceans, each of which has a strong bearing on the climate. South Africa is the most industrialized nation on the continent but still has large protected areas including the famous Kruger National Park and surrounding areas which occupy most of the lowveld. Covering some 471,445 square miles (1.2 million km²), South Africa is twice the size of Texas. English is the official language, with Zulu, Tswana, Xhosa, Sotho and Afrikaans all widely spoken. The population is estimated at around 45 million. Pretoria and Cape Town are the capital cities but Johannesburg is the business hub. Currency is the Rand (ZAR).

Cape Town and Environs

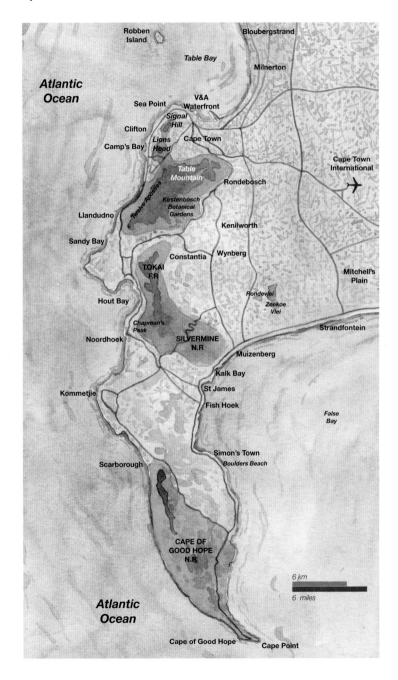

Robben Island

Bloubergstrand

Table Bay

Milnerton

Atlantic Ocean

Sea Point

V&A Waterfront

Signal Hill

Clifton

Lions Head

Cape Town

Camp's Bay

Cape Town International

Table Mountain

Rondebosch

Kirstenbosch Botanical Gardens

Llandudno

Twelve Apostles

Kenilworth

Sandy Bay

Constantia

Wynberg

TOKAI F.R

Mitchell's Plain

Hout Bay

Rondevlei

Zeekoe Vlei

Chapman's Peak

Strandfontein

Noordhoek

SILVERMINE N.R

Muizenberg

Kalk Bay

Kommetjie

St James

Fish Hoek

False Bay

Simon's Town

Scarborough

Boulders Beach

CAPE OF GOOD HOPE N.R

6 km

6 miles

Atlantic Ocean

Cape of Good Hope

Cape Point

Kgalagadi Transfrontier Park

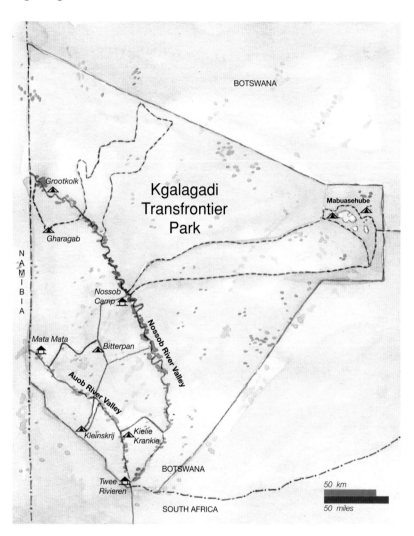

BOTSWANA

Grootkolk

Kgalagadi
Transfrontier
Park

Mabuasehube

Gharagab

N
A
M
I
B
I
A

Nossob
Camp

Mata Mata

Bitterpan

Nossob River Valley

Auob River Valley

Kleinskrij

Kielie
Krankie

BOTSWANA

Twee
Rivieren

SOUTH AFRICA

50 km

50 miles

Kruger National Park

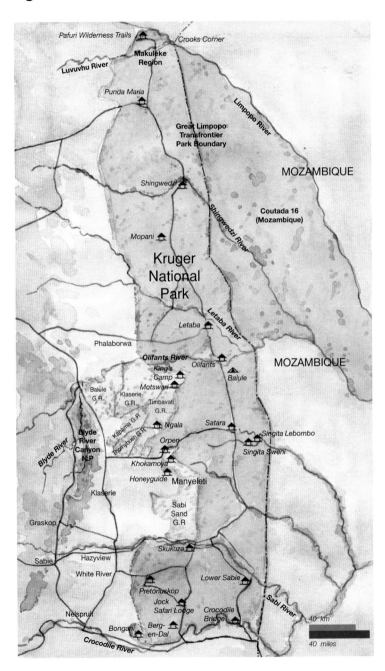

Sabi Sand Private Game Reserve

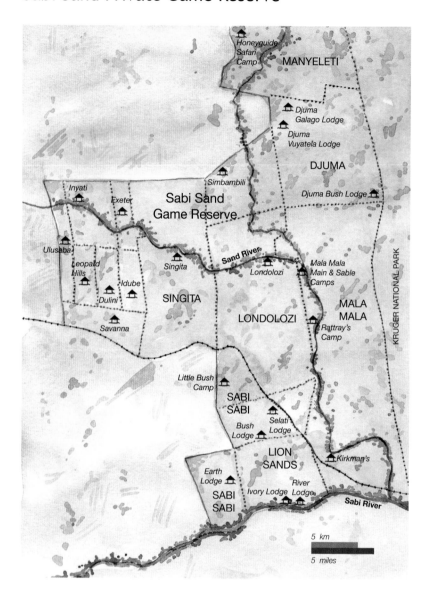

Kwa-Zulu Natal

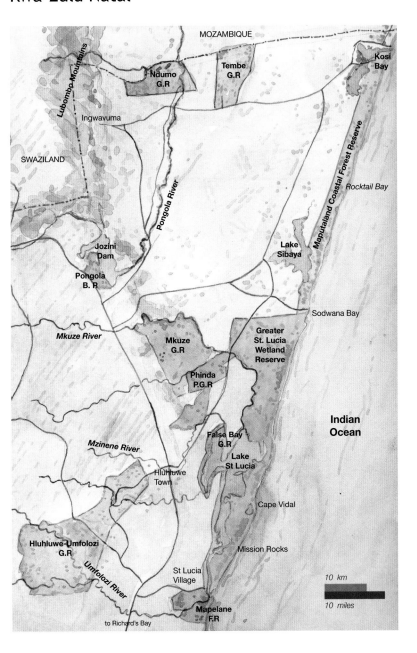

MOZAMBIQUE

Kosi Bay

Tembe G.R

Ndumo G.R

Lubombo Mountains

Ingwavuma

SWAZILAND

Pongola River

Maputaland Coastal Forest Reserve

Rocktail Bay

Jozini Dam

Lake Sibaya

Pongola B. R

Mkuze River

Sodwana Bay

Mkuze G.R

Greater St. Lucia Wetland Reserve

Phinda P.G.R

Mzinene River

False Bay G.R

Lake St Lucia

Indian Ocean

Hluhluwe Town

Cape Vidal

Hluhluwe-Umfolozi G.R

Mission Rocks

Umfolozi River

St Lucia Village

10 km

10 miles

to Richard's Bay

Mapelane F.R

Swaziland

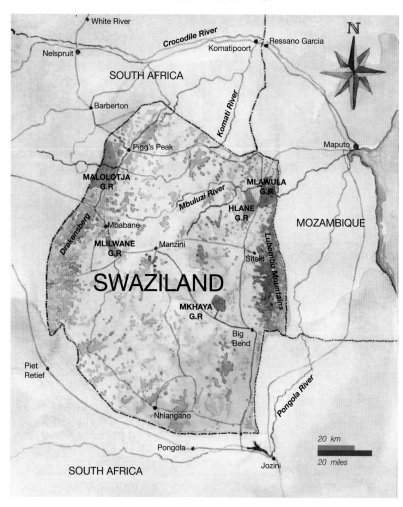

Swaziland is a small country divided into a temperate mountainous highveld in the west, and a subtropical lowveld in the east. The Lubombo hills form the eastern border with Mozambique. Elevation ranges from around 6,000 feet (1,829m) at Malolotja to 2,100 feet (640m) in the Komati River valley. With an area of 6,704 square miles (17,364km^2) Swaziland is about the size of New Jersey, and has a population of about 1.5 million. SiSwati and English are the languages. Mbabane is the capital city. Currency is the Lilangeni.

Tanzania

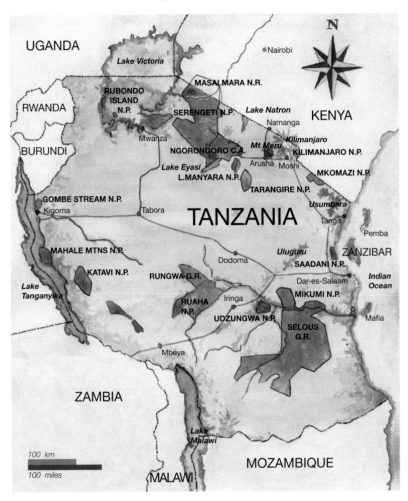

Set between the tropical Indian Ocean and the two arms of the Rift Valley, Tanzania is one of Africa's most scenically beautiful countries. It also has some of the most extensive protected areas including the fabled Serengeti. The landscape rises from sea level to 19,000 feet (5,894m) at the summit of Mt. Kilimajaro. Covering 365,000 square miles (945,000km²), Tanzania is about the same size as Texas and Oklahoma combined. The population numbers some 36 million, with Dodoma as the administrative capital. The famous port city of Dar es Salaam has been a key trading center for centuries. KiSwahili is the most widely spoken language, but English is also commonly used. Currency is the Tanzanian Shilling.

Northern Tanzania & Southern Kenya

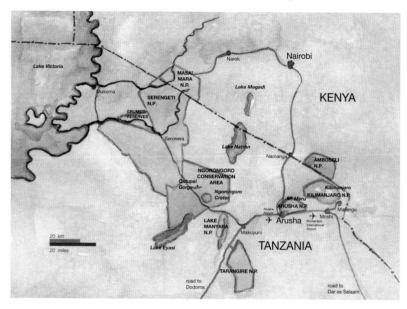

Arusha National Park

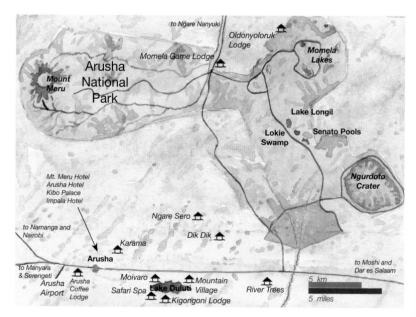

Mt. Kilimanjaro National Park

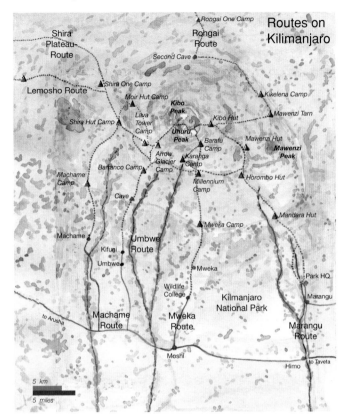

Routes on Kilimanjaro

Rongai One Camp
Rongai Route
Second Cave
Shira Plateau Route
Lemosho Route
Shira One Camp
Moir Hut Camp
Kibo Peak
Kibo Hut
Kikelena Camp
Mawenzi Tarn
Shira Hut Camp
Lava Tower Camp
Uhuru Peak
Barafu Camp
Mawenzi Hut
Mawenzi Peak
Arrow Glacier Camp
Karanga Camp
Barranco Camp
Horombo Hut
Machame Camp
Millennium Camp
Cave
Mandara Hut
Mweka Camp
Machame
Umbwe Route
Kifuni
Umbwe
Mweka
Park HQ
Marangu
Wildlife College
Kilmanjaro National Park
to Arusha
Machame Route
Mweka Route
Marangu Route
Moshi
Himo
to Taveta
5 km
5 miles

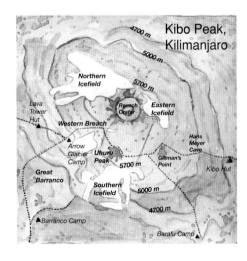

Kibo Peak, Kilimanjaro

4700 m
5000 m
5700 m
Northern Icefield
Reusch Crater
Eastern Icefield
Lava Tower Hut
Western Breach
Hans Meyer Cave
Arrow Glacier Camp
Uhuru Peak
5700 m
Gillman's Point
Kibo Hut
Great Barranco
Southern Icefield
5000 m
4700 m
Barranco Camp
Barafu Camp

Lake Manyara National Park

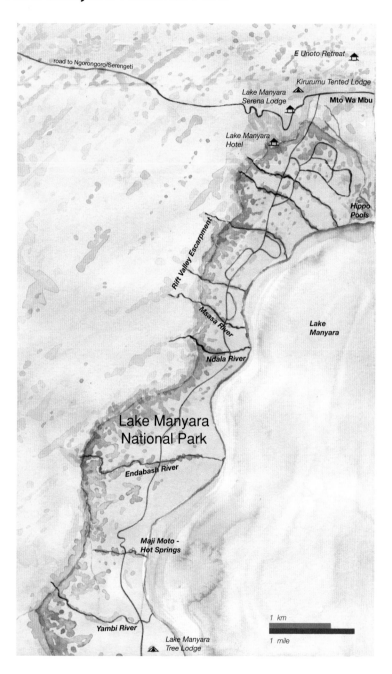

road to Ngorongoro/Serengeti

E Unoto Retreat

Kirurumu Tented Lodge

Lake Manyara
Serena Lodge

Mto Wa Mbu

Lake Manyara
Hotel

Hippo
Pools

Rift Valley Escarpment

Msasa River

Lake
Manyara

Ndala River

Lake Manyara
National Park

Endabash River

Maji Moto -
Hot Springs

1 km

1 mile

Yambi River

Lake Manyara
Tree Lodge

Ngorongoro Crater

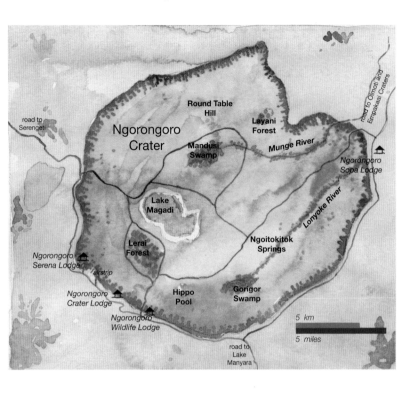

- Round Table Hill
- Layani Forest
- Ngorongoro Crater
- Mandusi Swamp
- Munge River
- road to Serengeti
- road to Olmoti and Empakaai Craters
- Ngorongoro Sopa Lodge
- Lake Magadi
- Lonyoke River
- Lerai Forest
- Ngoitokitok Springs
- Ngorongoro Serena Lodge
- airstrip
- Ngorongoro Crater Lodge
- Hippo Pool
- Gorigor Swamp
- Ngorongoro Wildlife Lodge
- road to Lake Manyara
- 5 km
- 5 miles

Black Rhinoceros

Ruaha National Park

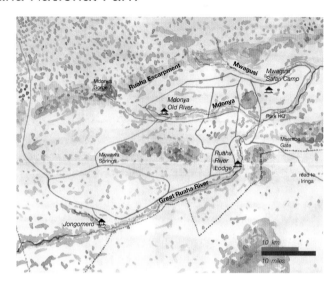

Selous Game Reserve

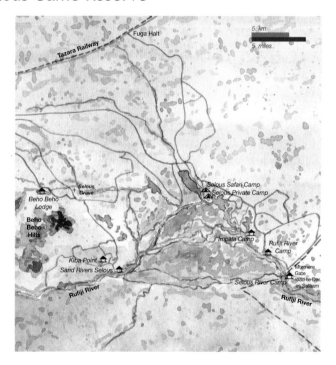

Serengeti National Park

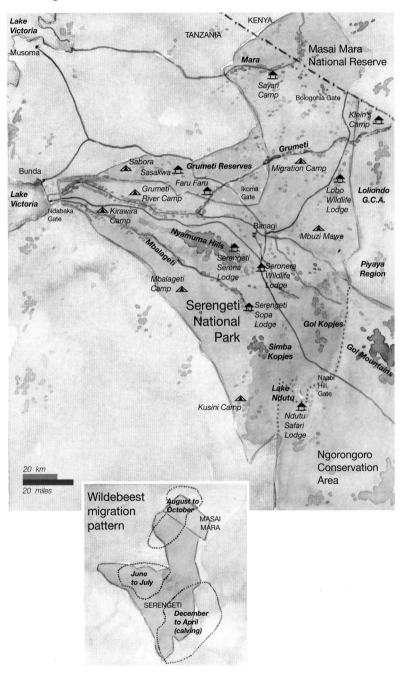

Lake Victoria

Musoma

KENYA

TANZANIA

Masai Mara National Reserve

Mara

Sayari Camp

Bologonia Gate

Klein's Camp

Bunda

Sabora

Sasakwa

Grumeti Reserves

Grumeti

Migration Camp

Lake Victoria

Grumeti River Camp

Faru Faru

Ikoma Gate

Lobo Wildlife Lodge

Loliondo G.C.A.

Ndabaka Gate

Kirawira Camp

Banagi

Mbuzi Mawe

Nyamuma Hills

Mbalageti

Serengeti Serena Lodge

Seronera Wildlife Lodge

Piyaya Region

Mbalageti Camp

Serengeti Sopa Lodge

Gol Kopjes

Serengeti National Park

Gol Mountains

Simba Kopjes

Naabi Hill Gate

Kusini Camp

Lake Ndutu

Ndutu Safari Lodge

Ngorongoro Conservation Area

20 km

20 miles

Wildebeest migration pattern

August to October

MASAI MARA

June to July

SERENGETI

December to April (calving)

Tarangire National Park

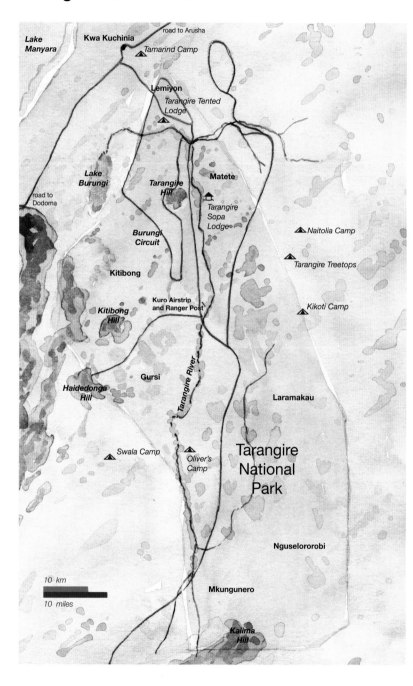

Lake Manyara

Kwa Kuchinia

road to Arusha

Tamarind Camp

Lemiyon

Tarangire Tented Lodge

Lake Burungi

road to Dodoma

Tarangire Hill

Matete

Tarangire Sopa Lodge

Naitolia Camp

Tarangire Treetops

Burungi Circuit

Kitibong

Kuro Airstrip and Ranger Post

Kikoti Camp

Kitibong Hill

Gursi

Haidedonga Hill

Tarangire River

Laramakau

Swala Camp

Oliver's Camp

Tarangire National Park

Nguselororobi

10 km

10 miles

Mkungunero

Kalima Hill

Zanzibar

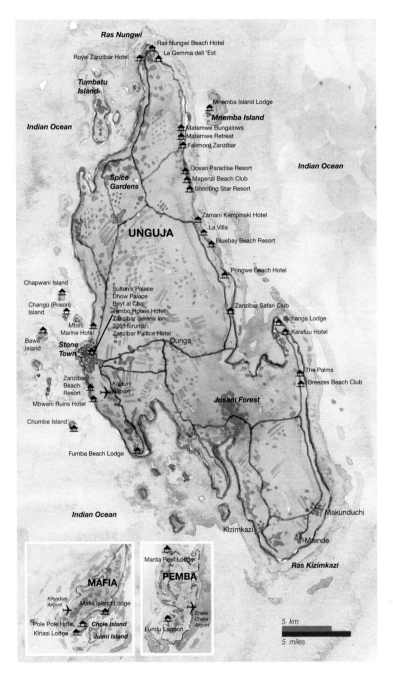

Ras Nungwi
Ras Nungwi Beach Hotel
La Gemma dell 'Est
Royal Zanzibar Hotel

Tumbatu
Island

Indian Ocean

Mnemba Island Lodge
Mnemba Island
Matemwe Bungalows
Matemwe Retreat
Fairmont Zanzibar

Ocean Paradise Resort
Mapenzi Beach Club
Shooting Star Resort

Indian Ocean

Spice
Gardens

UNGUJA

Zamani Kempinski Hotel
La Villa
Bluebay Beach Resort

Pongwe Beach Hotel

Chapwani Island

Changu (Prison)
Island

Mtoni
Marine Hotel

Bawe
Island

Stone
Town

Sultan's Palace
Dhow Palace
Beyt al Chai
Tembo House Hotel
Zanzibar Serena Inn
236 Hurumzi
Zanzibar Palace Hotel

Dunga

Zanzibar Safari Club

Kichanga Lodge
Karafuu Hotel

The Palms
Breezes Beach Club

Zanzibar
Beach
Resort

Kisauni
Airport

Mbweni Ruins Hotel

Josani Forest

Chumbe Island

Fumba Beach Lodge

Indian Ocean

Makunduchi

Kizimkazi

Mtende

Ras Kizimkazi

MAFIA

Manta Reef Lodge

PEMBA

Kilondoni
Airport

Mafia Island Lodge

Pole Pole Hotel
Kinasi Lodge

Chole Island
Juani Island

Chake
Chake
Airport

Fundu Lagoon

5 km

5 miles

Uganda

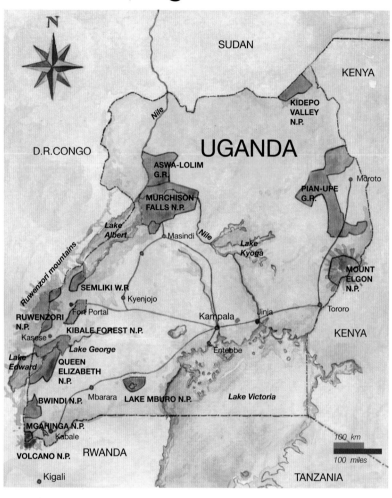

Straddling the equator, Uganda is a verdant country once referred to as the "Pearl of the British Empire." Most of Uganda is an upland plateau averaging 3,000 feet (1,000m) above sea level. With the enormous Lake Victoria occupying the south-eastern part of the country, and numerous other Rift Valley lakes as well as the mighty Nile River, one-sixth of Uganda is fresh water. Approximately the size of Oregon (or Great Britain) Uganda covers 93,000 square miles (240,000km²). Almost all of the 27 million population are either subsistence farmers or employed in agriculture. Kampala is the capital city with over 1.2 million inhabitants. KiSwahili and English are the main languages. Currency is the Ugandan Shilling.

Southwestern Uganda, Rwanda and Eastern Congo

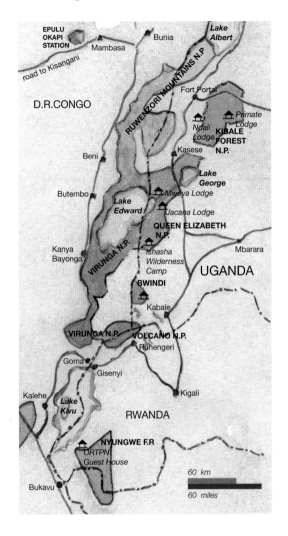

EPULU OKAPI STATION
Mambasa
road to Kisangani
Bunia
Lake Albert
RUWENZORI MOUNTAINS N.P.
Fort Portal
D.R.CONGO
Primate Lodge
Ndali Lodge
KIBALE FOREST N.P.
Kasese
Beni
Lake George
Butembo
Lake Edward
Mweya Lodge
Jacana Lodge
QUEEN ELIZABETH N.P.
Kanya Bayonga
VIRUNGA N.P.
Ishasha Wilderness Camp
Mbarara
UGANDA
BWINDI
Kabale
VIRUNGA N.P.
VOLCANO N.P.
Ruhengeri
Goma
Gisenyi
Kalehe
Lake Kivu
Kigali
RWANDA
NYUNGWE F.R
ORTPN Guest House
Bukavu

60 km
60 miles

Queen Elizabeth National Park

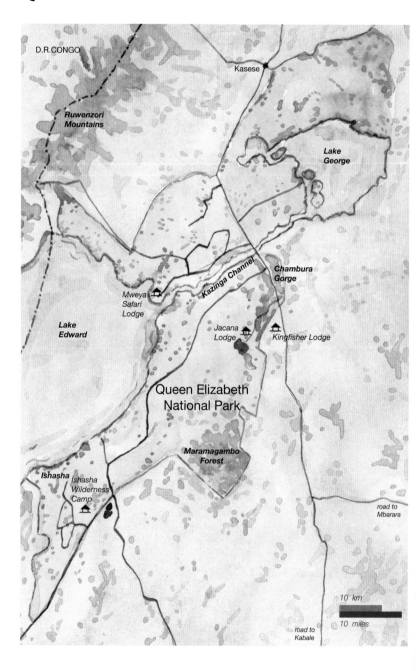

D.R.CONGO

Kasese

Ruwenzori
Mountains

Lake
George

Chambura
Gorge

Kazinga Channel

Mweya
Safari
Lodge

Jacana
Lodge

Kingfisher Lodge

Lake
Edward

Queen Elizabeth
National Park

Maramagambo
Forest

Ishasha
Ishasha
Wilderness
Camp

road to
Mbarara

10 km

10 miles

road to
Kabale

Ruwenzori Mountains

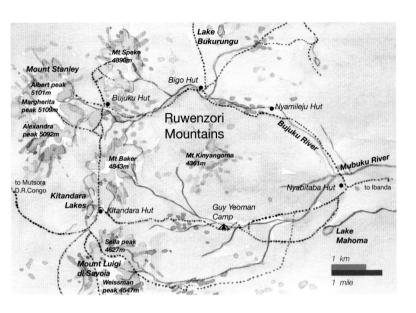

Lake Bukurungu

Mt Speke 4890m

Mount Stanley

Albert peak 5101m
Margherita peak 5109m

Bujuku Hut

Bigo Hut

Nyamileju Hut

Ruwenzori Mountains

Bujuku River

Alexandra peak 5092m

Mt Baker 4843m

Mt Kinyangoma 4361m

Mubuku River

to Mutsora D.R.Congo

Kitandara Lakes

Kitandara Hut

Guy Yeoman Camp

Nyabitaba Hut

to Ibanda

Lake Mahoma

Sella peak 4627m

1 km

Mount Luigi di Savoia

Weissman peak 4547m

1 mile

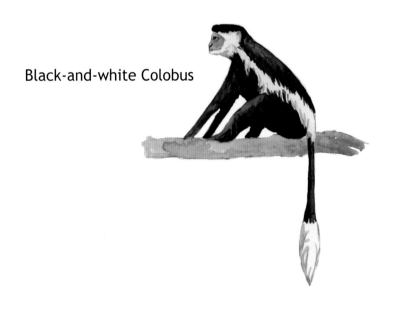

Black-and-white Colobus

Zambia

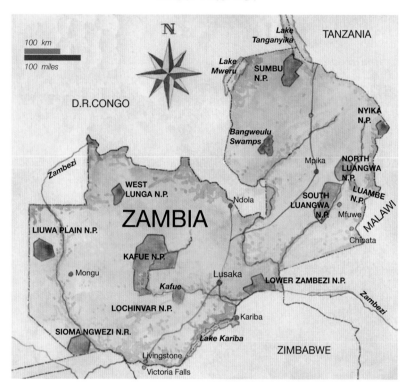

Zambia is one of Africa's least developed countries, with vast areas of wilderness and a comprehensive network of national parks protecting its wildlife. The landscape is an upland plateau ranging in altitude from 3,000 to 5,000 feet above sea level (915 to 1,525m) with dry savannah and miombo woodland predominating. Zambia's economy is based on copper mining, agriculture and tourism. At 290,586 square miles (752,614km^2), Zambia is larger than Texas (or France), but has a population of some 11 million. Lusaka is the capital city with 1.3 million inhabitants. English is the official language, with Bemba, Tonga, Ngoni and Lozi widely spoken. Currency is the Zambian Kwacha.

Kafue National Park

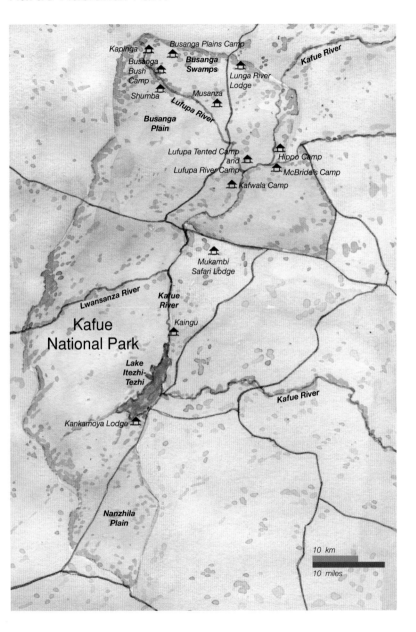

Kapinga
Busanga Plains Camp
Busanga
Bush
Camp
Busanga
Swamps
Lunga River
Lodge
Kafue River
Shumba
Musanza
Lufupa River
Busanga
Plain
Lufupa Tented Camp
and
Lufupa River Camp
Hippo Camp
McBride's Camp
Kafwala Camp

Mukambi
Safari Lodge

Lwansanza River
Kafue
River

Kafue
National Park
Kaingu

Lake
Itezhi-
Tezhi

Kafue River

Kankamoya Lodge

Nanzhila
Plain

10 km
10 miles

Lower Zambezi National Park

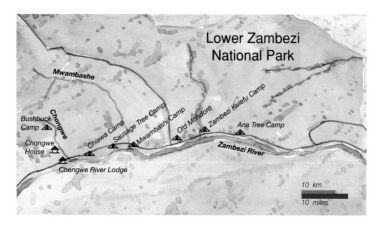

Lower Zambezi
National Park

Mwambashe

Chongwe

Bushbuck
Camp

Chongwe
House

Chongwe River Lodge

Chiawa Camp

Sausage Tree Camp

Mwambashi Camp

Old Mondoro

Zambezi Kulefu Camp

Ana Tree Camp

Zambezi River

10 km
10 miles

South Luangwa National Park

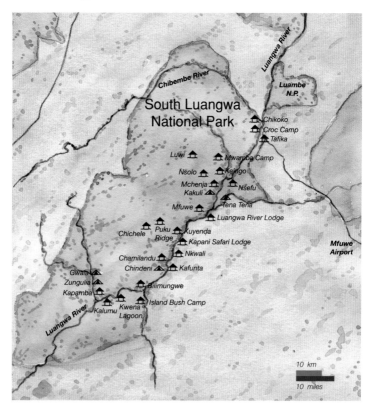

Luangwa River

Chibembe River

Luambe
N.P.

South Luangwa
National Park

Chikoko
Croc Camp
Tafika

Luwi

Mwamba Camp

Nsolo

Kaingo

Mchenja

Nsefu

Kakuli

Mfuwe

Tena Tena

Luangwa River Lodge

Chichele

Puku
Ridge

Kuyenda

Kapani Safari Lodge

Chamilandu

Nkwali

Chindeni

Kafunta

Gwala

Bilimungwe

Zungulia

Kapamba

Island Bush Camp

Luangwa River

Kalumu

Kwena
Lagoon

Mfuwe
Airport

10 km
10 miles

Zimbabwe

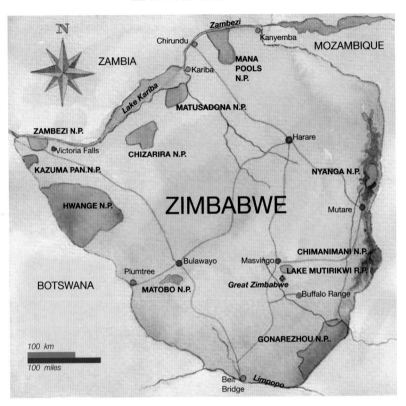

Zimbabwe is a scenic land consisting of a central plateau which drops down to the Zambezi and Limpopo river valleys in the north and south respectively. The average altitude is about 3,300 feet (1,000m) on the plateau, rising to 8,000 feet (2,440m) in the Eastern Highlands. The plateau is dominated by *brachystegia* (miombo) woodland, with acacia and mopane savanna in the larger valleys. A mosaic of grassland and forest occurs in the Eastern Highlands. With an area of 150,872 square miles (390,759km²), Zimbabwe is about the size of California (or Great Britain). The population is estimated at 11.5 million, with the capital of Harare having some 2 million inhabitants. Shona, Ndebele and English are the main languages. Currency is the Zimbabwean dollar.

Northwestern Zimbabwe

Hwange National Park

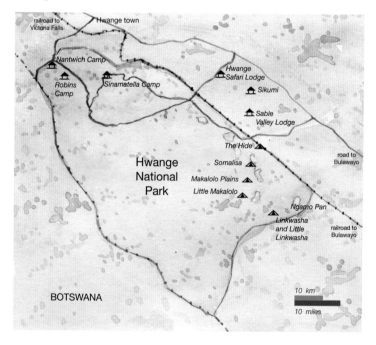

Mana Pools National Park

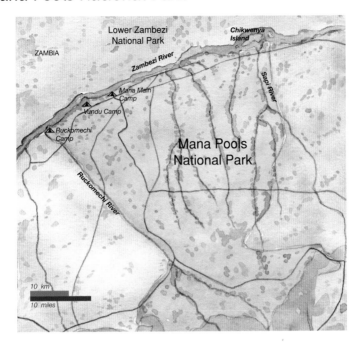

Matusadona National Park

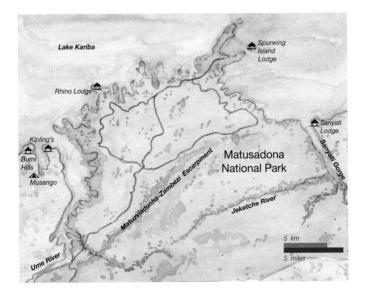

Victoria Falls and Upper Zambezi River

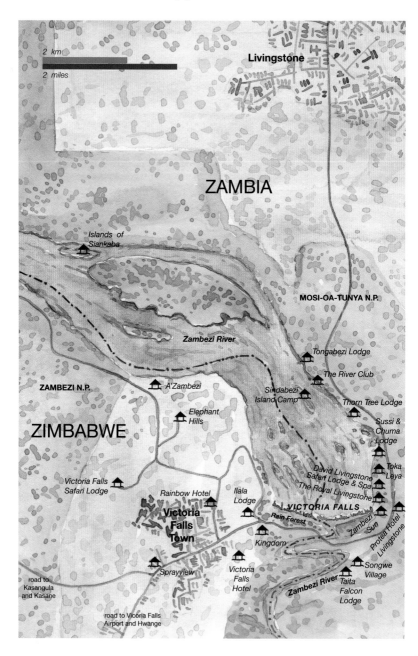

2 km

2 miles

Livingstone

ZAMBIA

Islands of
Siankaba

MOSI-OA-TUNYA N.P.

Zambezi River

Tongabezi Lodge

The River Club

ZAMBEZI N.P.   A'Zambezi

Sindabezi
Island Camp

Thorn Tree Lodge

Elephant
Hills

Sussi &
Chuma
Lodge

ZIMBABWE

Toka
Leya

David Livingstone
Safari Lodge & Spa

Victoria Falls
Safari Lodge

Rainbow Hotel

Ilala
Lodge

The Royal Livingstone

VICTORIA FALLS

Rain Forest

Zambezi

Protea Hotel
Livingstone

Sun

**Victoria
Falls
Town**

Kingdom

Songwe
Village

Sprayview

Victoria
Falls
Hotel

Zambezi River   Taita
Falcon
Lodge

road to
Kasangula
and Kasane

road to Victoria Falls
Airport and Hwange

French Words and Phrases

(CENTRAL AFRICA)

General Expressions

English	French	Phonetics
good morning	bon jour	bonjor
good day	bon jour	bonjor
good night	bonne nuit	bon nuee
How are you?	Comment allez-vous?	koman-tallay-voo
very well	très bien	tray-beeuh
good-bye (go well)	au revoir	o-revwour
mister	monsieur	muh seeuh
madam	madame	madam
yes/no	oui/non	wee/no
please	s'il vous plait	seal-voo-play
thank you	merci	mear see
very much	beaucoup	bo-koo
today	aujourd'hui	o jord wee
tomorrow	demain	duhma
yesterday	hier	ee year
toilet	toilette	twalet
left	gauche	gosh
right	droite	drwat
I want	je dèsire	juh dezeer
How much?	Combien?	komb ya
How many?	Combien?	komb ya
Where is?	Ou est?	oo-ay
When?	Quand?	kon
to eat	manger	mon-jay
food	nourriture	nureetur
water	eau	o
coffee	cafè	kafe
tea	thè	te
milk	lait	lay
beer	bière	be-year
bread	pain	pun
butter	beurre	burr
sugar	sucre	sukr
salt	sel	cell
pepper	poivre	pwavr
hot/fire	chaud/feu	show/fuh
cold	froid	frwa
ice	glace	glass

Numbers

English	French	Phonetics
one	un	uh
two	deux	duh
three	trois	trwa
four	quatre	katr
five	cinq	sank
six	six	sees
seven	sept	set
eight	huit	wheat
nine	neuf	nuhf
ten	dix	dees
eleven	onze	ownz
twenty	vingt	vuh
thirty	trente	trwant
forty	quarante	karant
fifty	cinquante	sank-ant
sixty	soixante	swa-sant
seventy	soixante-dix	swa-sant dees
eighty	quatre-vingt(s)	katr-vuh
ninety	quatre-vingt(s)-dix	katr-vuh dees
hundred	cent	san
thousand	mille	meal

Mammal Names

English	French	Phonetics
aardvark	fourmillier	foor mee lye
aardwolf	protèle	protel
antelope, roan	hippotrague rouanne	eepotrahguh-rwan
antelope, sable	hippotrague noir	eepotrahguh-nwar
baboon	babouin	bah bwa
bongo	bongo	bongo
buffalo, Cape	buffle d'Afrique	bufl-dafreek
bushbaby, greater	galago à guelle epaisse	galago-ah-kuh-aypass
bushbuck	antilope harnaché	onteelop-ahrnah shay
bushpig	potamochère d'Afrique	potahmoshare-dafreek
caracal	caracal	kahrahkahl
cheetah	guépard	gu-epahr
chimpanzee	chimpanzé	shamponzay
civet	civette	see vet
colobus, black-&-white	colobe guereza	kolob guerezah
dikdik, Kirk's	dikdik de Kirk	deek deek duh kirk
duiker, common or grey	cephalophe du Cap	sefahlof du kap
eland	élan	aylon
elephant	elephant d'Afrique	aylayfon-dafreek
fox, bat-eared	otocyon	otoseeon
gazelle, Grant's	gazelle de Grant	gahzel duh grant
gazelle, Thomson's	gazelle de Thomson	gahzel duh tomson
gemsbok	oryx	oreex
genet, large spotted	genette à grandes taches	juhnet-ah-grand-tash
gerenuk	gazelle giraffe	gahzel giraf
giraffe	giraffe	giraf

Mammal Names

English	French	Phonetics
gorilla	gorille	goreeyuh
grysbok, Sharpe's	grysbok	greesbok
hare, scrub	lièvre des buissons	lee-evr de bueessan
hartebeest, red	bubale	bubal
hedgehog	hérisson du cap	ayreessan du kap
hippopotamus	hippoptame	eepopotahm
hog, giant forest	hylochère géant	ee-lo-share gayan
honey badger	ratel	rahtel
hyena, brown	hyène brune	yen brun
hyena, spotted	hyène tachetée	yen ta shuhte
hyena, striped	hyène rayée	yen re ye
hyrax, tree	daman d'arbre	dahmon dahrbr
impala	pallah	pah lah
jackal, black-backed	chacal à chabraque	shah kahl-ah-shahbrak
jackal, side-striped	chacal à flancs rayé	shah kahl-ah-flon-ray-ye
klipspringer	oreotrague	orayo trah guh
kob, Uganda	cob de Buffon	kob duh bufon
kudu, greater	grand koudou	gran koo doo
lechwe, red	cobe lechwe	kobe lechwe
leopard	lèopard	lay opahr
lion	lion	leeown
meerkat	suricate	mangooz-fov
mongoose, banded	mangue rayée	mangooz-ray-ye
monkey, Syke's	cercopitheque	sare ko pee tek
monkey, vervet	grivet	gree vay
nyala	nyala	nee ah lah
oribi	ourébie	oo ray bee
otter, clawless	loutre à joues blanches	lootr-ah-jeur-blansh
pangolin, Temminck's	pangolin de Temminck	pangola-duh-taymeek
porcupine	porc-épique	pork-ay-peek
puku	puku	puku
reedbuck, common	redunca grande	ruhdunka grand
rhino, black	rhinocéros noir	reenosayros nwar
rhino, white	rhinocéros blanc	reenosayros blan
serval	serval	sair vahl
sitatunga	sitatunga	see tah tun gah
springbok	antidorcas	an tee dor kah
springhare	lièvre	leeevr
squirrel, tree	e'cureuil des bois	aykuroyl-de-bwa
steenbok	steenbok	steenbok
topi	damalisque	dah mah leesk
tsessebe	sassaby	sah sah bee
warthog	phacochère	fah ko share
waterbuck, common	cobe à croissant	kob-ah-krwasson
waterbuck, defassa	cobe defassa	kob-defahssah
wild dog	cynhyène	seen yen
wildebeest	gnou bleu	gnu-bluh
zebra, Burchell's	zèbre de steppe	zabr-duh-step
zebra, Grevy's	zèbre de Grévy	zabr-duh-grayvee
zorilla	zorille	zoreeyl

Shona Words and Phrases

(ZIMBABWE)

General Expressions

English	Shona	Phonetics
good morning	mangwanani	mä-gwä-nä'-nee
good day	masikati	mä-see-kä'-tee
good night	manheru	män-ay'-roo
How are you?	Makadini?	mä-kä-dee'-nee
very well	ndiripo zvangu	n-dee-ree'-po zwän'-goo
good-bye (go well)	chiendal zvenyu	chee-aan'-däee zwaan'-yoo
mister	baba	bä'-bä
madam	amai	ä-mä'-yee
yes/no	hongu/kwete	oon'-goo/kwâ-tâ
please	ndapota	n-dä-po'-tä
thank you	mazviita	mä-zwee'-tä
very much	kwazvo	kwä'-zo
today	nhasi	nää'-zee
tomorrow	mangwana	män-gwä-nä
yesterday	nezuro	nay-zoo-rö
toilet	chimbuzi	cheem-boo-zee
left	ruboshwa	roo-bô'-shwâ
right	rudyi	roo'-dee
I want	ndinoda	ndee-no'-dä
How much?	Zvakawanda sei?	zwä-kä-wän'-dä
How many?	Zvingani?	zween-gä-nee
Where is?	Ndekupi?	nday-koo'-pee
When?	Rini?	ree'-nee
to eat	kudya	koo'-deeä
food	chidyo	chee'-deeo
water	mvura	m-voo'-rä
coffee	kofi	ko'-fee
tea	tii	tee
milk	mukaka	moo-kä'-kä
beer	doro	do'-ro
bread	chingwa	cheen'-gwä
butter	bhata	bää'-tä
sugar	shuga, tsvigiri	shoo'-gä, tswee-gee'-ree
salt	munyu	moon'-yoo
hot/fire	inopisa/moto	e-no-pee'-sä/mo'-to
cold	inotonhora	e-no-ton-o-rä
ice	chando, aizi	chän'-do, äee'-zee

Numbers

English	Shona	Phonetics
one	potsi	po'-tsee
two	piri	pee'-ree
three	tatu	tä'-too
four	ini	e'-nee
five	shanu	shä'-noo
six	tanhatu	tän-ä-too
seven	nomwe	no'-mway
eight	tsere	tsay'-ray
nine	pfumbanmwe	foom-bä'-mway
ten	gumi	goo'-mee
eleven	gumi nerimwechere	goo'-mee nay-ray-mway'-ayayray
twenty	makumi maviri	mä-koo-mee mä-vee'-ree
thirty	makumi matatu	mä-koo-mee mä-tä'-too
forty	makumi mana	mä-koo-mee mä'-nä
fifty	makumi mashanu	mä-koo-mee mä-shä'-noo
sixty	makumi matanhatu	mä-koo-mee mä-tän'-ä-too
seventy	makumi manomwe	mä-koo-mee mä-no'-mway
eighty	makumi masere	mä-koo-mee mä-say'-ray
ninety	makumi mapfumbamwe	mä-koo-mee mä-foom-bä'-mway
hundred	zana	zä'-nä
thousand	chiuru	chee-oo'-roo

Mammal Names

English	Shona	Phonetics
aardvark	bikita, chikokoma	bee-kee'-tä, chee-ko-ko'-mä
aardwolf	mwena	mwi-nä
antelope, roan	chengu, ndunguza	chayn'-goo, n-doon-goo'-zä
antelope, sable	mharapara	m-ä'-rä-pä-rä
baboon	bveni/gudo	vay'-nee/goo'-doe
buffalo	nyati	n-yä-tee
bushbaby	chinhavira	cheen-ä-vee'-rä
bushbuck	dzoma	zoo'-mä
bushpig	humba	hoom'-bä
caracal	hwana, twana	hwä-nä, twä'-nä
cheetah	didingwe	dee-deen'-gway
civet	bvungo, jachacha	voon'-go, zhä-chä'-chä
duiker	mhembwo	maym'-bway
eland	mhofu	m-o'-foo
elephant	nzou	nzo'-oo
genet	tsimba, simba	tseem'-bä, seem'-bä
giraffe	furiramudenga	foo-ree'-rä-moo-dayn'-gä
hare	tsuro	tsoo'-ro
hartebeest	hwiranondo	whee-rä-nôn'-dô
hedgehog	shoni, tyoni	sho'-nee, too'-nee
hippopotamus	mvuu	m-voo'
honey badger	sere, tsere	say'-ray, tsay'-ray
hyena	bere, magondo	bay'-ray, mä-gôn'-do

Mammal Names

English	Shona	Phonetics
hyrax	mbira	m-be'-rä
impala	mhara	m-ä-rä
jackal	hungubwe	hoon-goo'-bwa
klipspringer	nguururu	n-goo-roo'-roo
kudu	nhoro	n-o'-ro
leopard	mbada	m-bä'-dä
lion	shumba	shoom'-bä
mongoose	hovo	ho'-vo
monkey, vervet	shoko, tsoko	sho'-ko, tso'-ko
nyala	nyara	n-yä'-rä
oribi	sinza, tsinza	seen'-zä, tseen'-zä
otter	binza, chipu, mbiti	been'-zä, chee'-poo, m-be'-tee
pangolin	haka	hä'-kä
porcupine	nungu	noon'-goo
reedbuck	bimha	beem'-hä
rhino	chipembere	chee-paym-bay-ray
serval	nzudzi, nzunza	n-zoo'-zhee,' n-zoon'-zä
squirrel	tsindi	tseen'-dee
steenbok	mhene	m-â-nâ
tsessebe	nondo	non'-do
warthog	njiri	n-zhee'-ree
waterbuck	dhumukwa	doo-moo'-kwä
wild dog	mhumbi	moom'-bee
wildebeest	mvumba, ngongoni	m-voom-bä,n-gon-go'-nee
zebra	mbizi	m-be-ze
zorilla	chidembo	chee-daym'-bo

Swahili Words and Phrases

(KENYA, TANZANIA AND UGANDA)

General Expressions

English	Swahili	Phonetics
hello	jambo	jä-mbô
How are you?	Habari?	hä-bä-ree
fine, good	nzuri	nzoo-ree
good-bye	kwaheri	kwä-hay-ree
mister	bwana	bwä-nä
madam	bibi	bee-bee
yes/no	ndio/hapana	ndee-ô/hä-pä-nä
please	tafadhali	itä-fä-dhä-lee
thank you	asante	ä-sä-ntay
very much	sana	sä-nä
today	leo	lay-ô
tomorrow	kesho	kay-shô
yesterday	jana	jä-nä
toilet	choo	chô-ô
left	kushoto	koo-shô-tô
right	kulia	koo-lee-ä
I want	nataka	nä-tä-kä
I would like	ningependa	nee-ngay-pee-ndä
How much?	Pesa ngapi?	pay-sä ngä-pee
How many?	Ngapi?	ngä-pee
Where is?	Iko wapi?	ee-kô wä-pee
When?	Lini?	lee-nee
to eat	kula	koo-lä
food	chakula	chä-koo-lä
water	maji	mä-jee
coffee	kahawa	kä-hä-wä
tea	chai	chä-ee
milk	maziwa	mä-zee-wä
beer	pombe	pô-mbay
bread	mkate	'm-kä-tay
butter	siagi	see-ä-gee
sugar	sukari	soo-kä-ree
salt	chumvi	choo-'m-vee
hot/fire	moto	mô-tô
cold	baridi	bä-ree-dee
ice	barafu	bä-rä-foo

Numbers

English	Swahili	Phonetics
one	moja	mô-jä
two	mbili	mbee-lee
three	tatu	tä-too
four	nne	'n-nay
five	tano	tä-nô
six	sita	see-tä
seven	saba	sä-bä
eight	nane	nä-nay
nine	tisa	tee-sä
ten	kumi	koo-mee
eleven	kumi na moja	koo-mee nä mô-jä
twenty	ishirini	eé-shee-ree-nee
thirty	thelathini	thay-lä-thee-nee
forty	arobaini	ä-rô-bä-ee-nee
fifty	hamsini	hä-m'-see-nee
sixty	sitini	see'-tee-nee
seventy	sabini	sä'-bee-nee
eighty	themanini	thay-mä-nee-nee
ninety	tisini	tee'-see-nee
hundred	mia	mee-ä
thousand	elf	ay-l'-foo

Mammal Names

English	Swahili	Phonetics
aardvark	muhanga	moo-hä-ngä
aardwolf	fisi ndogo	fee-see ndô-gô
antelope, roan	korongo	kô-rô-ngô
antelope, sable	palahala	pä-lä-hä-lä
baboon	nyani	nyä-nee
buffalo	nyati	nyä-tee
bushbaby	komba	kô-mbä
bushbuck	pongo	pô-ngô
bushpig	nguruwe	ngoo-roo-way
caracal	siba mangu	see-bä mä-ngoo
cheetah	duma	doo-mä
chimpanzee	sokwe mtu	sô-kway 'm-too
civet	fungo	foo-ngô
dikdik	dikidiki	dee-kee-dee-kee
duiker	naya	n-syä
eland	pofu	pô-foo
elephant	tembo	tay-mbô
fox, bat-eared	mbweha masikio	mbway-hä mä-see-ke
gazelle, Grant's	swala granti	swä-lä 'grä-ntee
gazelle, Thomson's	swala tomi	swä-lä tô-mee .
genet	kanu	kä-noo
giraffe	nguruwe, twiga	ngoo-roo-way, twee-gä
gorilla	makaku	mä-kä-koo
hare	sungura	soo-ngoo-rä
hartebeest	kongoni	kô-ngô-nee
hedgehog	kalunguyeye	kä-loo-ngoo-yay-yay

Mammal Names

English	Swahili	Phonetics
hippopotamus	kiboko	kee-bô-kô
hog, giant forest	nguruwe mwitu dume	ngoo-roo-we mwe-too doo-may
honey badger	nyegere	nyay-gay-ray
hyena	fisi	fee-see
hyrax	pimbi	pee-mbee
impala	swalapala	swä-lä-pä-lä
jackal	mbweha	mbway-hä
klipspringer	mbuzimawe	mboo-zee-mä-wee
kudu	tandala mdogo	tä-ndä-lä 'm-dô-gô
leopard	chui	choo-ee
lion	simba	see-mbä
mongoose	nguchiro	ngoo-chee-rô
monkey, colobus	mbega	mbay-gä
monkey, vervet	tumbili ngedere	too-mbee-lee ngay-day-ray
oribi	taya	tä-yä
oryx	choroa	chô-rô-ä
otter	fisi maji	fee-see mä-jee
pangolin	kakakuona	kä-kä-koo-ô-nä
porcupine	nunguri	noo-ngoo-ray
reedbuck	tohe	tô-hay
rhino	kifaru	kee-fä-roo
serval	mondo	mô-ndô
sitatunga	nzohe	nzô-hay
squirrel	kidiri	kee-dee-ree
steenbok	dondoro	dô-ndô-rô
topi	nyamera	nyä-may-rä
tsessebe	nyamera	nyä-may-rä
warthog	ngiri	ngee-ree
waterbuck	kuro	koo-rô
wild dog	mbwa mwitu	'mbwä mwee-too
wildebeest	nyumbu	nyoo-mboo
zebra	pundamilia	poo-nday-'mee-lee-ä
zorilla	kicheche	kee-chay-chay

Tswana Words and Phrases

(BOTSWANA)

General Expressions

English	Tswana	Phonetics
good morning	dumêla	doo-may'-lä
good day	dumêla	doo-may'-lä
good night	rôbala sentlê	rô-bä'-lä sin'-kla
How are you?	O tsogilê jang?	o tso-khee-lay zhäng
fine, thank you	ke tsogilê sentlê	ki tso-khee-lay sin'-klâ
good-bye (go well)	tsamaya sentlê	tsä-mä-yä sin'-kla
mister	rrê	r-ra'
madam	mmê	m-mô'
yes/no	êê/nnyaa	a'-a/n-nyä'
please	tswêê-tswêê	tswâ-tswâ
thank you	kea lêboga	ki'-ä lay-bo'-khä
very much	thata	tä'-tä
today	gompiêno	khom-pee-a'-no
tomorrow	kamosô	kä-mo'-sô
yesterday	maabane	mä-ä-bä'-ni
toilet	ntlwana ya boithomêlô	n-klwä'-nä yä bo-ee-toe-mô-lo
left	ntlha ya molêma	n-klhä yä mo-lô'-mä
right	ntlha ya go ja	n-klhä yä kho zhä
I want	ke batla	ki bä-klä
How much?	Bokae?	bo-kä'-i
How many?	Dikae?	dee-kä'-i
Which way is?	Tsela e kae?	tsela-a-kä'-i
When?	Leng?	li'-ng
to eat	go ja	kho zhä
food	dijô	dee'-zhô
water	mêtsi	may-tsee'
coffee	kôfi	ko'-fee
tea	tee	ti'-i
milk	maswi/mashi	mä-shwee/mä-shee
beer	bojalwa	bo-zhä'-lwä
bread	borôthô	bo-rô'-tô
butter	bôtôrô	bô-tô'-rô
sugar	sukiri	soo-kee'-ree
salt	letswai	li-tswä'-ee
fire (hot)	aa fisa/molelô	ä'-ä fee-sä/mo-li'-lô
cold	a tsididi	ä tsee-dee'-dee
ice	segagane	see-khä-khä'-ni

Numbers

English	Tswana	Phonetics
one	nngwe	n-ngwâ'
two	pedi	pay'-dee
three	tharo	tä'-ro
four	nne	n-nâ'
five	tlhano	klhä'-no
six	thataro	tä-tä'-ro
seven	supa	soo'-pä
eight	rôbêdi	ro-bay'-dee
nine	rôbongwe	ro-bo'-ngwâ
ten	lesomê	li-so'-mâ
eleven	lesomê le motsô	li-so'-mâ li mo-tsô
twenty	masomê mabêdi	mä-so'-mâ ä mä-bay'-de
thirty	masomê mararo	mä-so'-mâ ä mä-rä'-ro
forty	masomê manê	mä-so'-mâ ä mä'-nâ
fifty	masomê amatlhano	mä-so'-mâ ä mä-klhä'-no
sixty	masomê amarataro	mä-so'-mâ ä mä-rä-tä'-ro
seventy	masomê aa supa	mä-so'-mâ ä soo-pä
eighty	maomê aa rôbêdi	mä-so'-mâ ä ro-bay'-dee
ninety	masomê aa rôbongwe	mä-so'-mâ ä ro-bo-ngwe
hundred	lekgolo	li-kho'-lo
thousand	sekete	si-ki'-ti

Mammal Names

English	Tswana	Phonetics
aardvark	thakadu	tä-kä-doo
aardwolf	thukhwi	too-khwee
antelope, roan	kwalara êtsnêtiha	kw-lä-tä a tsâ'-klhä
antelope, sable	kwalata êntsho	kwä-lä'-tä a n-cho'
baboon	tshwêne	chway'-ni
buffalo	nare	nä'-ri
bushbaby	mogwele	mo-khwi'-li
bushbuck	serôlô-bolhoko	si-rô'-lô-bo-klo-ko
bushpig	kolobê	ko-lo'-bâ
caracal	thwane	twä'-ni
cheetah	letlôtse	li-ngä'-oo li-klô-tsâ
civet	tshipalore	tse-pä-lo-ri
duiker	photi	poo'-tee
eland	phôhu	po'-foo/po'-hoo
elephant	tlôu	klo'-oo
fox, bat-eared	(mo)tlhose	(mo) klho'-si
genet	tshipa	tse-pä
giraffe	thutlwa	too'-klwä
hare	mmutla	m-moo'-klä
hartebeest	kgama	khä'-mä
hedgehog	(se)tlhông	(si) klho'-ng
hippopotamus	kubu	koo'-boo
honey badger	magôgwê/matshwane	mä-khô-khwâ/mä-chwä'-ni

Mammal Names

English	Tswana	Phonetics
hyena, spotted	phiri	pe'-re
hyrax	pela	pi'-lä
impala	phala	pä'-lä
jackal	phokojwê	po-ko-zhwâ
klipspringer	mokabayane, kololo	mo-kä-bä-yä'-ni, ko-lo'-lo
kudu	thôlô	tô'-lô
lechwe	letswee	li-tswi'-i
leopard	nkwê	n-kwâ
lion	tau	tä-oo
mongoose, slender	kgano	khä'-no
monkey, vervet	kgabo	khä'-bo
oribi	phuduhudu kgamane	poo-doo-hoo-doo khä-mä-ni
oryx	kukama	koo-kä'-mä
otter	kônyana yanoka	kôn-yä-nä yä-no-kä
pangolin	kgaga	khä'-khä
porcupine	noko	no'-ko
reedbuck	sebogata, motsweema	si-boo'-gä-tä, mo-tsway-ay-mä
rhino	tshukudu	choo-koo'-doo
serval	tadi	tä'-de
sitatunga	sitatunga/nankông	si-tä-toon'-gä/nân-ko'-ng
springbok	tshêphê	tsâ'-pâ
squirrel, tree	setlhora	si-klho'-rä
steenbok	phuduhudu	poo-doo-hoo'-doo
tsessebe	tshêsêbê	tsâ-sä-bâ
warthog	kolobê yanaga	ko-lo-bâ yä nä'-khä
waterbuck	motumoga	mo-too-mo'-khä
wild dog	letlhalerwa	li-klhä-li-rwä
wildebeest, blue	kgôkông	kho-ko'-ng
zebra	pitse/yanaga	pe'-tsi
zorilla	nakêdi	nä-kay-dee

Zulu Words and Phrases

(SOUTH AFRICA)

General Expressions

English	Zulu	Phonetics
good morning	sawubona	sä-woo'-bo-nä
good day	sawubona	sä-woo'-bo-nä
good night	lala kahle	lä-lä kä'-klhay
How are you?	Kunjani?	koon-zhä'-nee
very well	kuhle	koo'-klhay
good-bye (go well)	hamba kahle	häm'-bä kä-klhay
mister	mnumzane	m-noom-zä-ni
madam	nkosazane	n-ko-s-ä-zä'-ni
yes/no	yebo/qua	yay'-bo/qwa
please	ngiyacela	n-gee-yä-câ'-lä
thank you	ngiyabonga	n-gee-yä-bon-gä
very much	kakhulu	kä-koo'-loo
today	namuhla	nä-moo'-klhä
tomorrow	kusasa	koo'-sä-sä
yesterday	izolo	e-zo'-lo
toilet	indlwana	een-dlwä'-nä
	yangaphandle	yän-gä-pän'-dlee
left	esokunxele	i-so-koo-nxay'-lay
right	esokudia	i-so-koo'-dlä
I want	ngifuna	n-gee-foo'-nä
How much?	Kangakanani?	kän-gä-kä-nä'-nee
How many?	Zingakanani?	zeen-gä-kä-nä'-nee
Where is?	Zikuphi?	zee-koo'-pee
When?	Nini?	nee'-nee
to eat	ukudla	oo-koo'-dlä
food	ukudla	oo-koo'-dlä
water	amanzi	ä-män'-zee
coffee	ikhofi	e-ko'-fee
tea	itiye	e-tee'-yay
milk	ubisi	oo-be'-see
beer	utshwala, ubhiya	oo-chwä'-lä, oo-be'-yä
bread	isinkwa	e-seen'-kwä
butter	ibhotela	e-bo-tay'-lä
sugar	ushukela	oo-shoo'-kay-lä
salt	itswayi, usawoti	e-tswä'-e, oo-sä-oo-tee
hot/fire	ayashisa/umlilo	ä-yä-she'-sä/oom-lee'-lo
cold	ayabanda	ä-yä-bän'-dä
ice	iqhwa	e'-qhwä

Numbers

English	Zulu	Phonetics
one	kunye	koon'-yay
two	kubili	koo-be'-lee
three	kutathu	koo-tä'-too
four	kune	koo'-nay
five	kuhlanu	koo-klä'-noo
six	isithupha	e-see-too'-pä
seven	isikhombisa	e-see-kom-be'-sä
eight	isithobambili	e-see-to'-bäm-be-lee
nine	isithobanye	e-see-to'-bän-yay
ten	ishumi	e-shoo'-me
eleven	ishumi nanye	e-shoo'-me nän-yay
twenty	amashumi amabili	ä-mä-shoo'-me ä mä-be'-lee
thirty	amashumi amathathu	ä-mä-shoo'-me ä mä-tä'-too
forty	amashumi amane	ä-mä-shoo'-me ä mä'-nay
fifty	amashumi amahlanu	ä-mä-shoo'-me ä mä-klhä'-noo
sixty	amashumi ayisithupha	ä-mä-shoo'-me ä ye-see-too'-pä
seventy	amashumi ayisikhombisa	ä-mä-shoo'-me ä ye-see-kom-be-sä
eighty	amashumi ayisithobambili	ä-mä-shoo'-me ä ye-see-to-bäm-be'-lee
ninety	amashumi ayisithoba	ä-mä-shoo'-me ä ye-see-to'-bä
hundred	ikhulu	e-koo'-loo
thousand	inkulungwane	een-koo-loon-gwä'-ni

Mammal Names

English	Zulu	Phonetics
aardvark	isambane	e-säm-bä'-ni
aardwolf	isingci	e-see'-ngcee
antelope, sable	impalampala	eem-pä-läm-pä
baboon	imfene	eem-fay'-nay
buffalo	inyathi	een-yä'-tee
bushbaby	insinkwe	e-seen'-kway
bushbuck	imbabala	eem-bä-bä'-lä
bushpig	ingulube	een-goo-loo'-bay
caracal	indabushe	e-dä-boo-she
cheetah	ingulule	een-goo-loo'-lay
civet	impica	eem-pee'-cä
duiker	impunzi	eem-poon'-zee
eland	impofu	eem-po'-foo
elephant	indlovu	een-dlo'-voo
genet	insimba	en-seem'-bä
giraffe	indiulamithi	een-dloo-lä-me'-tee
hare	unogwaja, umvundla	oo-no-gwä-zä, oom-voon'-dlä

Mammal Names

English	Zulu	Phonetics
hartebeest	indluzele, inkolongwane	een-dloo-zay'-lay, eenko-loon-gwä'-ni
hedgehog	inhloni	een-klo'-nee
hippopotamus	imvuvu	eem-voo'-boo
honey badger	insele	een-say'-lay
hyena	impisi	eem-pee'-see
hyrax	imbila	eem-be'-lä
impala	impala	eem-pä'-lä
jackal	impungutshe	eem-poon-goo'-tsee
klipspringer	igogo	e-go'-go
kudu	umgankla	oom-gän'-klä
leopard	ingwa	een'-gwä
lion	ingonyama, ibhubese	een-gon-yä'-mä, e-boo-bay'-see
mongoose	uchakide	oo-chä-kee'-day
monkey, vervet	inkawu	een-kä-woo
nyala	inyala	een-yä'-lä
oribi	iwula	e-woo'-lä
otter	umthini	oom-tee'-nee
pangolin	isambane	e-säm-bä'-ni
porcupine	inungu, ingungumbane	e-noon'-goo, een-goon-goom'-bä-ni
reedbuck	inhlangu	een-klhän'-goo
rhino	umkhombe, ubhejane	oom-koom'-bâ, oo-b-zhä'-ni
serval	indlozi	een-dlo'-zee
springbok	insephe	een-say'-pay
squirrel	intshindane	een-tseen-dä'-ni
steenbok	inqhina	e-qhee'-nä
warthog	indlovudawana, intibane	een-dloo-voo-dä-wä-nä, een-tee-bä'-ni
waterbuck	iphiva	e-pee-vä
wild dog	inkentshane	een-kane-tsä'-ni
wildebeest	inkonkoni	een-kone-ko'-nee
zebra	idube	e-doo'-bay
zorilla	iqaqa	e-qä'-aä

Giraffe

Mammal Checklist

Wildlife Reserve

								Mammal	Illustration page number
								aardvark (antbear)	152
								aardwolf	142
								antelope, roan	167
								antelope, sable	167
								baboon, chacma	133
								baboon, gelada	133
								baboon, Guinea	
								baboon, olive	132
								baboon, sacred	133
								baboon, yellow	
								badger, honey (ratel)	151
								bat, epauletted fruit	177
								bat, yellow-winged	177
								bongo	
								buffalo, African	161
								bushbuck	165
								bushpig	158
								caracal	143
								cat, African wild	143
								cat, black-footed	
								cheetah	144
								chimpanzee	137
								civet, African	150
								civet, African palm	
								dikdik, Kirk's	172
								dolphin, bottle-nosed	178
								dolphin, common	178
								duiker, blue	172
								duiker, common or grey	172
								duiker, red	172
								eland	165
								elephant, African	154

Mammal Checklist

Wildlife Reserve

									Mammal	Illustration page number
									fox, bat-eared	139
									fox, Cape	139
									galago, lesser (bushbaby)	131
									galago, greater (bushbaby)	131
									gazelle, Grant's	168
									gazelle, Thomson's	168
									genet, large-spotted	150
									gerenuk	169
									giraffe, Maasai	160
									giraffe, reticulated	160
									giraffe, Rothschild's	
									giraffe, southern	160
									gorilla, lowland	
									gorilla, mountain	136
									grysbok, Cape	
									grysbok, Sharpe's	
									hare, rock	
									hare, scrub	174
									hartebeest, Lichtenstein's	
									hartebeest, red (kongoni)	163
									hedgehog	176
									hippopotamus	155
									hog, giant forest	
									hyena, brown	142
									hyena, spotted	141
									hyena, striped	142
									hyrax, bush	
									hyrax, rock	153
									hyrax, tree	
									impala	165
									jackal, black-backed	138
									jackal, golden	138

Mammal Checklist

Wildlife Reserve

								Mammal	Illustration page number
								jackal, side-striped	138
								klipspringer	173
								kob, Uganda	171
								kudu, greater	164
								kudu, lesser	164
								lechwe, red	171
								leopard	145
								lion	146
								meerkat (suricate)	148
								mongoose, banded	148
								mongoose, dwarf	148
								mongoose, marsh	
								mongoose, Egyptian	149
								mongoose, slender	149
								mongoose, white-tailed	149
								mongoose, yellow	149
								monkey, Bale	
								monkey, blue	135
								monkey, colobus, black-and-white	135
								monkey, colobus, red	
								monkey, De Brazza	
								monkey, golden	
								monkey, grey-cheeked mangabey	
								monkey, Le Hoest's	
								monkey, patas	
								monkey, red-tailed	
								monkey, samango	
								monkey, Syke's	
								monkey, vervet	135
								mouse, striped	175
								nyala	164
								oribi	173

Mammal Checklist

Wildlife Reserve

									Mammal	Illustration page number
									oryx (gemsbok)	166
									otter, cape clawless	147
									pangolin, ground	152
									porcupine, African	175
									puku	
									reedbuck, Bohor	
									reedbuck, common	
									reedbuck, southern	170
									rhinoceros, black	157
									rhinoceros, white	156
									seal, Cape fur	147
									serval	143
									shrew, elephant (sengi)	176
									sitatunga	
									springbok	169
									springhare	175
									squirrel, bush	
									squirrel, ground	174
									steenbok	173
									suni	
									topi	163
									tsessebe	163
									warthog	158
									waterbuck, common	170
									waterbuck, Defassa	
									weasel, striped	151
									whale, humpback	
									whale, southern right	178
									wild (hunting) dog, African	140
									wildebeest, black	162
									wildebeest, common (gnu)	162
									wolf, Ethiopian	139

Mammal Checklist

Wildlife Reserve

									Mammal	Illustration page number
									zebra, Burchell's (plains)	159
									zebra, Grevy's	159
									zebra, mountain	
									zorilla (striped polecat)	151

Bird Checklist

Over 330 of the most common and conspicuous birds likely to be seen in eastern and southern Africa

	Bird	Illustration page number		Bird	Illustration page number
☐	albatross, black-browed	226	☐	buzzard, steppe	
☐	apalis, yellow-breasted		☐	canary, yellow-fronted	
☐	avocet		☐	chat, ant-eating	256
☐	babbler, arrow-marked		☐	chat, familiar	
☐	barbet, black-collared	255	☐	chat, mocking (cliff)	216
☐	barbet, crested	209	☐	chat, sooty	
☐	barbet, double-toothed	209	☐	chat, stone	
☐	barbet, red-and-yellow		☐	chatterer, rufous	215
☐	barbet, spot-flanked	209	☐	cisticola, fan-tailed	
☐	bateleur	193	☐	cisticola, rattling	257
☐	batis, chin-spot	218	☐	cisticola, fan-tailed	
☐	bee-eater, blue-cheeked		☐	cisticola, zitting	217
☐	bee-eater, southern carmine	210	☐	coot, red-knobbed	189
☐	bee-eater, European		☐	cordon-bleu, red-cheeked	
☐	bee-eater, little	210	☐	cormorant, great (white-breasted)	
☐	bee-eater, white-fronted				
☐	bishop, southern red	224	☐	cormorant, reed	181
☐	bittern, little		☐	coucal, Burchell's	253
☐	boubou, slate-colored		☐	coucal, Senegal	204
☐	boubou, tropical		☐	coucal, white-browed	
☐	broadbill, African	212	☐	courser, two-banded	
☐	brubru		☐	crake, black	189
☐	bulbul, black-eyed (common)	256	☐	crane, blue	
☐	bulbul, dark-capped	215	☐	crane, grey-crowned	187
☐	buffalo-weaver, red-billed		☐	crane, wattled	187
☐	buffalo-weaver, white-headed	223	☐	crombec, long-billed	217
☐	bunting, cinnamon-breasted rock		☐	crombec, red-faced	
			☐	crow, pied	
☐	bunting, golden-breasted		☐	cuckoo, common	
☐	bushshrike, grey-headed	220	☐	cuckoo, Diderik	204
☐	bustard, black-bellied		☐	cuckoo, Klaas's	
☐	bustard, kori	190	☐	cuckoo, red-chested	204
☐	buzzard, augur	194	☐	cuckooshrike, black	
☐	buzzard, common		☐	cuckooshrike, white-breasted	219
☐	buzzard, lizard		☐	darter, African	181
			☐	dikkop, water	

Bird Checklist

Bird	Illustration page number	Bird	Illustration page number
dove, African mourning	201	flycatcher, white-eyed slaty	218
dove, emerald-spotted wood	201	francolin, crested	191
dove, laughing		francolin, red-necked	
dove, Namaqua	201	francolin, Swainson's	
dove, red-eyed		frigatebird, greater	226
dove, ring-necked		gannet, Cape	226
dove, rock		go-away bird, bare-faced	
drongo, fork-tailed	219	go-away bird, grey (lourie)	205
duck, fulvous		go-away bird, white-bellied	
duck, knob-billed		goose, African pygmy	188
duck, white-faced	250	goose, Egyptian	188
duck, yellow-billed		goose, spur-winged	
eagle, African fish	193	goshawk, African	
eagle, bateleur	145	goshawk, dark chanting	
eagle, brown snake		goshawk, gabar	
eagle, crowned		goshawk, little banded	
eagle, long-crested		(shikra)	146
eagle, martial	193	goshawk, pale-chanting	
eagle, tawny	251	grebe, little (dabchick)	183
eagle, Verreaux's (black)	193	greenshank	198
eagle, Wahlberg's		grenadier, purple	
egret, black		guineafowl, crested	
egret, cattle	182	guineafowl, helmeted	191
egret, great white		guineafowl, vulturine	
egret, little		gull, grey-headed	202
falcon, lanner	196	gymnogene	
falcon, peregrine		hamerkop	183
falcon, pygmy	196	harrier, African marsh	
finfoot, African	189	harrier, Montago's	195
firefinch, red-billed	225	hawk, bat	
fiscal, common	257	helmetshrike, white-crested	220
fiscal, grey-backed		heron, black-headed	
flamingo, greater		heron, goliath	182
flamingo, lesser	186	heron, green-backed	182
flycatcher, African blue		heron, grey	182
flycatcher, African paradise	218	heron, purple	
flycatcher, northern black		honeyguide, greater	207
flycatcher, southern black		honeyguide, lesser	
flycatcher, spotted		hoopoe, African	207

Bird Checklist

Bird	Illustration page number	Bird	Illustration page number
hornbill, grey	255	nightjar, fiery-necked	206
hornbill, red-billed		nightjar, freckled	253
hornbill, silvery-cheeked	208	oriole, African golden	219
hornbill, southern ground	208	oriole, black-headed	
hornbill, trumpeter		osprey	195
hornbill, Von der Decken's	208	ostrich	190
hornbill, yellow-billed	255	owl, African scops	
ibis, glossy		owl, barn	206
ibis, hadeda	184	owl, Verreaux's (giant) eagle	206
ibis, sacred	184	owl, pearl-spotted	
jacana, African	199	owl, Pel's fishing	
kestrel, common (rock)		owl, spotted eagle	
kestrel, lesser	196	owlet, pearl-spotted	206
kingfisher, African pygmy		oxpecker, red-billed	221
kingfisher, giant	211	oxpecker, yellow-billed	
kingfisher, grey-headed		oystercatcher, African black	
kingfisher, malachite	211	parrot, brown (Meyer's)	203
kingfisher, pied	211	parrot, brown-headed	
kingfisher, striped		parrot, grey	203
kingfisher, woodland	211	parrot, orange-breasted	
kite, black-shouldered	194	pelican, great white	181
kite, yellow-billed (black)	252	pigeon, African	226
korhaan, red-crested	190	pigeon, African green	201
lapwing, blacksmith	197	pigeon, olive (rameron)	
lapwing, crowned	197	pigeon, speckled (rock)	
lark, red-capped		pipit, grassland (Richard's)	
lark, rufous-naped	213	plover, Kittlitz's	
lark, sabota		plover, three-banded	197
longclaw, rosy-breasted (pink-throated)	213	plover, white-fronted	197
		prinia, tawny-flanked	
longclaw, yellow-throated	256	puffback, black-backed	
lovebird, Fischer's	203	pytilia, green-winged (melba finch)	
lovebird, rosy-faced			
mannikin, bronze		quail, common	
moorhen, common		quelea, red-billed	223
mousebird, blue-naped	212	robin-chat, red-capped (Natal)	
mousebird, red-faced			
mousebird, speckled		robin-chat, white-browed	216
nicator, Eastern	215	roller, broad-billed	210

Bird Checklist

	Bird	Illustration page number		Bird	Illustration page number
☐	roller, European		☐	stork, European white	
☐	roller, lilac-breasted	210	☐	stork, marabou	185
☐	roller, rufous-crowned (purple)		☐	stork, openbill	
☐	sandgrouse, black-faced		☐	stork, saddle-billed	185
☐	sandgrouse, double-banded	200	☐	stork, yellow-billed	
☐	sandgrouse, Namaqua	200	☐	sunbird, collared	
☐	sandgrouse, yellow-throated	200	☐	sunbird, golden-winged	222
☐	sandpiper, common	198	☐	sunbird, scarlet-chested	258
☐	sandpiper, wood	198	☐	sunbird, white-bellied	222
☐	scimitarbill, Abyssinian		☐	swallow, barn (European)	
☐	scimitarbill, common		☐	swallow, lesser striped	214
☐	scrubrobin, white-browed		☐	swallow, wire-tailed	
☐	secretarybird	195	☐	swamphen, African purple	189
☐	shikra	194	☐	swift, little	214
☐	shoebill	183	☐	swift, African palm	214
☐	shrike, grey-headed bush		☐	tchagra, black-crowned	
☐	shrike, magpie	220	☐	teal, Capeteal, red-billed	188
☐	shrike, red-backed		☐	tern, Arctic	
☐	shrike, white-crowned		☐	tern, Caspian	
☐	silverbird	218	☐	tern, gull-billed	
☐	skimmer, African	202	☐	tern, whiskered	202
☐	snipe, African		☐	tern, white-winged	
☐	sparrow, grey-headed		☐	thick-knee, water	199
☐	sparrowhawk, little		☐	thrush, kurrichane	
☐	sparrow-lark, Fischer's		☐	thrush, spotted morning	216
☐	sparrow-weaver, white-browed		☐	tinker barbet, yellow-fronted	
☐	spoonbill, African	184	☐	tit, grey penduline	
☐	spurfowl, red-necked		☐	tit, red-throated	219
☐	starling, Burchell's		☐	tit, southern black	
☐	starling, greater blue-eared	221	☐	tit, white-bellied	
☐	starling, Hildebrandt's		☐	trogon, narina	212
☐	starling, red-winged	258	☐	turaco, knysna	205
☐	starling, Ruppell's long-tailed		☐	turaco, purple-crested	
☐	starling, superb	221	☐	(lourie)	253
☐	starling, violet-backed		☐	turaco, Ross's	205
☐	starling, wattled		☐	turaco, Ruspoli's	
☐	stilt, black-winged	199	☐	turaco, Schalow's	
☐	stork, Abdim's (white-bellied)	248	☐	twinspot, Peter's	225
☐	stork, African open-billed		☐	vulture, Egyptian	

Bird Checklist

Bird	Illustration page number	Bird	Illustration page number
vulture, hooded		weaver, rufous-tailed	
vulture, lappet-faced (Nubian)	192	weaver, sociable	223
vulture, Ruppell's griffon		weaver, village	223
vulture, white-backed	192	wheatear, capped	
vulture, white-headed	192	wheatear, mountain	216
wagtail, African pied	213	white-eye, cape	222
wagtail, yellow		whydah, pin-tailed	224
warbler, grey-backed bleating		widow, red-collared	
warbler, grey-capped	217	widow, white-winged	
warbler, willow		widowbird, Jackson's	224
wattle-eye, common		wood-hoopoe, green	207
waxbill, blue/cordonbleu	225	woodpecker, bearded	209
waxbill, common		woodpecker, cardinal	
waxbill, violet-eared	225	woodpecker, ground	
weaver, golden		woodpecker, Nubian	
weaver, lesser masked		wren-warbler, stierlings	217
weaver, red-headed			

Bird Checklist

Bird

Bird

Reptile Checklist

	Reptile	Illustration page number		Reptile	Illustration page number
☐	agama, tree	231	☐	monitor, Nile (leguaan)	229
☐	black mamba	230	☐	monitor, rock	
☐	boomslang	230	☐	puff adder	230
☐	brown house snake	230	☐	python, African rock	229
☐	chameleon, dwarf	231	☐	skink, striped	231
☐	crocodile, Nile	228	☐	terrapin	
☐	frog, foam-nest	233	☐	toad, guttoral	233
☐	frog, painted reed	233	☐	tortoise, leopard	232
☐	gecko, tropical house	231	☐	turtle, green	232
☐	lizard, agama	231	☐	vine (twig) snake	230
☐	mole snake		☐		

Insect Checklist

Insect	Illustration page number	Insect	Illustration page number
antlions	238	moths	235
ants	236	paper wasps	
butterflies	235	potter-wasps	
cuckoo-wasps		praying mantid	237
dragonflies	238	rhinoceros-beetles	
dung-beetles	235	spider-hunting wasps	
fig-wasps		termites	236
hornets		tiger-beetles	
longicorn beetles		wasps	237
mason-wasps			

Tree Checklist

	Tree	Illustration page number		Tree	Illustration page number
☐	acacia, apple ring		☐	leadwood tree	
☐	acacia, camel thorn		☐	mahogany, pod	244
☐	acacia, fevertree		☐	mangosteen	246
☐	acacia, stinkbark		☐	marula	245
☐	acacia, umbrella	240	☐	miombo	244
☐	acacia, yellow-barked (fever tree)		☐	monkey orange	245
			☐	mopane	244
☐	aloe spicata	243	☐	msasa	
☐	baobab	242	☐	palm, borassus	241
☐	bushwillow	245	☐	palm, coconut	
☐	candelabra		☐	palm, fan (Ilala)	
☐	chestnut, African star		☐	palm, raphia	
☐	cluster-leaf	246	☐	palm, wild date	
☐	coral tree	246	☐	rain tree	
☐	croton, lavender		☐	sausage tree	242
☐	date, desert		☐	sickle bush	245
☐	diospyros, ebony		☐	tamarind	244
☐	euphorbia ingens	241	☐	teak, Zambezi	
☐	fig, sycamore	243	☐	terminalia	
☐	gardenia, savannah		☐	thorn, wait-a-bit	
☐	jackalberry	246	☐	thorn, whistling	
☐			☐		
☐			☐		
☐			☐		
☐			☐		
☐			☐		
☐			☐		
☐			☐		
☐			☐		
☐			☐		
☐			☐		
☐			☐		
☐			☐		
☐			☐		
☐			☐		
☐			☐		
☐			☐		

AFRICA'S TOP WILDLIFE COUNTRIES Seventh Edition
$29.95 ISBN 978-0-939895-12-0
640 pp, 300+ photos

AFRICA'S TOP WILDLIFE COUNTRIES, 7th Edition
by Mark W. Nolting

Now in Full Color!

This guidebook is designed to help the reader decide the best time to go to the places that interest them most in a manner of travel that personally suits them best!

AFRICA'S TOP WILDLIFE COUNTRIES highlights and compares wildlife reserves and other major attractions in the continent's best countries for game viewing – making the planning of the journey of a lifetime easy! African countries, and the wildlife reserves within them, vary greatly as to the types and quality of safari experiences they offer. This is the only guidebook that effectively assists readers in choosing the best destinations for the kind of wildlife experience they would most enjoy by comparing travel options among all the top wildlife countries.

The complete guide for anyone traveling to Africa

* Jam-packed with information essential to the successful safari

* 18 countries, including the top safari countries of Tanzania, Kenya, Rwanda, Uganda, Botswana, Zambia, Zimbabwe, Namibia and South Africa, along with the Indian Ocean "Paradise" islands.

* 640 pages of color including hundreds of striking photographs

* 60 maps, detailing countries and major wildlife reserves

* 11 charts, including When's The Best Time to Go? and What Wildlife is Best Seen Where?

* Color wildlife illustrations and descriptions

* Accommodations graded for convenient selection

Detailed information on:

Photo Safaris	Mountain Climbing
Gorilla and Chimpanzee Safaris	Bird Watching
Canoe/Kayak/Boat Safaris	Scuba Diving & Snorkeling
Hot-Air Balloon Safaris	Night Game Drives
Walking and Horseback Safaris	White-water Rafting
Villa Vacations	Family Safaris
Honeymoon Safaris	Elephant Back Safaris

"Responsible travel to Africa is one of the best ways for individuals to contribute to the conservation of wildlife. Africa's wildlife and people will mark you indelibly, and I encourage you to see for yourself what the continent has to offer. Mark's book is an excellent tool to help you plan and make the most of your trip. I've been in Africa for over 20 years and I still turn to Mark's book as a valuable resource for travel."

Patrick Bergin, President
African Wildlife Foundation

"A trip to Africa is for most the trip of a lifetime. *Africa's Top Wildlife Countries* is an incredible guide that provides a wealth of information on everything you will need to help you best prepare for the adventure. It is full of wonderful tips on everything from where to stay, times to go, and the incredible wildlife that you can expect to see. Mark Nolting has taken his many years of experience in Africa and provided a resource that will be invaluable to anyone planning this dream vacation and hoping to get the most out of what this great continent has to offer. Don't go on safari before reading this book!"

Ron Magill
Communications & Media
Miami Metrozoo

"*Africa's Top Wildlife Countries* was my key reference book ten years ago when I first started traveling in Africa. It was a first rate, no nonsense resource then and it just keeps getting better with each edition. The book contains detailed information about each country and what it offers; it is content rich and very well organized, making it very easy to use a planning guide. Nolting's book covers all the things that matter most when traveling to Africa; where to go, when are the best times, what will you see, what activities are available in each country. Everything you need to know to plan your African Safari is covered in this fantastic book!"

Gene Eckhart – professional photographer and author of
"Mountain Gorillas: Biology, Conservation and Coexistence"

"*Africa's Top Wildlife Countries* is my main reference book for traveling to Africa…and has been for more than a decade. It told me about places I'd only heard of…and many I had NEVER heard of. To this day, I have used the book as a reference for planning almost a dozen 'trips of a lifetime' to Africa…and I plan to keep going on more!!"

Abby Lazar
Jamesville, NY

"I started traveling to Africa in 1993. Upon returning to New York from my second trip, I picked up a copy of *Africa's Top Wildlife Countries* and read it cover to cover as I knew I was hooked on the experience and could not wait to go again. I was very impressed with the depth of knowledge and information imparted in the book, and have used the last several editions to help me plan the 15 trips I have taken to Africa since!"

Iva Spitzer
New York, NY

The
Africa Adventure
Company

*"For a Safari
of a Lifetime"*

Tel: 800.882.9453
Tel: 954.491.8877
Fax: 954.491.9060

5353 North Federal Highway, Suite 300
Fort Lauderdale, Florida 33308 U.S.A.

safari@africanadventure.com
Look for us on the web!
www.africanadventure.com

The
Africa Adventure
Company

*"For a Safari
of a Lifetime"*

Tel: 800.882.9453
Tel: 954.491.8877
Fax: 954.491.9060

5353 North Federal Highway, Suite 300
Fort Lauderdale, Florida 33308 U.S.A.

safari@africanadventure.com
Look for us on the web!
www.africanadventure.com

The
Africa Adventure
Company

*"For a Safari
of a Lifetime"*

Tel: 800.882.9453
Tel: 954.491.8877
Fax: 954.491.9060

5353 North Federal Highway, Suite 300
Fort Lauderdale, Florida 33308 U.S.A.

safari@africanadventure.com
Look for us on the web!
www.africanadventure.com

The
Africa Adventure
Company

*"For a Safari
of a Lifetime"*

Tel: 800.882.9453
Tel: 954.491.8877
Fax: 954.491.9060

5353 North Federal Highway, Suite 300
Fort Lauderdale, Florida 33308 U.S.A.

safari@africanadventure.com
Look for us on the web!
www.africanadventure.com

Mark Nolting, author of
Africa's Top Wildlife Countries - 7th edition
ISBN: 978-0-939895-12-0
US $29.95

and the

African Safari Journal - 5th edition
ISBN: 978-0-939895-11-3
US $19.95

Available at bookstores and from
The Africa Adventure Company

Mark Nolting, author of
Africa's Top Wildlife Countries - 7th edition
ISBN: 978-0-939895-12-0
US $29.95

and the

African Safari Journal - 5th edition
ISBN: 978-0-939895-11-3
US $19.95

Available at bookstores and from
The Africa Adventure Company

Mark Nolting, author of
Africa's Top Wildlife Countries - 7th edition
ISBN: 978-0-939895-12-0
US $29.95

and the

African Safari Journal - 5th edition
ISBN: 978-0-939895-11-3
US $19.95

Available at bookstores and from
The Africa Adventure Company

Mark Nolting, author of
Africa's Top Wildlife Countries - 7th edition
ISBN: 978-0-939895-12-0
US $29.95

and the

African Safari Journal - 5th edition
ISBN: 978-0-939895-11-3
US $19.95

Available at bookstores and from
The Africa Adventure Company

PLEASE GIVE THESE TO ANYONE INTERESTED IN TRAVELING TO AFRICA